LITERATURE SALES ORDER FORM

NAME: _____

COMPANY: _____

ADDRESS: _____

CITY: _____ STATE: _____ ZIP: _____

COUNTRY: _____

PHONE NO.: (_____) _____

ORDER NO.	TITLE	QTY.	PRICE	TOTAL
☐☐☐☐☐☐	_____	____ ×	____ =	____
☐☐☐☐☐☐	_____	____ ×	____ =	____
☐☐☐☐☐☐	_____	____ ×	____ =	____
☐☐☐☐☐☐	_____	____ ×	____ =	____
☐☐☐☐☐☐	_____	____ ×	____ =	____
☐☐☐☐☐☐	_____	____ ×	____ =	____
☐☐☐☐☐☐	_____	____ ×	____ =	____
☐☐☐☐☐☐	_____	____ ×	____ =	____
☐☐☐☐☐☐	_____	____ ×	____ =	____
☐☐☐☐☐☐	_____	____ ×	____ =	____

Subtotal _____

Must Add Your
Local Sales Tax _____

Must add appropriate postage to subtotal (10% U.S. and Canada, 20% all other) ⟶ Postage _____

Total _____

Pay by Visa, MasterCard, American Express, Check, Money Order, or company purchase order payable to Intel Literature Sales. Allow 2-4 weeks for delivery.
☐ Visa ☐ MasterCard ☐ American Express Expiration Date _____

Account No. _____

Signature: _____

Mail To: Intel Literature Sales
P.O. Box 58130
Santa Clara, CA
95052-8130

International Customers outside the U.S. and Canada should contact their local Intel Sales Office or Distributor listed in the back of most Intel literature.

Call Toll Free: **(800) 548-4725** for phone orders

Prices good until 12/31/87.

Source HB

W9-BUC-316

intel®

80286
HARDWARE
REFERENCE
MANUAL

1987

PREFACE

The Intel 80286 microsystem is a high-performance microprocessing system based on the 80286 microprocessor.

This manual serves as the definitive hardware reference guide for 80286 system designs. It is written for system engineers and hardware designers who understand the operating principles of microprocessors and microcomputer systems. Readers of this manual should already be familiar with the 80286 architecture at the level described in the *Introduction to the iAPX 286* (Intel publication Order Number 210308).

In this manual, the 80286 microsystem is presented from a hardware perspective. Information on the software architecture, instruction set, and programming of the 80286 can be found in these related Intel publications:

* *80286 Programmer's Reference Manual*, Order Number 210498
* *ASM286 Assembly Language Reference Manual*, Order Number 121924
* *PL/M-286 User's Guide*, Order Number 121945
* *PL/M-286 User's Guide Pocket Reference*, Order Number 121946

Other related publications are the following:

* *80286 Operating System Writers Guide*, Order Number 121960
* *Microprocessor and Peripheral Handbook*, Order Number 210844
* *80287 Support Library Reference Manual*, Order Number 122129
* *8086 Software Toolbox Manual*, Order Number 122203 (includes information about 80287 Emulator Software)

These publications provide a complete description of the 80286 microsystem for hardware designers, software engineers, and all users of the 80286 systems.

ORGANIZATION OF THIS MANUAL

The information in this manual is divided into seven chapters. The material is introduced beginning with a system-level description of the 80286 microsystem, and continues with discussions of the detailed hardware design information needed to implement system designs using the actual 80286 components.

* Chapter One provides an overview of the 80286 microsystem.
* Chapter Two describes 80286 system architecture from the viewpoint of the system designer. Examples illustrate the many different system configurations that are possible within this architecture. Design tradeoffs for the various choices are discussed.

- Chapter Three discusses the 80286 local bus. Included in this chapter are detailed signal descriptions and timing for the 80286 and support components, a discussion of 80286 memory and I/O organization, and in-depth discussions of processor and local bus interface guidelines.

The next four chapters provide the information required to interface memory, peripheral devices, and processor extensions to the 80286 microprocessor.

- Chapter Four discusses techniques for designing memory subsystems for the 80286, and describes the effects of wait states on 80286 performance.
- Chapter Five explains how to interface I/O devices to an 80286 system.
- Chapter Six describes the interface between the 80286 and the 80287 Numeric Processor Extension, which greatly expands the mathematical processing power of the 80286 microsystem.
- Chapter Seven shows how an 80286 system can interface to the IEEE 796 Multibus, Intel's multi-master system bus.

ABOUT THIS MANUAL

Since the last publication of this manual in 1983, there have been a few updates. All calculations were repeated and updated to include 8, 10, and 12.5 MHz 80286 timings. Anyone wishing to reproduce the calculations in this manual should be aware of the following:

- All timing parameters used in this manual originated from the 80286 Data Sheet (210253-011), the 82C284 Data Sheet (210453-005), and the 82288 Data Sheet (210471-006). All of these Data Sheets can be found in the Intel publication *1987 Intel Microprocessor Handbook, Volume I* (230843-004).
- All AS-series timings used in this manual originated from the 1986 Texas Instruments publication *ALS/AS Logic Data Book 1986*.
- All Standard TTL, Schottky, and Low-Power Schottky timings used in this manual originated from the 1985 Texas Instruments publication *The TTL Data Book, Volume 2, Standard TTL, Schottky, Low-Power Schottky Circuits*.
- All FAST timings originated from the 1986 Signetics publication *Signetics FAST Data Manual, 1986*.

NOTE
Refer to the most recent data sheet for current component specs.

TABLE OF CONTENTS

Page

CHAPTER 4
MEMORY INTERFACING

Figures

Tables

CUSTOMER SUPPORT

CUSTOMER SUPPORT

Customer Support is Intel's complete support service that provides Intel customers with hardware support, software support, customer training, and consulting services. For more information contact your local sales offices.

After a customer purchases any system hardware or software product, service and support become major factors in determining whether that product will continue to meet a customer's expectations. Such support requires an international support organization and a breadth of programs to meet a variety of customer needs. As you might expect, Intel's customer support is quite extensive. It includes factory repair services and worldwide field service offices providing hardware repair services, software support services, customer training classes, and consulting services.

HARDWARE SUPPORT SERVICES

Intel is committed to providing an international service support package through a wide variety of service offerings available from Intel Hardware Support.

SOFTWARE SUPPORT SERVICES

Intel's software support consists of two levels of contracts. Standard support includes TIPS (Technical Information Phone Service), updates and subscription service (product-specific troubleshooting guides and COMMENTS Magazine). Basic support includes updates and the subscription service. Contracts are sold in environments which represent product groupings (i.e., iRMX environment).

CONSULTING SERVICES

Intel provides field systems engineering services for any phase of your development or support effort. You can use our systems engineers in a variety of ways ranging from assistance in using a new product, developing an application, personalizing training, and customizing or tailoring an Intel product to providing technical and management consulting. Systems Engineers are well versed in technical areas such as microcommunications, real-time applications, embedded microcontrollers, and network services. You know your application needs; we know our products. Working together we can help you get a successful product to market in the least possible time.

CUSTOMER TRAINING

Intel offers a wide range of instructional programs covering various aspects of system design and implementation. In just three to ten days a limited number of individuals learn more in a single workshop than in weeks of self-study. For optimum convenience, workshops are scheduled regularly at Training Centers worldwide or we can take our workshops to you for on-site instruction. Covering a wide variety of topics, Intel's major course categories include: architecture and assembly language, programming and operating systems, bitbus and LAN applications.

Introduction 1

CHAPTER 1
INTRODUCTION

The 80286 is a high-performance, VLSI microprocessor that supports multi-user repro-grammable and real-time multi-tasking applications. The 80286 microsystem includes the 80286 microprocessor, the 80287 processor extension, and additional support components. The 80286 system architecture specifies how these components relate to each other, and is the key to the versatility of the 80286 system.

80286 MICROSYSTEM COMPONENTS

The components that make up the 80286 microsystem are designed to work together in modular combinations within the overall framework of the 80286 architecture. System functions are distributed among specialized components, allowing designers to select an appropriate mix of components to fit the needs of their particular target system. This modular structure allows systems to grow in an orderly way to meet new needs, without adding unneeded capabilities or excessive cost.

Table 1-1 lists the components in the 80286 microsystem and describes their functions.

Microprocessors

At the center of the 80286 microsystem is the 80286 Central Processing Unit (CPU). The 80286 is a high-performance microprocessor with a 16-bit external data path and up to 16 megabytes of directly-addressable physical memory; up to one gigabyte of virtual memory space is available to each user. The standard operating speed of the 80286 is 8-MHz; 12.5-MHz, 10-MHz and 6-MHz versions of the 80286 are also available.

Table 1-1. 80286 Microsystem Components

Microprocessor	Description
80286 Central Processing Unit (CPU)	16-bit high performance microprocessor with on-chip memory management and memory protection
80287 Numeric Processor Extension (NPX)	High-performance numeric extension to the 80286 CPU
Support Component	**Description**
8259A Programmable Interrupt Controller	Provides interrupt control and priority management for the CPU
82C284 Clock Generator and Driver	Generates system timing functions, including system clock, RESET, and Ready synchronization
82288 Bus Controller	Generates bus command signals
82289 Bus Arbiter	Controls access of microprocessors to multi-master bus

The 80286 operates in two modes: Real-Address Mode and Protected Virtual-Address Mode.

- In Real-Address Mode, the 80286 is fully code-compatible with the 8086 and 8088 microprocessors. All 8086 and 8088 instructions execute on the 80286 at a much faster rate. An 8 MHz 80286 executes instructions up to six times faster than a 5-MHz 8086.

- In Protected Virtual-Address Mode, the 80286 is also compatible with the 8086 instruction set. Protected Virtual-Address Mode allows use of the 80286's built-in memory protection and management capabilities and virtual-memory support.

The 80287 Numeric Processor Extension is an 80286 processor extension that uses the 80286 to fetch instructions and transfer operands. The 80287 extends the numeric processing abilities of the 80286 to include 8-, 16-, 32-, 64-, and 80-bit integer and floating-point data types and to perform common transcendental functions. The 80287 is compatible with the IEEE 754 Floating-Point Standard.

Interrupt Controller

Interrupt management for an 80286 system is provided by the 8259A Programmable Interrupt Controller. Interrupts from up to eight sources are accepted by the 8259A; up to 64 requests can be accommodated by cascading several 8259A devices. The 8259A typically resolves priority between active interrupts, interrupts the CPU, and passes a code to the CPU to identify the interrupting source. Programmable features of this device allow it to be used in a variety of ways to fit the interrupt requirements of the particular system.

Bus Interface Components

Bus interface components connect the 80286 processors to memory and peripheral devices. The use of these components in a system is based on the requirements of the particular configuration.

The 82C284 Clock Generator is a CMOS device that generates timing for the 80286 processors and support components. The device supplies the internal clock to the processors and also provides a TTL-level half-frequency peripheral clock signal to other devices in the system. The Clock Generator also synchronizes RESET and Ready signals for the processors and support devices.

The 82288 Bus Controller is an HMOS device that decodes status lines from the 80286 CPU to generate bus command signals. These command signals identify and control the bus cycles that are performed. The 82288 also provides address latch and data buffer control signals for Address Latches and Bus Transceivers. The Bus Controller's command outputs provide the high AC and DC drive required for large systems, while control inputs allow tailoring of the command timing to accommodate a wide variety of timing requirements.

Access by the 80286 system to a multi-master system bus is controlled by the HMOS 82289 Bus Arbiter. A multi-master system bus connects memory and peripheral resources that are shared by two or more processing elements. Bus Arbiters for each processor can use one of several priority-resolving techniques to ensure that only one processor is driving the bus at any given time. The 82289 Bus Arbiter supports bus arbitration signals that are fully-compatible with the IEEE 796 MULTIBUS standard.

80286 System Architecture

2

CHAPTER 2
80286 SYSTEM ARCHITECTURE

The 80286 microsystem supports a very flexible architecture that opens up a wide range of possibilities for system designers. This chapter describes the 80286 system architecture and examines some of the possible configurations this architecture supports.

- The first section of this chapter describes the organization of the 80286 bus. This parallel bus structure forms the basis for many of the configuration possibilities of the 80286 system architecture.

- The second section introduces memory subsystems for the 80286 system. Memory is a crucial part of every microprocessing system; it is used for the storage of program instructions and for the holding of processing data and information.

- The third section discusses the possible I/O configurations of an 80286 system. The 80286 can directly address a large number of peripheral devices, or alternatively, I/O processing tasks can be off-loaded to dedicated processing subsystems.

- The fourth section introduces the 80287 Numeric Processor Extension and briefly describes how the 80287 operates in conjunction with the 80286 CPU.

- The final section of this chapter describes the architectural features of the 80286 microsystem which support multi-processing. Multi-processing provides virtually limitless possibilities for increasing the performance of 80286 systems through the modular expansion of processing capabilities.

80286 BUS ORGANIZATION

The 80286 system architecture is centered around a parallel bus structure that connects the 80286 processor to memory and I/O resources. Across this bus, the 80286 processor fetches program instructions, manipulates stored information, and interacts with external I/O devices. Figure 2-1 shows this basic 80286 bus architecture.

The 80286 architecture contains two types of buses: the local bus and the system bus.

- The local bus connects the 80286 processor with processor extensions and other processing elements. Private memory and I/O devices connect to a buffered version of this local bus, and are available only to processing elements residing on the local bus.

- The system bus connects the 80286 microsystems processor to public memory and I/O resources. These public resources are typically shared among the 80286 processor and other bus masters that also connect to the system bus.

Specialized bus interface components connect the 80286 local bus to both the buffered local bus and the system bus. These interface components process the signals that come from the 80286 local bus and generate appropriate signals for use on the buffered local bus or the public system bus.

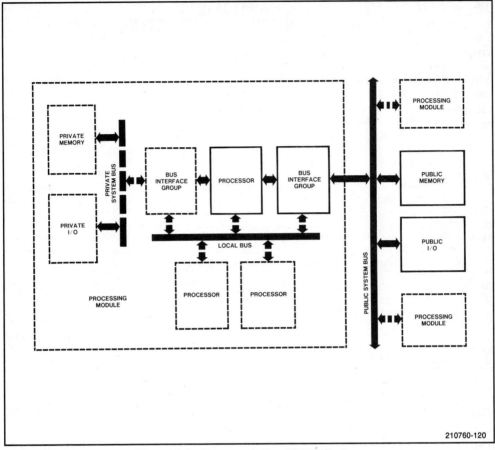

Figure 2-1. Representative 80286 System

The 80286 Local Bus

The 80286 microsystem local bus is formed from the signals generated by the 80286 CPU. These signals include address, data and control or status information that directs the operation of the local bus. All 80286 systems have at least one local bus driven by the 80286 CPU.

The 80286 provides on-chip arbitration logic and external control signals that allow it to share the local bus with other processing elements. Examples of other processing elements that connect to the local bus are processor extensions, Direct Memory Access (DMA) devices, or other specialized processors. These arbitration functions provide a cost-effective way to structure a small, multi-processing system, since the same bus interface components are shared by all of the processing elements on the local bus. Additional arbitration logic is not required for additional processors on the local bus.

The Buffered Local Bus

A buffered local bus is just that: a buffered version of the 80286 local bus which contains private memory and I/O resources that are accessible only to processors on that local bus. All but the smallest of 80286 systems contain a buffered version of the local bus. Since the buffered local bus takes full advantage of the 80286 local bus timing, and since the 80286 processor does not have to contend with other system processing elements for the use of these resources, the maximum system performance is typically obtained when the 80286 is executing programs from memory that resides on this buffered local bus.

The System Bus

The system bus, like the buffered local bus, is composed of buffered versions of the local bus signals. Unlike a buffered local bus, the public system bus connects memory and I/O resources that are shared among processors belonging to more than one local bus.

By providing easy shared access to processing resources on the system bus, the public system bus allows multi-processor systems to communicate among themselves and to avoid a needless duplication of resources.

Bus Interface Groups

Specialized bus interface components are used to translate the 80286 local bus signals onto the buffered bus to connect the 80286 local bus to either a buffered local bus or to a public system bus.

These bus interface components include the 82288 Bus Controller, the 82289 Bus Arbiter, Octal Transparent Address Latches such as the 74AS373 and 74AS533, and Octal Bus Transceivers such as the 74AS245 and 74LS640. These components can be mixed and matched as required to connect the 80286 to buffered local or system buses. In fact, the modular nature of the 80286 bus structure allows as many local and system buses as required by the target system.

Figure 2-2 shows an example of an 80286 connected to a multi-master (more than one processor) public system bus. Address latches and data transceivers transfer the local bus address and data onto the system bus, respectively. The 82288 Bus Controller translates the 80286 local bus signals to provide the system bus command signals. The 82289 Bus Arbiter provides the arbitration and control functions necessary to ensure that only one master has control of the system bus at any given time.

Figure 2-3 shows an 80286 connected to both a multi-master system bus and to a buffered local bus. Separate Bus Controllers, address latches, and data transceivers are used to implement each of the two bus interfaces. No Bus Arbiter is required for the buffered local bus interface, because the 80286 has exclusive control of the buffered local bus.

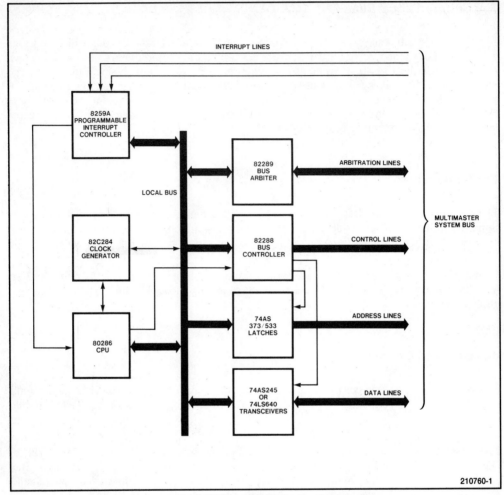

Figure 2-2. 80286 on Multi-Master System Bus

In a system having more than one bus, address decoders typically select which of the available buses is being requested when the 80286 performs a bus operation. The appropriate Bus Controller and Bus Arbiter, if any, are activated and the 80286 bus operation continues to completion.

Chapter Three describes the operation of the 80286 local bus in more detail. Chapter Seven discusses the considerations for designing interfaces between the 80286 and a public system bus.

The following sections provide a closer look at some of the configuration possibilities for 80286 systems.

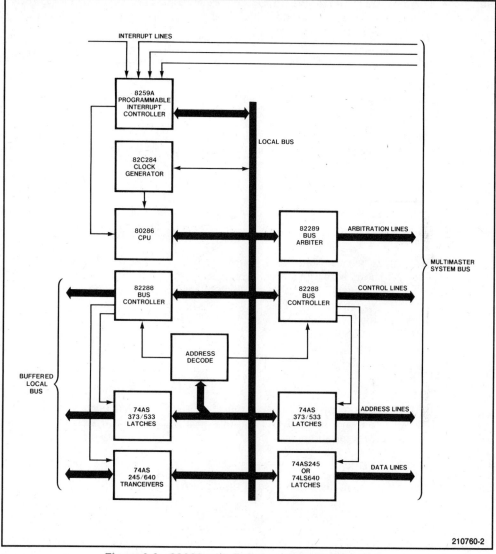

Figure 2-3. 80286 with Both Local and System Buses

MEMORY SUBSYSTEMS FOR THE 80286

An 80286 processor operating in Protected Virtual-Address mode can directly address as much as 16 megabytes of physical memory. This large physical address space can be segmented into a number of separate memory subsystems, with each having different characteristics and functions, but with all memory subsystems directly accessible by the 80286 processor.

Individual memory systems for the 80286 can be configured either as local memory, accessible by an 80286 and other processors on a single local bus, or as system memory shared by multiple independent processors having their own local buses.

- Local memory resides on a buffered local bus and is available to processors on that local bus only.

- System memory resides on a public system bus and is available to all processors that interface to the public bus.

- A third alternative that combines the advantages of both local and system memory is to configure the same memory to be accessible both as local memory from a local bus, and as system memory from a public system bus. Such a memory system is called a dual-port memory.

The 80286 architecture allows any of these configurations to be used in a single system; the use of one or all memory approaches depends on the needs of the target system.

Typical 80286 systems will use some combination of both local and system memory (the system in Figure 2-1 shows both). In systems configured with memory on both the buffered local bus and the system bus, the selection of which bus is accessed during a given memory operation is based on the memory or I/O address. Figure 2-4 shows an example memory and I/O address map for the 80286 system shown in Figure 2-1.

Local Memory

Local memory provides a processor with private memory space that is not accessible to other processors (except those that share the processor's local bus). This physical isolation of memory areas can assure program and data security in high-reliability multi-processor systems.

The use of local memory can maximize system throughput in several ways:

- Local memory permits the 80286 to take advantage of its pipelined address timing, making the most efficient use of the bus and performing memory operations in the least possible time.

- Since the local memory is not shared with other processors, no access delays are incurred, whereas access delays usually happen when several processors contend for use of the same resources.

- In systems where each of several processors has its own private memory space, multiple tasks can execute in parallel because each processor is fetching instructions on a separate data path.

The tradeoffs associated with using local memory in multi-processor systems include the cost of implementing a separate memory subsystem for each processor.

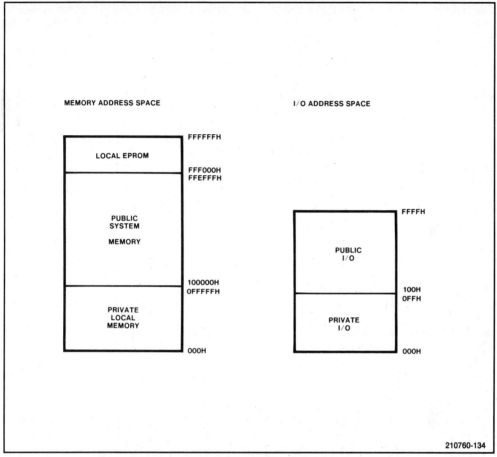

MEMORY ADDRESS SPACE

I/O ADDRESS SPACE

FFFFFFH

LOCAL EPROM

FFF000H
FFEFFFH

PUBLIC
SYSTEM
MEMORY

FFFFH

PUBLIC
I/O

100000H
OFFFFFH

100H
OFFH

PRIVATE
LOCAL
MEMORY

PRIVATE
I/O

000H

000H

210760-134

Figure 2-4. Representative 80286 System Memory Map

System Memory

System memory provides a shared memory space that can be accessed by all processors connected to a public system bus. This shared memory allows multiple processors to communicate with one another and efficiently pass blocks of data between their separate tasks.

Shared system memory is often a cost-effective alternative to using local memory when individual processors may occasionally require a relatively large physical memory space. Since the same memory is shared between multiple processors, the total system cost can be considerably less than if local memory for each processor were sized to accommodate their largest respective memory requirements.

Since system memory typically can be expanded simply by installing additional memory boards, this modular flexibility makes system memory attractive for many applications.

The tradeoffs associated with using shared system memory instead of local memory in multi-processor systems include the fact that access to system memory may be slower than access to local memory because processors must contend with each other for access to the system bus.

When several processors require use of the same memory resources at the same time, memory access time (and therefore system throughput) can be significantly reduced.

The risk of data corruption with system memory is also greater in systems that use other processors along with an 80286 because one processor can possibly overwrite data being used by another processor. However, the use of software protocols usually eliminates this problem.

Dual-Port Memory

Dual-port memory is a single memory subsystem that combines many of the advantages of both local and system memory. Dual-port memory appears both as local memory to processors on a single local bus, and as system memory to other processors in the system. Figure 2-5 shows an 80286 system that uses dual-port memory.

Dual-port memory permits the local processor to have high-speed access to the dual-port memory without tying up the public system bus. In this way, 80286 systems can access the dual-port memory as local cache memory without affecting other processors using other system resources on the system bus.

The dual-port memory is also accessible by other processors using the system bus, providing a shared memory space that can be used for inter-processor communications or other functions.

If necessary, address-mapping circuitry can make the memory appear in different address ranges for local and system bus processors. Address-mapping can also be used to permit other system processors access to only a portion of the dual-port memory, reserving portions of the memory array for exclusive use by the local processor.

Offsetting these advantages is the fact that dual-port memory typically is more complex than a (single-port) local or system memory subsystem. Dual-port memories require arbitration logic to ensure that only one of the two buses serving the memory can gain access at one time. Figure 2-6 gives a visualization of this arbitration requirement. Fortunately, the Intel 8207 Advanced Dynamic RAM Controller (ADRC) greatly simplifies design of dual-port memory subsystems.

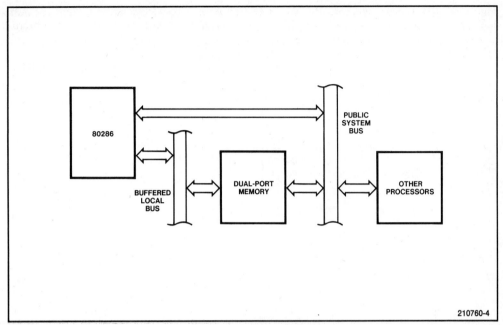

Figure 2-5. Dual-Port Memory

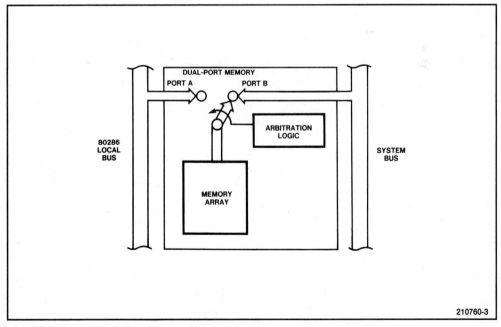

Figure 2-6. Arbitration Logic for a Dual-Port Memory

The 8207 Advanced Dynamic RAM Controller is a high-performance dynmic RAM controller designed to easily interface 16K, 64K, and 265K dynamic RAM devices to microprocessor systems. On-chip arbitration and synchronization logic implements the dual-port function, allowing two different buses to independently access the RAM array. The 8207 DRAM controller has a synchronous mode of operation that specifically supports the 80286 processor.

By combining RAM control and dual-port arbitration functions on a single chip, the 8207 ADRC provides an easy way to implement dual-port memory in an 80286 system. Figure 2-7 shows an 8207-based dual-port memory subsystem connected to an 80286 subsystem and a Multibus system bus interface.

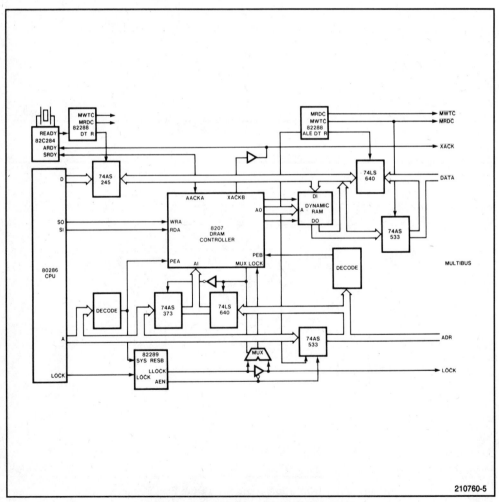

210760-5

Figure 2-7. 8207 Dual-Port Subsystem

The advantages of dual-port memories, described above, make dual-port memory a more effective choice for multi-processor applications where using strictly local or system memory would significantly impact system cost and/or performance. Chapter Four describes the design of memory subsystems for the 80286 in more detail.

I/O SUBSYSTEMS FOR THE 80286

The 80286 processor can directly address as many as 32,768 16-bit I/O devices, or 65,536 8-bit I/O devices, or combinations of the two. This large I/O address space is completely separate from the memory address space, as shown previously in Figure 2-4.

In addition to accessing individual peripheral devices, an 80286 system that requires extensive I/O capability can offload its I/O processing tasks to one or more dedicated, independent processors. An independent processor is one that executes an instruction stream separate from the 80286 CPU. Examples of independent processors include the 8086 and 8088 CPU's, the 8089 Input/Output Processor, and the 80186 High Integration Microprocessor.

An independent processor typically executes out of its own local memory and uses shared or dual-port memory for communicating with the 80286. Since the 8207 ADRC is compatible with both the 80286 and the independent processors already mentioned, it is ideal for implementing this type of I/O subsystem.

Figure 2-8 shows an 80286 system that includes such an I/O subsystem. The subsystem consists of either an 80186 or an 8086 CPU and 8089 IOP. For the second case, the 8089 is local to the 8086. For both cases, the processors are isolated from the 80286. Inter-processor communication between the 80286 and either the 186 or 8086/8089 is performed through the 8207-controlled dual-port memory.

This configuration protects the resources of each processing module from the other. The private memory and I/O space of the I/O subsystem is protected from the 80286 CPU; the private memory space of the 80286 is protected from incursion by the I/O subsystem processors.

When this level of protection is not required, the 80286 and the I/O subsystem may be configured on the same system bus. This type of multi-processing system is described later in this chapter, along with other types of multi-processing systems. Chapter Five describes the design of I/O subsystems for the 80286 in more detail.

PROCESSOR EXTENSIONS

A processor extension such as the 80287 Numeric Processor Extension (NPX) is a specialized processor that obtains its instructions from the 80286 CPU. By performing high-precision numeric instructions in parallel with the 80286 CPU, the 80287 extends the instruction set available to the 80286 and greatly increases the performance of the 80286 system over that of an 80286 processor without the 80287 processor extension.

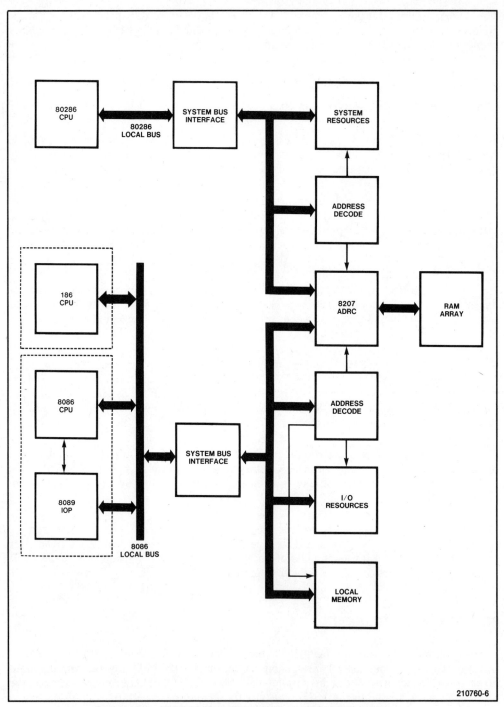

Figure 2-8. 80286 with 8086/8089 or 186 IOP Subsystems

210760-6

The 80287 monitors instructions fetched by the 80286 and automatically executes any numeric instructions as they are encountered by the 80286. The 80287 uses a special Processor Extension Data Channel within the 80286 to request operand fetches and to store the results of operations. Two of the processor extension's signal lines allow the 80287 to indicate error and status conditions.

Figure 2-9 shows an 80286 CPU and an 80287 NPX configured on a buffered local bus. Chapter Six describes in detail the design of 80286 systems using the 80287 Numeric Processor Extension.

MULTI-PROCESSING OVERVIEW

A single 80286 can provide a performance increase of up to 6 times that of a single 8086 CPU. In large systems requiring even greater performance, system throughput can be increased even further by employing multiple processors. By distributing system functions among multiple processors, significant advantages can be gained:

- System tasks can be allocated to special-purpose processors whose designs are optimized to perform those tasks simply and efficiently.
- Very high levels of performance can be attained when multiple processors execute simultaneously (parallel processing).
- System reliability can be improved by isolating system functions so that a failure or error which occurs in one part of the system has a limited effect on the rest of the system.
- Multi-processing promotes partitioning the system into modules, breaking system development into more manageable tasks and permitting the parallel development of subsystems. Partitioning also helps to isolate the effects of system modifications to a specific module.

Designers of multi-processing systems typically have been faced with the two classic problems whenever more than one processor shares a common bus: bus arbitration and mutual exclusion. The 80286 system architecture provides built-in solutions that virtually eliminate these problems.

Bus Arbitration

Bus arbitration is the means whereby one processing element gains control of a shared common bus from another processing element. In an 80286 system, this shared bus may be either the 80286 microsystem local bus (if more than one processor is configured on the local bus), or a public system bus that is shared between multiple processing elements. Bus arbitration for the control of the local bus is performed directly by the 80286 CPU. For the control of a public system bus, specialized support devices are used to provide the arbitration function.

At the local bus level, the 80286 provides bus arbitration through its on-chip arbitration logic and control signals. Two control signals, called HOLD and HLDA (hold and hold acknowledge), are provided, and are typically used with dedicated bus masters such as a Direct Memory Access (DMA) Controller.

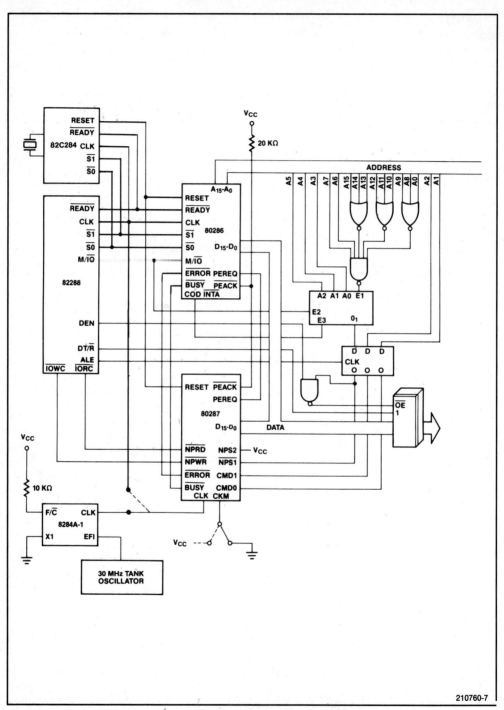

Figure 2-9. 80286/80287 System Configuration

Figure 2-10 shows an 80286 configured with an 82258 Advanced DMA Coprocessor on the local bus. The DMA coprocessor requests control of the local bus by asserting the HOLD signal to the 80286. The CPU responds by relinquishing control of the bus and sending the controller an acknowledge signal (HLDA).

At the system bus level, bus arbitration for 80286 systems typically is performed by the 82289 Bus Arbiter. The Bus Arbiter connects to the 80286 CPU and controls 80286 access to a multi-master system bus such as the IEEE 796 MULTIBUS. The 82289 supports a number of techniques for resolving requests from multiple masters on the system bus, including both serial and parallel priority resolution. Each 80286 subsystem connected to the public system bus has its own Bus Arbiter.

For other (non-80286) processors connected to the public system bus, the 8289 Bus Arbiter provides the necessary bus arbitration functions. The 8289 Bus Arbiter supports the 8086 and 8088 CPU's, the 80186 High Integration Microprocessor, and the 8089 Input/Output Processor. The 8289 Bus Arbiter is compatible with the 82289 bus control signals and the MULTIBUS interface.

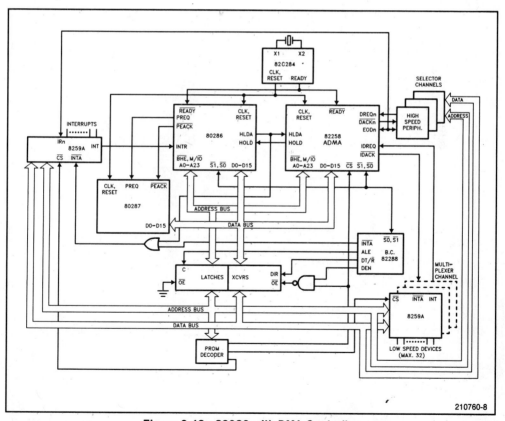

Figure 2-10. 80286 with DMA Controller

Figure 2-11 illustrates the use of the 82289 Bus Arbiter in implementing a system bus interface. 80286 system designs using the 82289 Bus Arbiter are described in greater detail in Chapter Seven.

Mutual Exclusion

Mutual exclusion is a property of a shared resource which assures that only one processing element uses the resource at one time. Typically, mutual exclusion means that one processor has the ability to prevent other processing elements from accessing a shared resource (such as the bus) until the processor has finished using the resource.

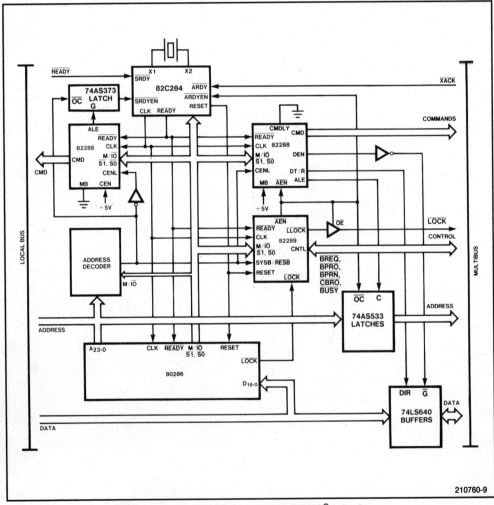

Figure 2-11. 80286 on the MULTIBUS® Interface

In many cases, mutual exclusion can be accomplished in software through the use of semaphores. In other cases, however, such as when several memory operations must be completed as a unit, support for mutual exclusion must be provided in hardware. The 80286 microsystem provides basic hardware support for mutual exclusion through the 80286 $\overline{\text{LOCK}}$ signal.

The 80286 $\overline{\text{LOCK}}$ signal is activated automatically during specific CPU operations, or explicitly through use of the ASM-286 LOCK prefix instruction, to prevent other processors from accessing a shared resource. The CPU operations which assert an active LOCK signal include interrupt-acknowledge sequences, the ASM-286 XCHG instruction, and some descriptor-table accesses. The LOCK prefix may be used with the following ASM-286 assembly instructions: MOVS, INS, OUTS, and rotate memory.

The 82289 Bus Arbiter and 8207 Advanced Dynamic RAM Controller both have inputs that connect to the 80286 $\overline{\text{LOCK}}$ signal. When its Lock input is active, the Bus Arbiter will not relinquish control of the system bus, preventing other system processors from using the system bus. In a dual-port memory subsystem, the 8207 ADRC $\overline{\text{LOCK}}$ input restricts memory access to a single processor and so prevents other processors from altering memory. Public system buses such as the IEEE 796 MULTIBUS define a similar LOCK signal, which is used to restrict access to the system bus resources.

The ability to exclude other processors from a shared resource in selected situations can provide a high level of performance and integrity in an 80286 system. For example, context switching and descriptor-table loading can be performed quickly and safely by $\overline{\text{LOCK}}$ing the transfer sequence because delays due to bus contention on the system bus are minimized and all data is protected from other processors until the sequence is complete. Interrupt responses, semaphore accesses, and $\overline{\text{LOCK}}$ed data transfers are also fast and reliable in an 80286 system.

The use of the $\overline{\text{LOCK}}$ signal with both a public system bus and a dual-port memory subsystem is described in greater detail in Chapter Seven.

Using the 80286 with the IEEE 796 MULTIBUS®

The Intel MULTIBUS (IEEE 796 Standard) is an example of a proven, industry-standard system bus that specifically supports multi-processing, and is well-tailored for 80286 systems. A wide variety of MULTIBUS-compatible I/O subsystems, memory subsystems, general-purpose processing boards, and dedicated-function boards are available from Intel and a variety of other manufacturers to speed product development while ensuring bus-level compatibility.

The job of interfacing an 80286 subsystem to the MULTIBUS is made relatively simple by using several Intel components specially suited for handling the MULTIBUS protocols. These bus interface components are the same components described previously, and include:

- The 82288 Bus Controller
- The 82289 Bus Arbiter
- Inverting Data Transceivers

- Inverting Latches
- The 8259A Programmable Interrupt Controller

These devices are functionally and electrically compatible with the MULTIBUS specifications. Figure 2-11 shows how these components interconnect to interface the 80286 to the Multibus public system bus. Chapter Seven describes in greater detail how these components can be used to provide a Multibus interface for an 80286 subsystem.

A Multi-Processing Design Example

Dedicated I/O subsystems as well as other multi-processing design techniques described in this chapter can be used to construct multi-processing systems that vary widely in function and complexity. Each processor module in the system can be optimized to perform its portion of the system task.

Figure 2-12 shows a system that distributes functions among several processor modules. For simplicity, bus interface components are not shown.

The supervisor module consists of a single 80286 CPU and local memory. The supervisor controls the system, primarily responding to interrupts and dispatching tasks to the other modules. The supervisor executes code out of local memory that is inaccessible to the other processors in the system. System memory, accessible to all of the processors connected to the public system bus, is used for messages and common buffers.

Each graphics module supports a graphics CRT terminal and contains an 80286 CPU and 80287, local memory, and local I/O.

The database module is responsible for maintaining all system files; it consists of an 80286 CPU with an 8086 CPU and 8089 IOP subsystem that controls the actual storage devices. Both the 80286 processor and the 8086 subsystem in the database module have their own local memory. A dual-port memory connects the 80286 to the subsystem processors.

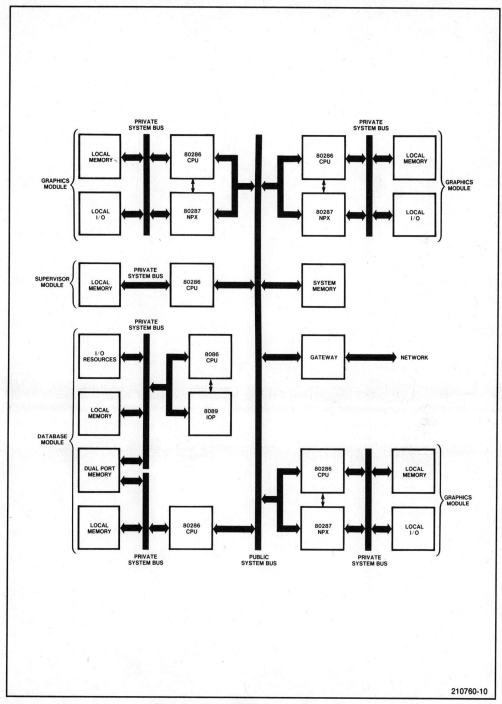

Figure 2-12. 80286 Design Example

210760-10

The 80286 Local Bus

CHAPTER 3
THE 80286 LOCAL BUS

The 80286 local bus connects the 80286 processor to memory and peripheral devices, and forms the backbone of any 80286 system. This chapter introduces the 80286 processor and describes the operation of the 80286 local bus:

- The first section of this chapter introduces the 80286 processor. The four internal processing units that make up the 80286 processor are described, as are the two operating modes of the 80286.

- The second section introduces the 80286 local bus, and gives an overview of the principles used by the 80286 in managing resources on the local bus:
  - The organization of the bus is described first, covering memory addressing, I/O, and interrupts.
  - The timing of the local bus is described, starting with a description of the local bus states, describing the 80286 bus operations that are composed of two or more bus states, and finally describing the way in which the 80286 uses the various bus operations.
  - Finally, specific bus interface components are introduced which greatly ease the design of 80286 local bus systems. Two of these interface components are the 82C284 Clock Generator and the 82288 Bus Controller.

- The third section contains specific design information on generating timing for an 80286 local bus, using the 82C284 Clock Generator. The generation of the three principle timing signals (the system CLK, RESET, and $\overline{\text{READY}}$) is described in detail.

- The fourth section describes how to generate 80286 local bus control signals using the 82288 Bus Controller.

- The fifth section describes additional design alternatives concerning the connection of memory, I/O, and other devices to the local bus. These design considerations include:
  - Address decoding and data buffering.
  - Connecting other bus masters to the local bus.
  - Initializing the 80286.
  - Detailed local bus timing.
  - Physical design considerations including layout, packaging, power and ground connections.

- Finally, the last section of this chapter introduces the iLBX™ bus, a high-performance local bus standard to allow the modular expansion of the 80286 local bus onto multiple boards.

INTRODUCTION TO THE 80286 CENTRAL PROCESSING UNIT

The 80286 Central Processing Unit (CPU) is an advanced, high-performance 16-bit microprocessor that is optimized for use in multiple-user and multi-tasking systems. The 80286 has built-in memory management and protection capabilities which permit operating system and task isolation as well as program and data isolation within tasks. In addition, a highly-efficient pipeline architecture in both the CPU itself and in the local bus protocols serves to maximize 80286 system throughput and performance, while minimizing the impact on bus- and memory-speed requirements.

Processor Architecture

As shown in Figure 3-1, the pipelined 80286 architecture consists of four independent processing units; these four units operate in parallel to maximize CPU performance.

THE BUS UNIT

The Bus Unit (BU) performs all bus operations for the CPU, generating the address, data, and command signals required to access external memory and I/O. The Bus Unit also controls the interface to processor extensions and other local bus masters. Most of the local bus signals interface directly to the BU.

When not performing other bus duties, the Bus Unit "looks ahead" and pre-fetches instructions from memory. When prefetching, the Bus Unit assumes that program execution proceeds sequentially; that is, the next instruction follows the preceding one in memory. When the prefetcher reaches the limit of the code segment, it stops prefetching instructions. If a program transfer causes execution to continue from a new program location, the Bus Unit resets the queue and immediately begins fetching instructions from the new program location.

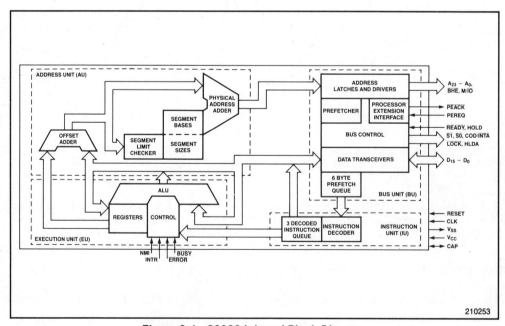

Figure 3-1. 80286 Internal Block Diagram

The Bus Unit stores these instructions in a 6-byte prefetch queue to be used later by the Instruction Unit. By prefetching instructions, the BU eliminates the idle time that can occur when the CPU must wait for the next sequential instruction to be fetched from memory.

THE INSTRUCTION UNIT

The Instruction Unit (IU) receives instructions from the prefetch queue, decodes them, and places these fully-decoded instructions into a 3-deep instruction queue for use by the Execution Unit.

THE EXECUTION UNIT

Decoded instructions from the Instruction Unit are fetched by the Execution Unit (EU) and executed. The EU uses the Bus Unit to perform data transfers to or from memory and I/O.

THE ADDRESS UNIT

The Address Unit (AU) provides the memory management and protection services for the CPU and translates logical addresses into physical addresses for use by the Bus Unit. A register cache in the AU contains the information used to perform the various memory translation and protection checks for each bus cycle.

THE EFFECTS OF PIPELINING

The four 80286 processing units operate independently and in parallel with one another, overlapping instruction fetches, decoding, and execution to maximize processor throughput and bus utilization. Figure 3-2 shows how this pipelined architecture results in substantially increased performance relative to a processor that fetches and executes instructions sequentially.

Operating Modes

The 80286 processor operates in one of two modes: 8086 Real-Address mode, and Protected Virtual-Address mode. In both modes, the 80286 executes a superset of the 8086 instruction set.

In 8086 Real-Address mode, the 80286 addresses up to one megabyte of address space using a twenty-bit physical address. In Protected Virtual-Address mode, programs executing on the 80286 can address up to a gigabyte of virtual address space, which the 80286 automatically maps into 16 megabytes of physical address space using a twenty-four-bit physical address.

From a hardware standpoint, these two operating modes differ only in that the upper four address lines (A_{23} through A_{20}) must be ignored when the 80286 is operating in Real-Address mode, and must be decoded along with the other address lines when the 80286 is operating in Protected Virtual-Address mode.

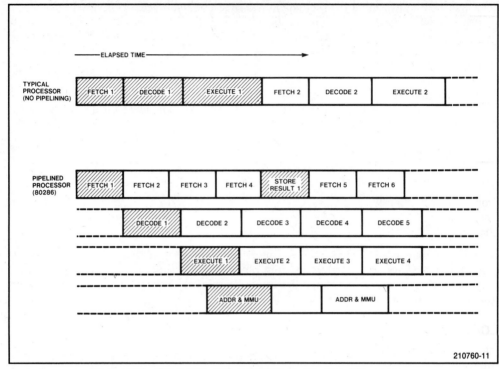

Figure 3-2. Operation of Sequential vs. Pipelined Processors

The 80286 Bus Interface

The 80286 CPU connects to external memory, I/O, and other devices using a parallel bus interface. This bus interface consists of a 24-bit address bus, a separate 16-bit data bus, and a number of control and status lines to control the transfer of information across the bus. Taken together, and with additional control signals derived from this basic set, these address, data, and control signals form the basis for the 80286 local bus.

Four status signals from the 80286 are used to control the operation of the local bus: the $COD/\overline{INTA}$, $M/\overline{IO}$, $\overline{S1}$, and $\overline{S0}$ signals. These signals are not latched and are only valid through the first half of each bus cycle. Table 3-1 shows the decoding of these status lines to identify the current bus cycle. Status combinations not shown in the table are reserved and will not be encountered in normal operation.

Additional control signals, along with on-chip arbitration logic, allow the 80286 to support processor extensions and other local bus masters. These signals for "handshaking" with other bus masters are controlled by the 80286 Bus Unit. Standard HOLD, HLDA protocol is used for other bus masters, while special processor extension request and acknowledge signals are used to support processor extensions.

An $\overline{ERROR}$ signal from a processor extension inputs directly into the 80286 Execution Unit as do the maskable (INTR) and non-maskable (NMI) interrupt signals. The $\overline{BUSY}$ signal

Table 3-1. 80286 Bus Cycle Status Decoding

$\overline{S1}$	$\overline{S0}$	COD/$\overline{INTA}$	M/$\overline{IO}$	Bus Cycle Initiated
L	L	L	L	Interrupt Acknowledge
L	L	L	H	If A1 = 1 then Halt; else Shutdown
L	H	L	H	Memory Data Read
L	H	H	L	I/O Data Read
L	H	H	H	Memory Instruction Read
H	L	L	H	Memory Data Write
H	L	H	L	I/O Data Write

from a processor extension indicates the processor extension status to the 80286. The RESET and CLK signals affect the 80286 processor as a whole; these signals do not interface with the device through a specific processing unit.

The following sections describe the 80286 local bus interface in greater detail. First, an overview of the 80286 local bus is given, explaining the relevant concepts and relationships that are involved. This general description is followed by a discussion of specific issues that must be considered when designing an 80286 system.

LOCAL BUS OVERVIEW

The 80286 local bus connects memory and I/O resources to the 80286 processor, using 24 separate address lines, 16 data lines, and a number of status and control signals. Together, these address, data, and control signals allow the 80286 processor to fetch and execute instructions, to manipulate information from both memory and I/O devices, and to respond to interrupts, processor extension requests, and requests from other bus masters.

In many respects, the principles and protocols used in the 80286 local bus are similar to those commonly used in other parallel bus systems. In some respects, however, the 80286 local bus is a high-performance bus that differs somewhat from typical bus patterns. The following sections describe how the 80286 local bus is organized and how it operates to assure the efficient transmission of information between all of the devices on the bus.

Organization of Physical Memory and I/O

The principal use of the local bus is to connect the 80286 processor to memory and I/O devices. When operating in Real-Address mode, the 80286 can directly address up to 1 megabyte of physical memory, while in Protected Virtual-Address mode, the 80286 can address up to 16 megabytes of physical memory. These two operating modes of the 80286 have already been described. Except for the differences in memory size, the organization of memory and I/O is identical for both Real-Address mode and Protected Virtual-Address mode.

In addition to its memory-addressing capabilities, the 80286 can also directly address up to 65,536 8-bit I/O ports or up to 32,768 16-bit I/O ports mapped into a separate I/O address space, in either operating mode. Figure 3-3 illustrates these separate memory and I/O address spaces.

MEMORY ORGANIZATION

The programmer views the memory address space of the 80286 as a sequence of (8-bit) bytes in which any byte may contain an 8-bit data element and any two consecutive bytes may contain a 16-bit (word) data element. Both byte and word information can be assigned to either even or odd addresses—there is no constraint on word boundaries.

As shown in Figure 3-4, the address space is physically implemented on a 16-bit data bus by dividing the address space into two banks of up to 512K bytes (in Real-Address mode)

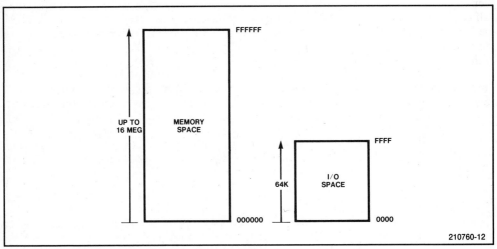

Figure 3-3. Separate Memory and I/O Spaces

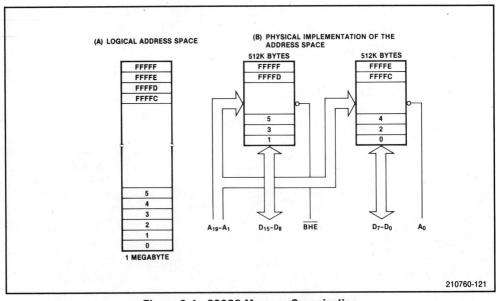

Figure 3-4. 80286 Memory Organization

or 8 Mbytes (in Protected mode). The lower half of the data bus (D7-D0) is connected to one bank of memory, and accesses even-addressed bytes (A0=0). The upper half of the data bus (D15-D8) connects to the other bank and contains odd-addressed bytes (A0=1). Address line A0 and Bus High Enable ($\overline{BHE}$) enable the appropriate banks of memory, while the remaining address lines select a specific byte within each bank. (When operating in Real-Address mode, address lines A23-A20 should be ignored, and address lines A19-A1 select the specific byte.)

To perform byte transfers to even addresses (Figure 3-5A), the CPU transfers information over the lower half of the data bus (D7-D0). A0 enables the bank connected to the lower half of the data bus to participate in the transfer. Bus High Enable ($\overline{BHE}$ active low), disables the bank on the upper half of the data bus from participating in the transfer. Disabling the upper bank is necessary to prevent a write operation to the lower bank from destroying data in the upper bank. During the transfer, the upper half of the data bus is undefined.

To perform byte transfers to odd addresses (Figure 3-5B), the CPU transfers information over the upper half of the data bus (D15-D8) while $\overline{BHE}$ (active low) enables the upper bank, and A0 disables the lower bank. The lower half of the data bus is undefined.

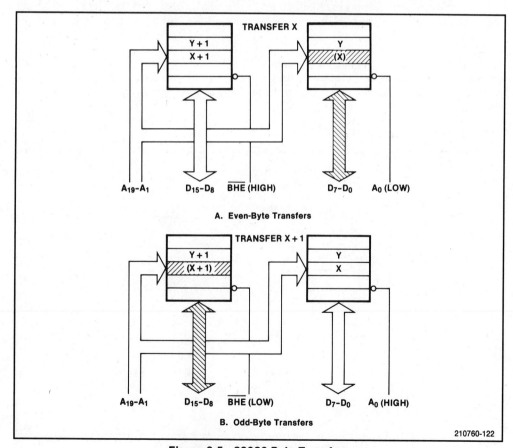

Figure 3-5. 80286 Byte Transfers

The 80286 automatically routes bytes between the appropriate half of the data bus and the upper or lower half of its internal data path, as well as activating $\overline{\text{BHE}}$ or A0 accordingly. The loading of a data byte from an odd-addressed memory location into the CL register (lower half of the CX register) illustrates this routing. The data is transferred into the 80286 over the upper half of the data bus, then automatically redirected to the lower half of the 80286 internal data path and stored into the CL register. This automatic routing ability also allows byte-I/O transfers between the AL register and 8-bit I/O devices that are connected to either half of the 16-bit data bus.

To access even-addressed 16-bit words (two consecutive bytes with the least significant byte at an even byte address), A0 (low) and $\overline{\text{BHE}}$ (low) enable both banks simultaneously, while the remaining address lines select the appropriate byte from each bank. Figure 3-6 illustrates this operation.

To access 16-bit word data beginning at an odd address, the 80286 automatically performs two byte accesses. As shown in Figure 3-7, the least significant byte addressed by the address lines is first transferred over the upper half of the data bus. The address is then incremented and a second byte transfer is executed, this time over the lower half of the data bus. This two-byte transfer sequence is executed automatically whenever a word transfer is performed to an odd address, with the CPU automatically routing the two bytes onto the appropriate halves of the data bus.

When the Bus Unit is prefetching instructions, however, the Bus Unit always performs word fetches on even boundaries. If the program transfers control to an odd address, the Bus Unit automatically performs a word fetch from the next-lower word-boundary, ignoring the lower byte of this first instruction fetch.

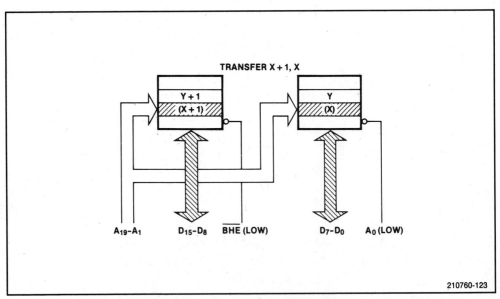

Figure 3-6. Even-Addressed Word Transfer

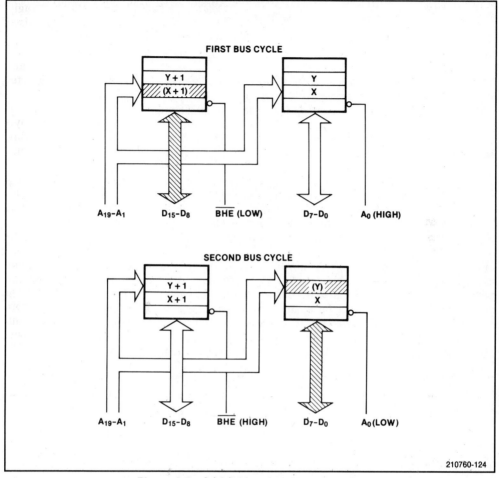

Figure 3-7. Odd-Addressed Word Transfer

I/O ORGANIZATION

The 80286 is capable of interfacing with 8-bit and 16-bit I/O devices that are mapped into a separate 64K I/O space (memory-mapped I/O is also supported, and is described in Chapter Six). The 80286 I/O space is organized as 65,536 8-bit ports or 32,768 16-bit ports or some combination of the two.

For 8-bit I/O devices, ports on the upper half of the data bus, have odd I/O addresses, while ports on the lower half of the data bus have even I/O addresses. To access an 8-bit I/O device, A0 and $\overline{\text{BHE}}$ select the appropriate half of the data bus, and address lines A15-A1 select one of the 32K I/O addresses. During any I/O transfer, address lines A23-A20 are always low.

Sixteen-bit I/O devices always have even addresses to permit the CPU to select and access the entire 16-bit port in a single operation. To access a 16-bit I/O device, address lines

A15-A1 select the particular I/O address, while A0 and $\overline{\text{BHE}}$ condition the chip select to ensure that a 16-bit transfer is being performed.

Interrupt Organization

The 80286 recognizes a variety of both hardware-generated and software-generated interrupts that alter the programmed execution of the 80286. Hardware-generated interrupts occur in response to an active input on one of the two 80286 interrupt request pins. Software-generated interrupts occur due to an $\overline{\text{INT}}$ instruction or one of several possible instruction exceptions. Software-generated interrupts are described in the *80286 Programmer's Reference Manual* (Order Number 210498); they are not described here.

The two hardware interrupt request inputs to the 80286 consist of a non-maskable interrupt request (NMI), and a maskable interrupt request (INTR). The maskable interrupt request INTR can be "masked" or ignored by the 80286 under software control, while a non-maskable interrupt request NMI will always invoke a response from the 80286 unless a previous NMI interrupt has occurred and is being serviced.

When the 80286 encounters an interrupt of any kind, it automatically transfers program execution to one of 256 possible interrupt service routines. A table stored in memory contains pointers defining the proper interrupt service routine for each interrupt. Once the 80286 has determined the type or vector for a particular interrupt (an index into the table corresponding to the appropriate service routine), the servicing of software- or hardware-interrupts proceeds identically. Figure 3-8 shows the structure of this interrupt descriptor table for an 80286 operating in both Real-Address mode and in Protected Virtual-Address mode.

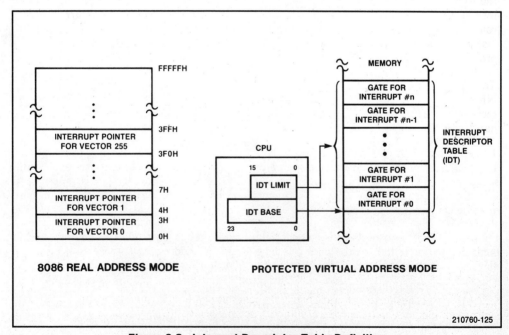

Figure 3-8. Interrupt Descriptor Table Definition

Table 3-2. Processing Order for Simultaneous Interrupts

Processing Order	Interrupt Source
1 (first)	Processor Exception
2	Single Step
3	NMI (Non-Maskable Interrupt Request)
4	Processor Extension Segment Overrun
5	INTR (Maskable Interrupt Request)
6 (last)	INT Instruction

INTERRUPT PRIORITIES

When an interrupt or exception occurs, the 80286 automatically transfers program control to the appropriate interrupt service routine, even if the 80286 is in the middle of processing a previous interrupt. In this manner, the last interrupt processed is the first one serviced.

The single exception to this rule is the 80286 treatment of the INTR interrupt input. When operating in Real-Address mode, any interrupt or exception automatically causes the 80286 to mask any INTR requests for the duration of the interrupt service routine until the occurrence of an IRET instruction or until the service routine explicitly enables INTR interrupts. When the 80286 is operating in Protected mode, the individual task gate for each interrupt service routine specifies whether INTR interrupts are to be masked for the duration of the interrupt service routine.

In the case of simultaneous interrupt or exception requests, the interrupts are processed in the fixed order shown in Table 3-2. Interrupt processing involves saving the flags and the return address, and setting CS:IP to point to the first instruction of the interrupt service routine. If other interrupt requests remain pending, they are processed before the first instruction of the current interrupt handler is executed. In this way, the last interrupt processed is the first one serviced.

To illustrate the information contained in the table, consider what occurs when both an NMI (non-maskable interrupt) request and an INTR (maskable interrupt) request are received simultaneously by an 80286 operating in Real-Address mode. The interrupts are handled in the following order:

1. The NMI interrupt will be processed first, saving the current status and pointing to the first instruction of the NMI service routine.

2. The INTR interrupt request will be masked, since the NMI interrupt causes the 80286 to mask INTR interrupts.

3. If no other exceptions occur, the NMI interrupt service routine will be executed until it is completed.

4. After the NMI service routine has completed, an IRET instruction will be executed to exit from the service routine. This IRET instruction re-enables INTR interrupts.

5. If the INTR interrupt request line is still active, the processor will then respond to the interrupt with two interrupt-acknowledge bus cycles, and then proceed to execute the appropriate interrupt service routine. Any subsequent NMI interrupts that occur during the execution of this service routine will immediately be serviced before execution of the INTR service routine continues.

6. Finally, after all interrupts have been serviced, program control will revert to the original interrupted program.

The following sections describe the 80286 system's different responses to the two hardware-generated interrupt requests, NMI and INTR.

NON-MASKABLE INTERRUPT REQUEST (NMI)

The non-maskable interrupt request (NMI) input to the 80286 is edge-triggered (on a low-to-high transition) and is generally used to signal the CPU of a "catastrophic" event such as the imminent loss of power, memory error, or bus-parity error.

Interrupt requests arriving on the NMI pin are latched by the CPU and cannot be disabled. The NMI input is asynchronous and, in order to ensure that it is recognized, is required to have been low for four system clock cycles before the transition and to remain high for a minimum of four additional clock cycles. To guarantee that the NMI input is recognized on a particular clock transition, the required set-up time for NMI is shown in Figure 3-9.

The NMI is recognized only on an instruction boundary in the 80286 execution unit and only after meeting the conditions previously described. Once recognized, the processor must finish executing the current instruction before it can start execution of the interrupt. The NMI automatically causes the 80286 to transfer control to the service routine corresponding to interrupt type 2; this interrupt vector is internally supplied and generates no external interrupt acknowledge sequence.

The total time required to service an NMI interrupt is determined by several factors. The total processing time includes:

• The time the interrupt was waiting to be recognized. While servicing one NMI, the 80286 will not acknowledge another NMI until an IRET instruction is executed.

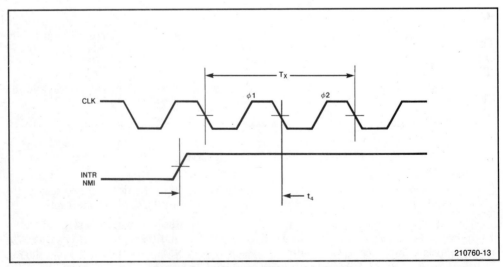

210760-13

Figure 3-9. NMI and INTR Input Timing

- Additional time allowed for the completion of the instruction currently being executed by the 80286. These instructions could be IRET, MUL, or task-switch instructions.
- Time required for saving the CS, IP, and Flags registers.
- Any time required by the interrupt service routine to save the contents of additional registers not automatically saved by the 80286.

Since the NMI interrupt will be recognized only on an instruction boundary, the time required for the CPU to recognize the request (interrupt latency) depends on how many clock periods remain in the execution of the current instruction.

On the average, the longest latency can occur if the interrupt request arrives while task-switch is being executed in Protected mode. Other instructions resulting in long interrupt latencies are multiplications and divisions. In the case of an instruction that loads the Stack Segment register, the interrupt will not be recognized until after the following instruction is executed, to allow loading of the entire stack pointer without intervening interrupts.

While executing an NMI service routine, the 80286 will not service additional NMI interrupts or processor extension segment-overrun interrupts until an interrupt return (IRET) instruction is executed or the CPU is reset. If an NMI interrupt request occurs while the 80286 is servicing a prior NMI request, the occurrence of the second NMI request will be saved and the request will be serviced after the CPU executes an IRET instruction.

During the NMI service routine, an 80286 operating in Real-Address mode automatically masks any INTR interrupt requests. In Protected mode, the NMI service routine is entered through either an interrupt gate or a task gate. The new task context may be defined with INTR interrupts either enabled or disabled. To re-enable INTR interrupts during the NMI service routine, the 80286 Interrupt (IF) flag can be set true. In any case, the IF flag is automatically restored to its original state when the service routine is completed (when the Flags register is restored following the first IRET instruction).

MASKABLE INTERRUPT REQUEST (INTR)

The INTR (Interrupt Request) line allows external devices to interrupt 80286 program execution. INTR is usually driven by an Intel 8259A Programmable Interrupt Controller (PIC), which, in turn, is connected to devices that require interrupt servicing.

The 8259A is a very flexible device that is controlled by software commands from the 80286 (the 8259A PIC appears to the CPU as a set of I/O ports). Its main job is to accept interrupt requests from devices connected to it, to determine which request has the highest priority, and then activate the INTR line to interrupt the CPU and supply an appropriate interrupt vector.

Figure 3-10 shows a block diagram of a multiple 8259A subsystem that uses a master interrupt controller driven by slave interrupt controllers. Chapter Five contains detailed information on interfacing the 8259A to an 80286 system.

The INTR input to the 80286 is level-sensitive and can be asynchronous to the system clock. INTR must be active for at least two processor clock cycles before the current instruction ends in order to interrupt before the next instruction begins. When the 80286's Interrupt

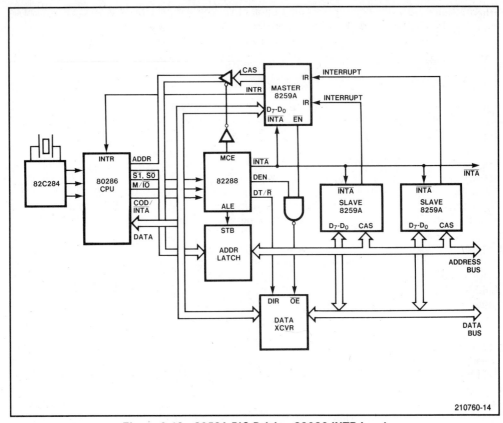

Figure 3-10. 8259A PIC Driving 80286 INTR Input

Flag (IF) is enabled and the INTR signal is driven active high, the 80286 will acknowledge the interrupt on the next instruction boundary. To guarantee recognition on a particular clock cycle, INTR must be set-up a minimum of 20 ns before the start of the clock cycle. INTR should remain active until the first INTA bus cycle to guarantee that the CPU responds to the interrupt. Figure 3-9 shows the required timing of the INTR input.

The 80286 acknowledges an INTR interrupt request by executing two interrupt-acknowledge (INTA) bus cycles (INTA bus cycles are described in a later section). The first INTA cycle signals all 8259As that the interrupt request has been honored. During the second INTA cycle, the 8259A with the highest-priority interrupt pending responds by placing a byte containing the interrupt type (0-255) onto the data bus to be read by the 80286. This interrupt type must have been previously programmed into the 8259A to correspond to the service routine for the particular device requesting service.

Following the second INTA cycle, the 80286 automatically transfers control to the interrupt service routine corresponding to that particular interrupt.

During the interrupt-acknowledge cycles, any bus hold requests arriving via the 80286 HOLD line are not honored until the interrupt-acknowledge cycles have been completed. In addition, the CPU activates its LOCK signal during the first of these cycles to prevent other bus masters from taking control of the bus.

As for the NMI interrupt, the total time required to service an INTR interrupt is determined by the type of instructions used and how long interrupts are disabled. The total servicing time is comprised of the same elements as described for the NMI interrupt.

Since INTR requests will be acknowledged only by the 80286 on an instruction boundary, the time required for the CPU to recognize the request (interrupt latency) depends on how many clock periods remain in the execution of the current instruction.

The same factors affecting interrupt latency for the NMI interrupt affect the latency of the INTR interrupt request. Specific instructions resulting in long interrupt latencies are multiplications, divisions, task switches in Protected mode, or instructions that load the Stack Segment register, as described for the NMI interrupt.

Pipelined Address Timing

The 80286 local bus differs most from a typical microprocessor bus in its use of pipelined address timing. To achieve high bus throughput, the pipelined address timing used by the 80286 allows overlapped bus cycles when accessing memory and I/O. The resulting increase in bus throughput is achieved without requiring a proportional increase in memory speed.

This pipelined timing differs from that of a typical microprocessor bus cycle. During transfers for typical processors, an address is transmitted at the start of the bus cycle and held valid during the entire cycle.

Using pipelined timing, the 80286 places the address for the next memory or I/O operation on the bus even before the previous bus operation has completed. This overlapping (pipelining) of successive bus operations permits the maximum address setup time before data is required by the CPU or memory.

Figure 3-11 illustrates how this address pipelining results in improved bus throughput, even though the address and data setup times for individual memory operations are identical for the two examples shown. For an 8-MHz 80286 system executing word transfers with zero wait states, data can be transferred at the rate of 8 Megabytes per second while still allowing individual address access times of 242 ns.

In the following sections, the complete 80286 bus cycle is described, and the implementation of pipelined timing is shown in greater detail. In a later section of this chapter, specific design considerations and components are described for building high-performance 80286 systems that take advantage of this pipelined address timing.

80286 Local Bus States

The 80286 CPU uses a double-frequency system clock (CLK) to control bus timing. The CPU internally divides the system CLK by two to produce the internal processor clock, which determines the local bus state. Each processor clock cycle is composed of two system CLK cycles, called Phase 1 and Phase 2. The 82C284 Clock Generator produces a peripheral clock output (PCLK) that identifies the phase of the internal processor clock. Figure 3-12 shows the relationship between the system CLK and the peripheral clock (PCLK).

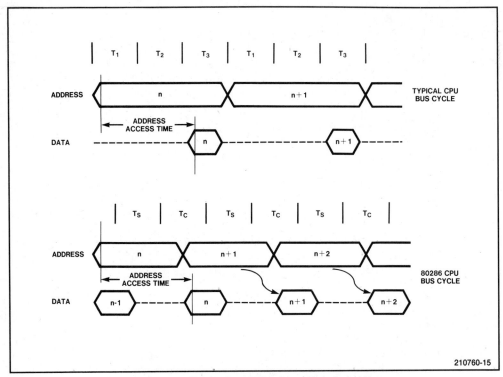

Figure 3-11. Typical and Pipelined Bus Operations

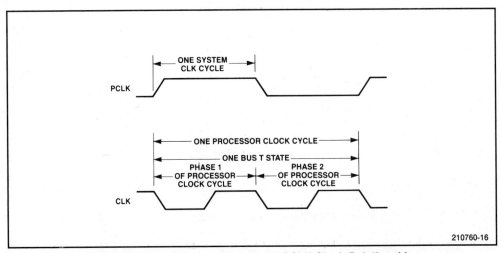

Figure 3-12. System and Peripheral/PCLK Clock Relationships

The 80286 local bus has three basic states: Idle (T_i), Send-Status (T_s), and Perform-Command (T_c). The 80286 CPU also has a fourth state called Hold (T_h). A T_h state indicates that the 80286 has surrendered control of the local bus to another bus master in response to a HOLD request. Each bus state is one processor clock long. Figure 3-13 shows the 80286 CPU states and the allowed transitions.

The Idle (T_i) state indicates that no data transfers are in progress. T_i states typically occur during execution of an instruction that does not require a bus cycle (assuming instruction and pre-fetch queues are full). A T_i state will also occur before the 80286 relinquishes control of the bus to another bus master, entering the T_h (Hold) state.

T_s is the first active state after T_i. T_s is signalled by either status line $\overline{S1}$ or $\overline{S0}$ from the 80286 going low ($\overline{S1}$ or $\overline{S0}$ going low also identifies Phase 1 of the processor clock). During T_s, the command encoding and data (for a write operation) are available on the 80286 output pins. If the address is not already valid prior to entering the T_s state, the address also becomes valid. The 82288 bus controller decodes the 80286 status signals to generate read/write commands and local transceiver-control signals.

After T_s, the perform command (T_c) state is entered. Memory or I/O devices are expected to respond to the bus operation during T_c, either transferring read data to the CPU or accepting write data. The $\overline{READY}$ input to the 80286 either terminates the bus cycle or causes the T_c state to be repeated. T_c states may be repeated as many times as necessary to assure sufficient time for the memory or I/O device to respond.

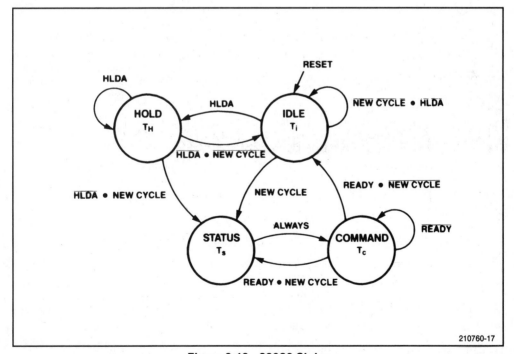

Figure 3-13. 80286 States

Following a T_c state, the bus may enter immediately into a T_s state, beginning another bus operation, or may enter the T_i (Idle) state. This ability to immediately execute back-to-back bus operations leads to high bus utilization and contributes to the 80286's high performance.

If another bus master requests and is granted control of the local bus, the 80286 will enter the T_h (Hold) state. If the 80286 is in the T_c state when the HOLD request is received, the bus will pass through one T_i (Idle) state before the 80286 grants control to the requesting bus master. During Hold (T_h), the 80286 floats all address, data, and status output pins, allowing the requesting bus master to control the local bus. The 80286 HLDA output signal acknowledges the HOLD request and indicates that the CPU has entered the T_h state.

80286 Bus Operations

The 80286 Bus Unit executes bus operations whenever the Execution Unit requires a bus operation as part of an instruction execution, whenever a processor extension requests a bus operation, or when sufficient room becomes available in the instruction pre-fetch queue. When no bus operations are in progress or requested, the local bus remains in the idle state.

Each local bus operation consists of one or more bus cycles. Each bus cycle consists of one Send-Status (T_s) state followed by one or more Perform-Command (T_c) states. At maximum speed, the local bus alternates between the T_s and T_c states, transferring one word of information every two processor clock cycles.

The 80286 local bus supports six types of bus operations: memory read, memory write, I/O read, I/O write, interrupt-acknowledge, and halt/shutdown operations. The signal timing during a bus cycle differs between read, write, interrupt-acknowledge, and halt/shutdown cycles. Bus timing is also dependent on the configuration of the bus controller, memory and I/O speed, and in the case of back-to-back bus cycles, the type of cycle previously performed. The following paragraphs describe what occurs during each of these bus cycles performed by the 80286 CPU.

READ CYCLES

Figure 3-14 shows the timing for a single read cycle without command delays or wait states; this cycle may be preceded and succeeded by any type of bus cycle, including other read cycles, write cycles, or bus idle (T_i) states. The sequence of signals that constitute a read cycle are as follows:

A. At the start of phase 2 of the bus state preceding the read cycle, the CPU transmits the memory or I/O address and drives the M/$\overline{IO}$ and COD/$\overline{INTA}$ signals to indicate a memory or I/O bus cycle. Address-decode logic begins operation.

B. At the start of phase 1 of the T_s state, the CPU drives status lines $\overline{S1}$ high and $\overline{S0}$ low to indicate that the cycle is read. The CPU also drives $\overline{BHE}$ high or low to indicate whether or not the upper half of the data bus will be used (D15-D8). Note that the $\overline{BHE}$ timing is slightly different than address timing.

C. Phase 2 of T_s begins with ALE from the bus controller going high to capture the address into any external address latches.

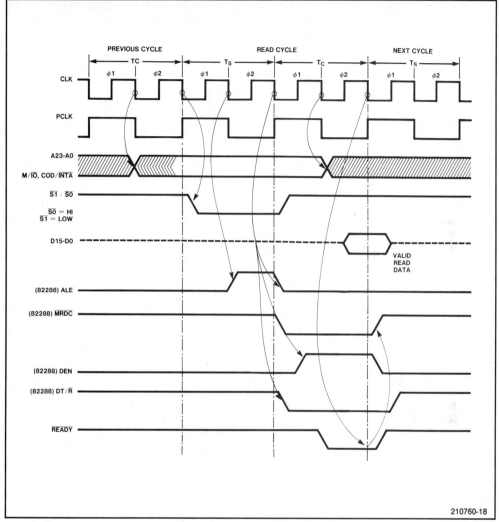

Figure 3-14. 80286 Read Cycle

D. At the start of the first T_c state, ALE goes low to latch the address and chip selects for the remainder of the bus cycle. The bus controller drives $DT/\overline{R}$ and $\overline{MRDC}$ low to condition the direction of the data transceivers and enable the memory or I/O location to be read. DEN from the bus controller then goes active (high) to enable the data transceivers. Status ($\overline{S1}$ or $\overline{S0}$) is removed in preparation for the next cycle.

E. At the start of Phase 2 of T_c, the address, $M/\overline{IO}$, and $COD/\overline{INTA}$ lines change to reflect the following bus operation (or enter the tri-state OFF condition if the following bus state is an INTA cycle or a T_i state before bus-hold acknowledge).

F. At the end of T_c, the $\overline{READY}$ signal is sampled. If $\overline{READY}$ is low, the input data is assumed to be valid at the CPU data pins. The CPU reads the data from the bus and the bus controller deactivates $\overline{\text{MRDC}}$ and DEN, returning DT/$\overline{\text{R}}$ to its normal active-high state. If $\overline{\text{READY}}$ is sampled high, additional T_c states will be executed until $\overline{\text{READY}}$ is sampled low.

WRITE CYCLES

Figure 3-15 shows the timing for a single write cycle without command delays or wait states; the timing of this write cycle is very much the same as for the read cycle just described, although the control signalling is of course different. The sequence of signals that constitute a write cycle are as follows:

A. As in the case of read cycles, the CPU drives the address, M/$\overline{\text{IO}}$, and COD/$\overline{\text{INTA}}$ signals at the start of phase 2 of the state preceding the bus cycle. Address decode logic begins operating.

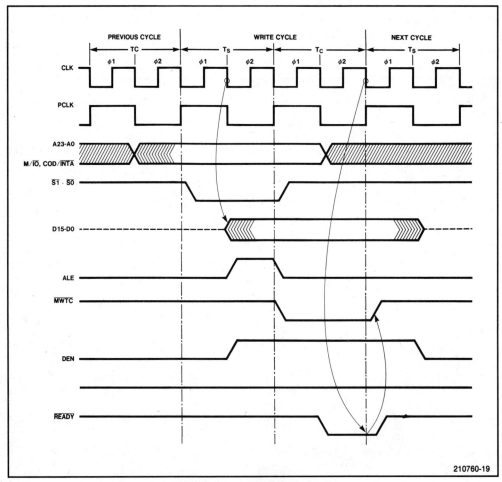

Figure 3-15. 80286 Write Cycle

B. At the start of T_s, the CPU drives $\overline{S1}$ low and $\overline{S0}$ high to indicate a write cycle. $\overline{BHE}$ is driven high or low to enable or disable the high byte of the data bus (D15-D0).

C. At the start of phase 2 of T_s, the CPU outputs the data to be written to memory or I/O while the bus controller drives ALE and DEN high to capture the address in external address latches and to enable the data transceivers. $DT/\overline{R}$ is normally conditioned to transmit write data through the transceivers; $DT/\overline{R}$ does not change at this time.

D. At the start of the first T_c, the CPU removes its status signals. The bus controller drives MWTC and ALE low to enable a memory or I/O write and to latch the address and chip selects for the rest of the bus cycle.

E. At the start of Phase 2 of T_c, the address, $M/\overline{IO}$, and $COD/\overline{INTA}$ lines change to reflect the following bus operation (or enter the tri-state OFF condition if the following bus state is an INTA cycle or a T_i state before bus-hold acknowledge).

F. At the end of T_c, the $\overline{READY}$ input is sampled. If $\overline{READY}$ is low, the bus controller drives MWTC high to latch data into the selected memory or I/O device. If $\overline{READY}$ is sampled high, additional T_c states are executed until $\overline{READY}$ is sampled low.

G. At the start of Phase 2 of the following T_s or T_i bus state, the DEN signal is disabled, and the data bus may change to reflect either new write data or enter the tri-state OFF condition. In this way, write data is held active well into the following bus cycle to provide sufficient data-hold time following termination of the write command.

INTERRUPT-ACKNOWLEDGE CYCLES

Interrupt-acknowledge cycles are performed by the CPU in response to an external interrupt request asserted via the INTR input pin. After recognizing the external interrupt request, the CPU executes a sequence of two back-to-back interrupt-acknowledge ($\overline{INTA}$) cycles to input an 8-bit vector that identifies the interrupting source and directs the 80286 to an interrupt handling routine. Figure 3-16 shows the sequence of signals that constitute the interrupt-acknowledge sequence:

A. At the start of phase 2 of the state preceding the first interrupt-acknowledge cycle, the address lines enter the tri-state OFF condition and $M/\overline{IO}$ and $COD/\overline{INTA}$ are driven low to identify the coming interrupt-acknowledge cycle.

B. At the start of T_s, $\overline{LOCK}$ and status lines $\overline{S1}$ and $\overline{S0}$ are driven low. $\overline{LOCK}$ prevents another bus master in a multi-master system from gaining control of the bus between the two interrupt-acknowledge ($\overline{INTA}$) cycles.

C. At the start of Phase 2 of T_s, the bus controller drives MCE and ALE high. MCE (Master Cascade Enable) enables the master 8259A interrupt controller (in a system that uses multiple interrupt controllers) to drive the cascade address onto the local address bus for distribution to any slave interrupt controllers.

D. At the start of the first T_c, the CPU drives status lines $\overline{S1}$ and $\overline{S0}$ high. The bus controller drives $\overline{INTA}$, ALE, and $DT/\overline{R}$ low. This first INTA signal freezes the contents of the interrupt controller; ALE latches the cascade address onto the system address bus for use by the slave interrupt controllers; and $DT/\overline{R}$ places the data transceivers into the receiver mode (any data on the data bus is ignored during this first $\overline{INTA}$ cycle). The bus controller drives DEN high to enable the data transceivers.

E. Halfway through the first T_c state, the CPU removes the $M/\overline{IO}$ and $COD/\overline{INTA}$ signals while the bus controller drives MCE low (ALE has already fallen low to latch the cascade address onto the address bus). $\overline{READY}$ is high to force a second T_c state (two T_c states are required to meet the minimum 8259A $\overline{INTA}$ pulse width).

F. At the start of the second T_c state, the CPU drives $\overline{LOCK}$ high. If the system bus was used for the first $\overline{INTA}$ cycle, the 82289 Bus Arbiter will not relinquish the bus until the second $\overline{INTA}$ cycle is complete.

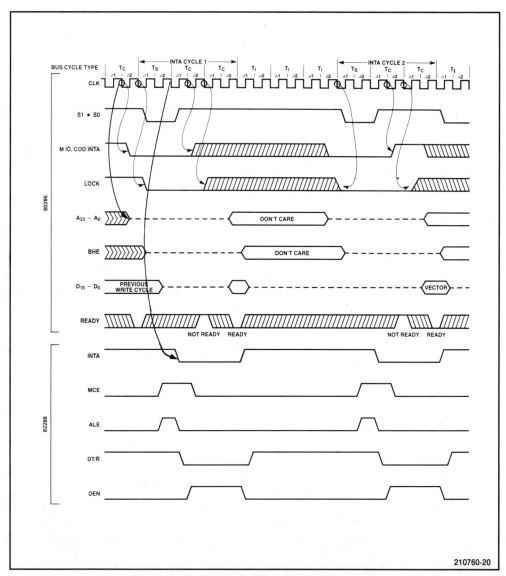

Figure 3-16. Interrupt-Acknowledge Sequence

G. $\overline{\text{READY}}$ going low at the start of phase 2 of T_c terminates the cycle at the end of T_c. The Bus Controller drives $\overline{\text{INTA}}$ and DT/$\overline{\text{R}}$ high and DEN low. The CPU drives the address pins out of TRI-STATE off during the second half of the second T_c.

H. Three idle states (T_i) are automatically inserted between the two $\overline{\text{INTA}}$ bus cycles to allow for the minimum 8259A $\overline{\text{INTA}}$-to-$\overline{\text{INTA}}$ time and CAS (Cascade Address) output delay.

I. In terms of signal timing, the second $\overline{\text{INTA}}$ cycle is almost identical to the first. $\overline{\text{LOCK}}$ remains high during the second cycle, and the interrupt vector is read from the lower half of the data bus at the end of the second T_c state. At least five idle states (T_i) are automatically inserted after the last T_c, which allows the 80286 to prepare for the rest of the interrupt cycle. The CPU does not start driving the bus until the second phase of the last T_i cycle.

HALT/SHUTDOWN CYCLES

The 80286 externally indicates halt and shutdown conditions as a bus operation. These two conditions occur due either to a HLT instruction or multiple protection exceptions while attempting to execute one instruction.

A halt or shutdown bus operation is signalled when $\overline{\text{S1}}$, $\overline{\text{S0}}$, and COD/$\overline{\text{INTA}}$ are low and M/$\overline{\text{IO}}$ is high. The address line A1 distinguishes between a halt or shutdown condition; A1 high indicates a halt condition, and A1 low indicates a shutdown condition. The 82288 does not issue ALE, nor is $\overline{\text{READY}}$ required to terminate a halt or shutdown bus operation.

During a halt condition, the 80286 may service processor extension requests (PEREQ) or HOLD requests. The 80286 will remain in the halt state until an NMI, RESET, processor extension segment overrun exception, or INTR interrupt (if interrupts are enabled) forces the processor out of halt.

During a shutdown condition, the 80286 may similarly service processor extension requests or HOLD requests, except that a processor extension segment overrun exception during shutdown will inhibit further servicing of processor extension requests. Only a non-maskable interrupt (NMI) or RESET can force the 80286 out of the shutdown condition.

80286 Bus Usage

The previous sections described the characteristics of read and write cycles that can occur on the 80286 local bus. These bus cycles are initiated by the 80286 Bus Unit in order to perform various functions. These functions include:

- prefetching instructions ahead of the current instruction that is executing
- transferring data required by an executing instruction
- transferring data for a processor extension through the processor extension data channel

The following sections describe the rules and conditions that determine which bus operation will be performed next by the 80286. These rules help to better explain the way in which the 80286 uses its local bus.

LOCAL BUS USAGE PRIORITIES

The 80286 local bus is shared between the 80286 internal Bus Unit and external HOLD requests. In the course of performing the three types of bus operations listed above, the 80286 Bus Unit also must contend with transactions that require more than one bus operation to complete. Table 3-3 shows the priorities followed by the 80286 Bus Unit in honoring simultaneous requests for the local bus.

PREFETCH OPERATIONS

The Bus Unit prefetches instructions when the local bus would otherwise be idle. When prefetching instructions, the BU obeys the following general rules:

- A prefetch bus cycle is requested when at least two bytes of the 6-byte prefetch queue are empty.
- Prefetches normally occur to the next consecutive address indicated by the Code Segment Instruction Pointer.
- The prefetcher normally performs word prefetches independent of the byte-alignment of the code segment base in physical memory.
- The prefetcher performs only a byte code-fetch operation for control transfers to an instruction beginning on an odd physical address.
- Prefetching stops whenever a control transfer or HLT instruction is decoded by the IU and placed into the instruction queue.
- In Real-Address mode, the prefetcher may fetch up to six bytes beyond the end of a code segment. In Protected Virtual Address mode, no prefetching occurs beyond the end of a code segment.

Table 3-3. Local Bus Usage Priorities

Priority	Operations Requesting the Local Bus
1 (Highest)	Any data transfer that asserts $\overline{LOCK}$ either explicitly (via the $\overline{LOCK}$ instruction prefix) or implicitly (segment descriptor access, interrupt-acknowledge sequences, or an XCHG with memory).
2	The second of the two byte-transfers required to transfer a word operand at an odd physical address, or the second transfer required to perform a processor extension data channel transfer.
3	A request for the local bus via the HOLD input.
4	A processor extension data channel transfer via the PEREQ input.
5	A data transfer requested by the EU as part of an instruction.
6 (Lowest)	An instruction prefetch performed by the BU. The EU will inhibit prefetching two processor clocks in advance of any data transfers to minimize waiting by the EU for a prefetch to complete.

- In Protected mode, the prefetcher will never cause a segment-overrun exception. The prefetcher stops at the last physical word in the code segment. Exception 13 will occur if the program attempts to execute beyond the last full instruction in the code segment.

- If the last byte of a code segment appears on an even physical memory address, the prefetcher will read the next physical byte of memory (perform a word code fetch). The value of the additional byte is ignored and any attempt to execute it causes exception 13.

- Instruction prefetch operations can occur back-to-back with other prefetches or other bus cycles, with no idle clocks on the bus.

DATA OPERATIONS

The Bus Unit performs data operations when the Execution Unit (EU) needs to read or write data to main memory or I/O. When performing data operations, the Bus Unit obeys the following general rules:

- Since the EU must wait on data reads, data operations have priority over prefetch operations when both data and prefetch operations are ready to begin. A data operation, however, will not interrupt a prefetch operation that has already started.

- If the bus is currently in use when the EU requests a write cycle, the address and data for the write cycle are stored by the Bus Unit in temporary registers until the current bus cycle completes. This allows the EU to begin executing the next instruction without having to wait for a prefetch or other bus operation to finish.

- Only one write operation can be buffered by the Bus Unit. If the EU requests a write cycle while these temporary buffers are full, the EU must wait for the buffers to empty before it can continue executing instructions.

- Any combination of data read and write operations can occur back-to-back with other bus operations, with no idle bus cycles. The string move or I/O instructions in particular transfer data with no idle states on the bus.

DATA CHANNEL TRANSFERS

The 80286 Bus Unit contains a processor extension data channel that supports data transfers between memory and processor extensions like the 80287 Numeric Processor Extension. Transfers are requested by the processor extension and performed by the CPU Bus Unit. Chapter Six describes the 80286 processor extension interface in more detail. The following guidelines govern data channel activity:

- Data channel transfers have priority over prefetch and execution data cycles if all three operations are requested at the same time.

- The transfers require at least two bus cycles to complete. For example, to transfer a word operand to the 80287, the CPU performs the first cycle to read the operand from memory. A second transfer writes the word to the 80287.

- The bus timing of these transfers is the same as any other bus read or write cycle.

- Data channel transfers are treated as indivisable operations by the 80286. The Bus Unit will not execute a data or prefetch operation until a data channel word transfer between memory and the 80287 is complete.

- Data channel transfers to or from the 80287 are always word transfers. No single-byte transfers are required by the 80287, nor are they performed by the 80286.

- Word transfers to an odd-addressed memory location are performed as two byte-transfers. This results in three bus cycles (one word-transfer from the processor extension, and two byte-transfers to memory).

BUS UTILIZATION

Many features of the 80286 contribute to a high utilization of the 80286 local bus. These features include:

- partitioning of CPU functions into individual processing units
- the Bus Unit guidelines for prefetch cycles, data cycles, and data channel transfers
- temporary Bus Unit address and data registers
- pipelined timing to allow back-to-back and overlapped bus operations

Depending on the particular program that is being executed and the speed of local memory, these architectural features can result in very high local bus utilization and bus efficiency. For typical types of software, about 60% to 70% of all bus operations will be instruction prefetches, and about 75%-85% of all bus clocks will be utilized by the CPU (assuming that memory responds with zero wait-states). If memories having one or more wait states are used, better than 90% of all available bus clocks will be used by the CPU. Long sequences of back-to-back bus operations are possible without the bus being idle, especially if a program involves string operations.

Designers can best take advantage of the high local bus throughput offered by pipelined timing and other features of the 80286 when interfacing the 80286 to local memory. The software tasks and data that are requested most often can reside in local memory where they can be quickly accessed. Less-used tasks and data can reside in remote memory on a public system bus, where access delays may be incurred due to bus arbitration and additional address and data buffers. Chapter Four discusses the performance tradeoffs of interfacing to fast vs. slow memories.

Bus Interface Components

The job of implementing an 80286 local bus around an 80286 CPU is made relatively simple by using several components specifically adapted to supporting the pipelined timing and status signals of the 80286. These interface components include:

- The 82C284 CHMOS Clock Generator, to generate the proper clock input for the 80286 CPU, to selectively enable and synchronize the 80286 $\overline{\text{READY}}$ input, and to handle the conditioning of the system RESET signal.

- The 82288 Bus Controller, to decode the 80286 status signals and to generate appropriate memory and I/O read/write commands, and data transceiver and address buffer control signals.

- Octal latches for latching local bus address lines or chip selects.
- Data transceivers for buffering the local bus data lines.

These devices support the pipelined timing of the 80286 local bus and combine functions that would take several dozen discrete components to perform. The remaining sections of this chapter describe how these circuits may be used to implement an 80286 local bus.

GENERATING TIMING USING THE 82C284 CHMOS CLOCK GENERATOR

The 82C284 Clock Generator provides the clock generation, $\overline{\text{READY}}$ timing, and RESET timing functions for the 80286 CPU and other 80286 support devices. Figure 3-17 illustrates how the 82C284 Clock Generator connects to an 80286 CPU.

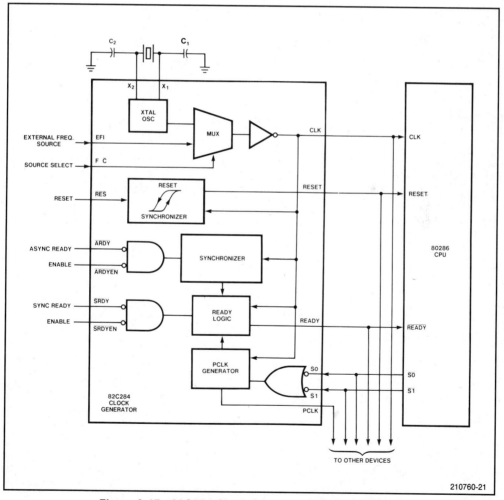

210760-21

Figure 3-17. 82C284 Clock Generator with an 80286 CPU

In generating the clock signal for the system, the 82C284 can use either a crystal or an external TTL-level signal as its frequency source. The CLK output signal is equal to the 80286 input source frequency and is double the specified processor clock frequency. The status lines $\overline{S0}$ and $\overline{S1}$ from the CPU are decoded by the 82C284 to synchronize the 82C284's PCLK (peripheral clock) output. This PCLK output is normally in phase with the 80286 internal processor clock.

The 82C284 generates the $\overline{READY}$ input to the 80286, which the CPU uses either to insert wait states into bus operations or to terminate successful bus operations. This $\overline{READY}$ output is synchronized to the system clock, and can be selectively generated from either an asynchronous or a synchronous ready input to the 82C284.

The third timing function of the 82C284 Clock Generator is the generation of the 80286 RESET, or system RESET signal. The 82C284 accepts an active-low $\overline{RES}$ input signal from a simple RC circuit or other reset source, synchronizes it with the system CLK, and drives its RESET output to properly initialize the 80286 CPU and other system components.

The following sections describe each of these functions of the 82C284 Clock Generator, and discuss some of the alternatives and considerations in designing an 80286 system using the 82C284.

Generating the System Clock

The 80286 requires a clock signal with fast rise and fall times (10 ns max) between low and high voltages of 0.6V low and 3.8V high. Since the 80286 internally uses dynamic cells, a minimum clock input frequency of 4 MHz is required to maintain the state of the CPU. Due to this minimum frequency requirement, the 80286 cannot be single-stepped by disabling the clock. The timing and voltage requirements for the CPU clock are shown in Figure 3-18.

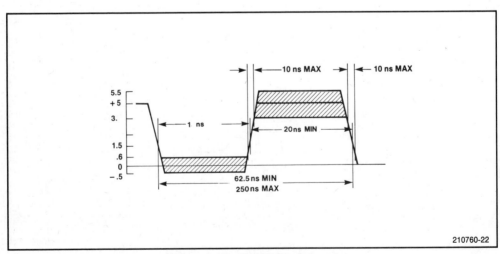

Figure 3-18. 80286 Clock Input

Using the 82C284 Clock Generator, an optimum 50% duty-cycle clock with the required MOS-level voltages and transition times can easily be obtained. Since the 80286 CLK is a double-frequency clock signal, the selected source must oscillate at twice the specified processor clock rate.

Either an external frequency source or a crystal can be used to drive the 82C284. The frequency source is selected by strapping the 82C284's F/C̄ input to indicate the appropriate frequency source.

To select the crystal inputs of the 82C284 as the frequency source for clock generation, the F/C̄ input to the 82C284 must be strapped to ground. The crystal, a parallel-resonant, fundamental mode crystal, connects to the X1 and X2 pins on the 82C284 and should have a typical capacitance load of 32 pF. Two loading capacitors are recommended to ensure stable operation of the 82C284's linear Pierce oscillator with the proper duty cycle, as shown in Figure 3-19. The sum of the board capacitance and the loading capacitors should equal the values shown in Table 3-4.

If a high-accuracy frequency source, externally-variable frequency source, or a common source for driving multiple 82C284's is desired, the External Frequency Input (EFI) of the 82C284 can be selected by pulling the F/C̄ input to 5 volts through a 1K ohm resistor (Figure 3-20). The external frequency source should be TTL-compatible, have a 50% duty cycle, and oscillate at the system clock rate (twice the processor clock rate).

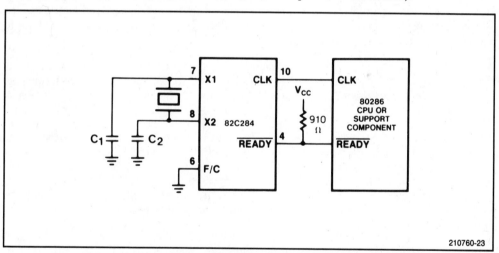

210760-23

Figure 3-19. Recommended Crystal Connections to the 82C284

Table 3-4. 82C284 Crystal Loading Capacitance Values

Crystal Frequency	C1 Capacitance (pin 7)	C2 Capacitance (pin 8)
1 - 8 MHz	60 pF	40 pF
8 - 20 MHz	25 pF	15 pF
above 20 MHz	15 pF	15 pF

NOTE: Capacitance values must include board capacitance.

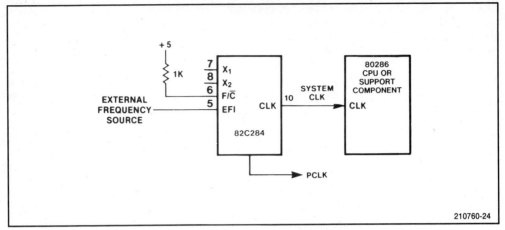

Figure 3-20. 82C284 with External Frequency Source

If several sources of CLK are needed (in a multi-processor system, for example), multiple 82C284 Clock Generators can be used, driven by a common frequency source. When multiple 82C284's driven by a common source are distributed throughout a system, each 82C284 should be driven by its own line from the source. To minimize noise in the system, each line should be a twisted pair driven by buffers like the 74LS04 with the ground of the twisted pair connecting the grounds of the source and receiver. To minimize clock skew, the lines to each 82C284 should be of equal length.

A simple technique for generating a master frequency source for additional 82C284's is shown in Figure 3-21. One 82C284 with a crystal is used to generate the desired frequency. The CLK output from this 82C284 drives the EFI input to the other 82C284 Clock Generators in the system.

Since the CLK output is delayed from the EFI input by up to 25 ns, the CLK output of the master 82C284 should not be used to drive both an 80286 and the EFI input of another 82C284 (for a second 80286) if the two CPUs are to be synchronized. The variation on EFI-to-CLK delay over a range of 82C284s may approach 10 to 15 ns. If, however, all 82C284s are of the same package type, and have the same relative supply voltage, and operate in the same temperature environment, the variation will be reduced to between 5 and 10 ns.

When multiple processors share a common local bus, they should be driven with the same system CLK to optimize the transfer of bus control. A single 82C284 Clock Generator can be used in this configuration, as shown in Figure 3-22. Each of the processors can share the common READY signal, since only one processor is permitted to use the bus at any given time. Processors that are not in control of the local bus will ignore any READY input.

The 82C284 Clock Generator has two clock outputs: the system clock (CLK), which drives the CPU and support devices, and a peripheral clock (PCLK), which runs at one-half the frequency of the system CLK and is normally synchronized to the 80286 internal processor clock. CLK has a 50% duty cycle, matching its input, and so does PCLK. CLK has MOS-level drive characteristics, while PCLK is a TTL-level signal at half the frequency of the CLK output.

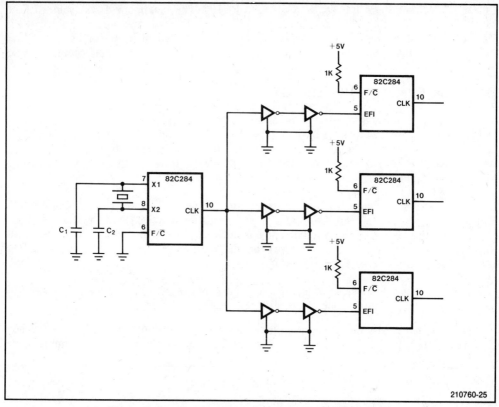

Figure 3-21. External Frequency for Multiple 82C284s

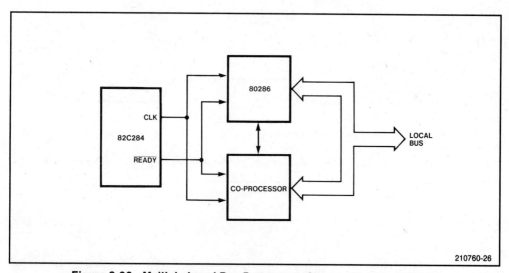

Figure 3-22. Multiple Local Bus Processors Share a Common 82C284

Figure 3-23 shows the relationship of CLK to PCLK. The maximum delay from CLK to PCLK is 45 ns. The 82C284 synchronizes PCLK to the CPU internal processor clock at the start of the first bus operation following a RESET, as detected by $\overline{S1}$ or $\overline{S0}$ going low. Following this first bus cycle, PCLK will remain in phase with the internal processor clock.

Timing Bus Operations Using $\overline{READY}$

As described previously in the discussion of 80286 bus operations, the $\overline{READY}$ input is used by the 80286 to insert wait states into a bus cycle, to accommodate memory and I/O devices that cannot transfer information at the maximum 80286 bus bandwidth. In multi-processor systems, $\overline{READY}$ is also used when the CPU must wait for access to the system bus or MULTIBUS interface.

To insert a wait state (an additional T_c state) into the bus cycle, the $\overline{READY}$ signal to the CPU, Bus Controller, and Bus Arbiter (if present) must be inactive (high) by the end of the current T_c state. To terminate the current bus cycle and avoid insertion of any additional wait states, $\overline{READY}$ must be low (active) for the specified set-up time prior to the falling edge of CLK at the end of T_c.

Depending on the size and characteristics of a particular system, designers may choose to implement a Ready signal in one of two different ways:

1. The classical Ready implementation is to have the system "normally not ready." When the selected device receives a command and has had sufficient time to complete the

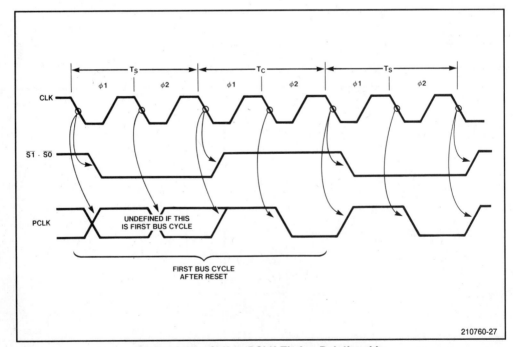

Figure 3-23. CLK to PCLK Timing Relationship

command, it activates Ready to the CPU and Bus Controller to terminate the bus cycle. This implementation is characteristic of large multi-processor, Multibus systems or systems where propagation delays, bus access delays, and device characteristics inherently slow down the system. For maximum performance, devices that can run with no wait states must return Ready within the specified time limit. Failure to respond in time will result in the insertion of one or more wait states.

2. An alternate technique is to have the system "normally ready." All devices are assumed to operate at the maximum CPU bus bandwidth. Devices that do not meet the requirement must disable Ready by the end of T_c to guarantee the insertion of wait states. This implementation is typically applied to small, single-CPU systems and reduces the logic required to control the READY signal. Since the failure of a device requiring wait states to disable Ready by the end of T_c will result in premature termination of the bus cycle, system timing must be carefully analyzed before using this approach.

As shown in Figure 3-24, the timing requirements for the CPU, Bus Controller, and Bus Arbiter READY inputs are identical regardless of which method of ready implementation is used. Set-up time for READY is 38 ns before the falling edge of CLK at the end of T_c; READY hold time is 25 ns from the falling edge of CLK (for an 8 MHz system).

To generate a stable READY output that satisfies the required setup and hold times, the 82C284 Clock Generator provides two ready inputs: a Synchronous Ready (SRDY) and an

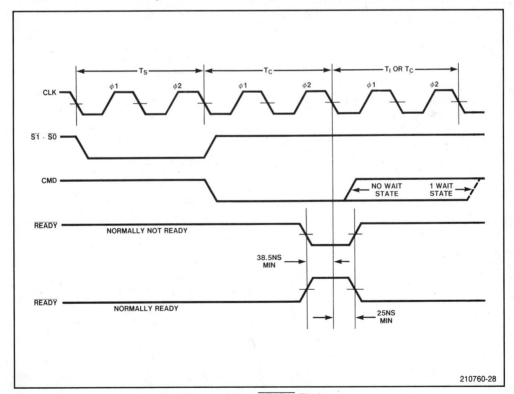

Figure 3-24. READY Timing

Asynchronous Ready ($\overline{\text{ARDY}}$) input. Typically, one or both of these inputs will be driven by external timing logic to determine an appropriate Ready condition. The two Ready inputs are qualified by separate Enable signals ($\overline{\text{SRDYEN}}$ and $\overline{\text{ARDYEN}}$) to selectively enable one of the two Ready inputs (Figure 3-25).

The two Ready inputs allow more flexibility in designing an 80286 system; although the $\overline{\text{SRDY}}$ input must be synchronized to the system CLK, it permits more time for the external Ready logic; the $\overline{\text{ARDY}}$ input need not be synchronized, but it permits less time for the Ready-timing logic to function.

Figure 3-26 shows the timing of the $\overline{\text{SRDY}}$ signal. When $\overline{\text{SRDYEN}}$ is low, $\overline{\text{SRDY}}$ is sampled on the falling edge of CLK at the end of Phase 1 of T_c. When $\overline{\text{SRDY}}$ is sampled low, the 82C284 immediately drives the $\overline{\text{READY}}$ output low (24 ns max. delay from the falling edge of CLK). The setup times for $\overline{\text{SRDY}}$ and $\overline{\text{SRDYEN}}$ are 15 ns before the falling edge of CLK.

Figure 3-27 shows the function of the $\overline{\text{ARDY}}$ input. When $\overline{\text{ARDYEN}}$ is low, $\overline{\text{ARDY}}$ is sampled on the falling edge of CLK at the start of T_c (one CLK cycle earlier than $\overline{\text{SRDY}}$). This allows one full CLK cycle for the 82C284 to resolve the state of $\overline{\text{ARDY}}$. When $\overline{\text{ARDY}}$ is sampled low, the $\overline{\text{READY}}$ output of the 82C284 is driven active-low following the falling edge of CLK at the end of phase 1 of T_c (24 ns max delay from the falling edge of CLK).

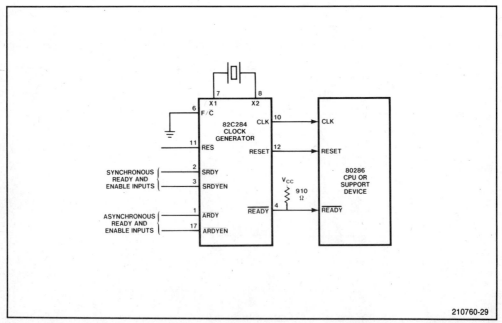

210760-29

Figure 3-25. Ready Inputs to the 82C284 and Output to the 80286 and 82288

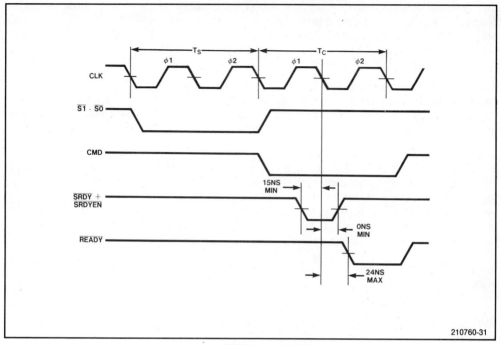

Figure 3-26. $\overline{SRDY}$ and $\overline{READY}$ Timing

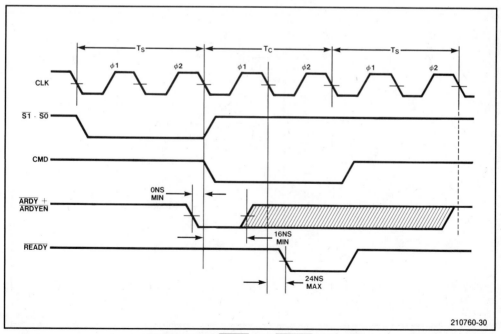

Figure 3-27. $\overline{ARDY}$ and $\overline{READY}$ Timing

To insert a wait state, *both* $\overline{\text{ARDY}}$ and $\overline{\text{SRDY}}$ must either be sampled inactive, or else be disabled using the appropriate Enable pin. Note that once both $\overline{\text{ARDY}}$ and $\overline{\text{ARDYEN}}$ have been resolved active low, the 82C284 ignores the condition of $\overline{\text{SRDY}}$ for the remainder of that bus cycle.

When only one Ready input is required, the associated Ready Enable signal can be tied to ground while the other Ready Enable signal is connected to 5 volts through a 1K ohm resistor (Figure 3-28). When both Ready inputs are used, the proper Ready Enable can typically be selected by latched outputs from address decode logic (Figure 3-29).

As shown in Figure 3-30, the $\overline{\text{READY}}$ output has an open-collector driver to allow other Ready circuits to be connected with it in a wired-OR configuration. This configuration requires the use of an external pull-up resistor on the $\overline{\text{READY}}$ signal. At the start of a bus cycle, indicated by $\overline{\text{S1}}$ or $\overline{\text{S0}}$ going low (Figure 3-31), the Clock Generator floats the $\overline{\text{READY}}$ output. The pull-up resistor has three system CLK cycles to raise the voltage on the $\overline{\text{READY}}$ line to the inactive (high) state before it is sampled by the 80286 CPU. When the selected 82C284 Ready input is active, the $\overline{\text{READY}}$ line is forced low. $\overline{\text{READY}}$ remains low until the next bus cycle is started ($\overline{\text{S1}}$ or $\overline{\text{S0}}$ going low) or until the selected Ready input is detected high.

During RESET, the Clock Generator pulls $\overline{\text{READY}}$ low to force the Bus Controller into the idle state.

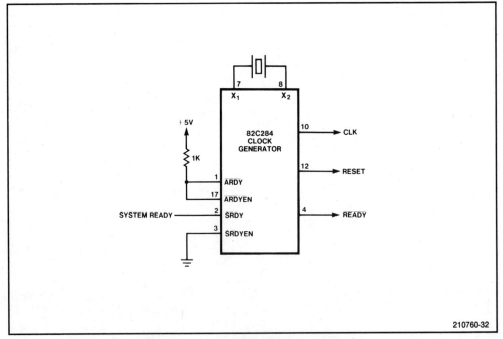

210760-32

Figure 3-28. Using Only One Ready Input

WAIT-STATE TIMING LOGIC

In the previous section, the operation of the $\overline{SRDY}$ and $\overline{ARDY}$ inputs to the Clock Generator were described. In this section, the wait-state timing logic that drives these Ready inputs are discussed, with specific examples for generating a fixed number of wait states.

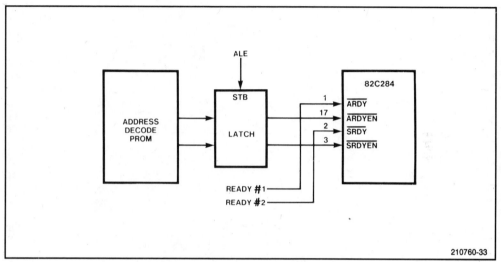

Figure 3-29. Selecting the Ready Input

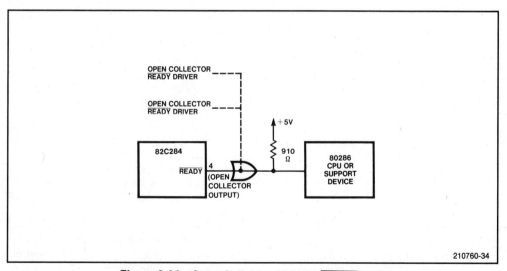

Figure 3-30. Open-Collector 82C284 $\overline{READY}$ Output

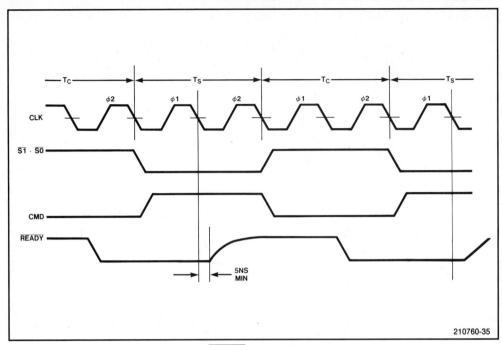

Figure 3-31. $\overline{\text{READY}}$ Output Characteristics

With an 8-MHz 80286 CPU, fast memory and peripherals can typically operate with 0 or 1 wait states. In most cases, address-decode logic can be used to select the number of wait states required by a particular device. This address-decode logic is also used to generate the appropriate chip selects.

Figure 3-32 shows a simple method for generating one wait state in an 80286 system. The timing for a typical bus cycle incorporating this single wait state is shown in Figure 3-33.

In the circuit shown, the output of the first flip-flop becomes active at the end of T_s. The output of the second flip-flop does not become activated until Phase 2 of the first T_c, after the 82C284 has sampled $\overline{\text{SRDY}}$ high and caused the insertion of an additional wait state. During the following T_c state, the 82C284 samples $\overline{\text{SRDY}}$ low and terminates the bus cycle by setting $\overline{\text{READY}}$ low. $\overline{\text{READY}}$ also resets the wait-state timing circuit in preparation for the following bus cycle.

For many existing memory and peripheral devices, one or more wait states will be required to operate with an 8-MHz 80286 CPU. Some peripheral devices may require more than two wait states. The circuit in Figure 3-34 shows a wait-state generator that inserts from 0 to 3 wait states into each bus cycle. This circuit can be extended to incorporate any number of wait states by adding an additional flip-flop for each wait state.

In the circuit shown, an address-decoder PROM selects the appropriate Ready signal to generate the proper number of wait states. The timing for this circuit is identical to that of the previous circuit, simply adding an additional wait state for each successive flip-flop.

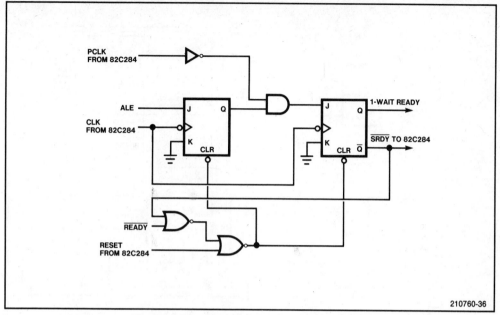

210760-36

Figure 3-32. Generating a Single Wait State

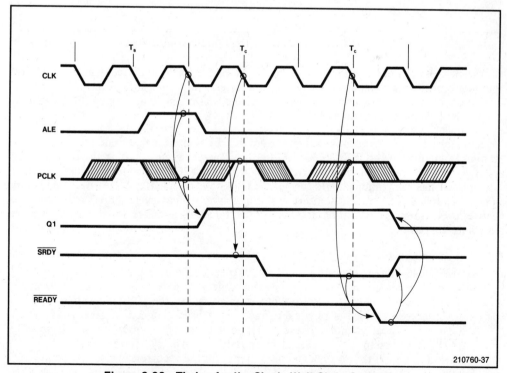

210760-37

Figure 3-33. Timing for the Single Wait-State Generator

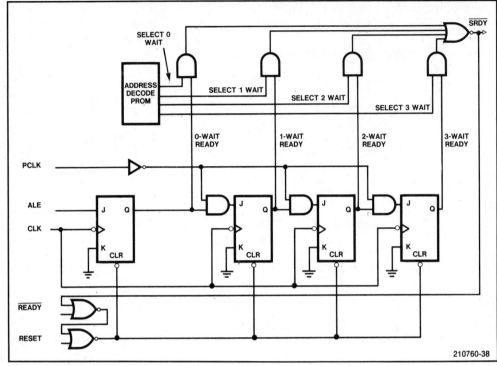

Figure 3-34. Generating from 0 to 3 Wait States

These circuits are sufficient for generating $\overline{SRDY}$ timing for local devices when the required number of wait states is known. For device addresses that are not local, e.g. for devices that reside on a system bus or require other timing, the $\overline{SRDYEN}$ Enable signal to the 82C284 should be driven inactive (high).

Memory and I/O devices configured on the MULTIBUS interface generate their own Ready timing through the MULTIBUS $\overline{XACK}$ signal (shown in Figure 3-41 in the next section). $\overline{XACK}$ can be used to drive the $\overline{ARDY}$ input to the 82C284, while an address-decoder recognizes addresses mapped onto the MULTIBUS and selects the $\overline{ARDYEN}$ Enable line. The 82C284 will automatically insert wait states into the bus cycle until $\overline{XACK}$ becomes active low. More information on designing a MULTIBUS interface for the 80286 is given in Chapter Seven.

NOTE

If the 80286 system operating in Real-Address mode is "normally not Ready," programmers should not assign executable code to the last six bytes of physical memory. Since the 80286 CPU prefetches instructions, the CPU may attempt to prefetch beyond the end of physical memory when executing code in Real Mode at the end of physical memory. If the access to non-existent memory fails to enable $\overline{READY}$, the system will be caught in an indefinite wait. Chapter Seven shows a bus-timeout circuit that is typically used to prevent the occurrence of such an indefinite wait.

Generating the Proper RESET Timing

As described previously, the third timing function of the 82C284 Clock Generator is to generate the system RESET signal to properly initialize the 80286 CPU and other system components.

The system RESET signal provides an orderly way to start or restart an 80286 system. When the 80286 processor detects the positive-going edge of RESET, it terminates all external activities. When the RESET signal falls low, the 80286 is initialized to a known internal state, and the CPU then begins fetching instructions from absolute address FFFFF0H.

To properly initialize the 80286 CPU, the high-to-low transition of RESET must be synchronized to the system CLK. This signal can easily be generated using the 82C284 Clock Generator. The 82C284 has a Schmitt-trigger $\overline{RES}$ input that can be used to generate RESET from an active-low external pulse. The hysteresis on this Schmitt-trigger input prevents the $\overline{RES}$ signal from entering an indeterminate state, and allows a simple RC circuit to be used to generate the $\overline{RES}$ signal upon power-up.

The specifications on the $\overline{RES}$ input circuit show that RESET will not become active until the $\overline{RES}$ input reaches at least 1.05 volts.

To guarantee RESET upon power-up, the $\overline{RES}$ input must remain below 1.05 volts for 5 milliseconds after Vcc reaches the minimum supply voltage of 4.5 volts. Following this event, $\overline{RES}$ must still remain below 1.05 volts for 16 processor clock cycles to allow for initializing the CPU. Figure 3-35 shows a simple RC circuit that will keep $\overline{RES}$ low long enough to satisfy both requirements.

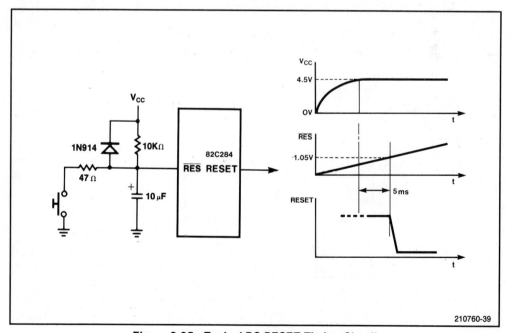

Figure 3-35. Typical RC RESET Timing Circuit

The 82C284 RESET output meets all of the requirements for the 80286 CPU RESET input. The RESET output is also available as a system RESET to other devices in the system, as shown in Figure 3-36.

During RESET, the 80286 internal processor clock is initialized (the divide by two counter is reset). Following the rising edge of RESET, the next CLK cycle will start Phase 2 of a processor clock cycle (see Figure 3-37). The 82C284 synchronizes the 82C284 PCLK output to the 80286 internal processor clock at the start of the first bus cycle after RESET.

Since the 82C284 synchronizes RESET to the system CLK, a delay of one or two clock cycles is introduced before the RESET output is driven high. The 82C284 will attempt to synchronize the rising edge of RESET if Vcc and CLK are correct at that time (Figure 3-38). However, since the rising edge of RESET may occur during power-up, when Vcc and CLK are not valid, the rising edge of RESET may be asynchronous to the CLK. A synchronized rising-edge of RESET is necessary only for clock-synchronous, multiprocessor systems.

Synchronizing Processor Clocks in a Multi-Processor System

In a multi-processor system where each processor must be clock-synchronous, all of the processor clocks must be synchronized following the initial power-up RESET. Since the CPU does not normally see the rising edge of a RESET signal during power-up due to delays between the time the voltage is applied and the time that the processor is functioning properly, a second RESET pulse must be generated.

This second RESET pulse cannot be provided directly by the 82C284 Clock Generator; additional logic is required. Figure 3-39 shows a circuit that provides a fully-synchronous RESET signal by generating a second RESET pulse that is triggered by the completion of the power-on reset. Timing for the circuit is shown in Figure 3-40.

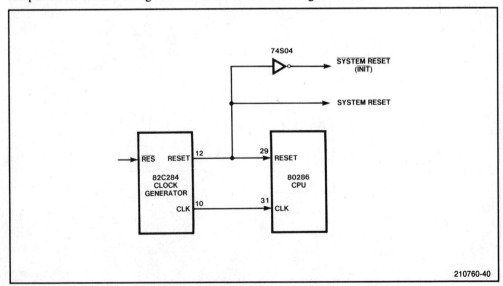

Figure 3-36. 80286 Reset and System Reset

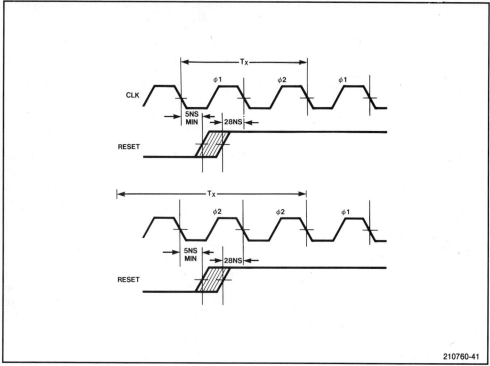

Figure 3-37. Processor Clock Synchronization

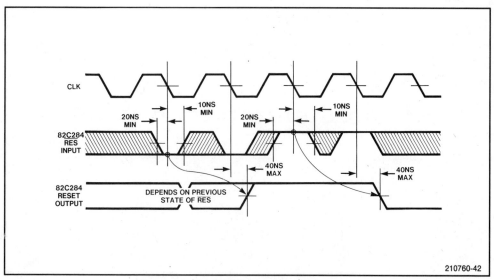

Figure 3-38. RESET Synchronized to CLK

The circuit actually provides two individual reset signals: CPU RESET, a synchronous reset signal that drives the 80286 CPU's in the system, and SYSTEM RESET, providing only a single RESET pulse for peripheral devices that need not be synchronized to the processor clock. The circuit also generates PCLK for the system (the 82C284 PCLK signal should be ignored).

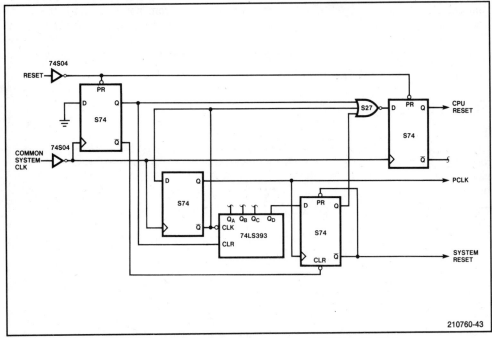

Figure 3-39. Generating a Synchronous RESET to Multiple 80286 CPUs

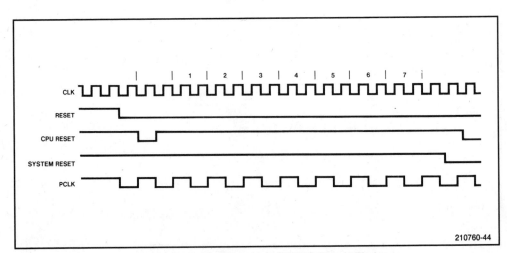

Figure 3-40. Synchronous RESET Circuit Timing

In operation, the normal power-on RESET occurs with the rising edge of CPU RESET not being seen by the processors. When the RESET input goes low, the circuit automatically initiates a second RESET that is synchronous to the system clock. The CPU RESET output goes low for one CLK cycle and then goes high for seventeen cycles (the 80286 requires a minimum RESET pulse width of sixteen CLK cycles subsequent to power-up reset). Both edges of this second reset pulse are synchronous to CLK and to PCLK (the pulse is derived from the PCLK signal). SYSTEM RESET remains high from power-up until the CLK cycle before the falling edge of the second CPU RESET pulse. Since the synchronous reset guarantees that PCLK is in phase with the processor clock, it is not necessary to synchronize PCLK to the processor clock via $\overline{S1}$ or $\overline{S0}$ going low at the start of the first bus cycle (as is done with the 82C284 PCLK signal).

CONTROLLING THE LOCAL BUS USING THE 82288 BUS CONTROLLER

The 82288 Bus Controller decodes the 80286 status signals and generates appropriate commands for controlling an 80286 local bus. By decoding the $\overline{S1}$, $\overline{S0}$, and M/$\overline{IO}$ signals from the 80286, the 82288 generates memory and I/O read/write commands, interrupt-acknowledge controls, and data transceiver and address latch controls. Figure 3-41 shows how the 82288 Bus Controller connects to the 80286 CPU.

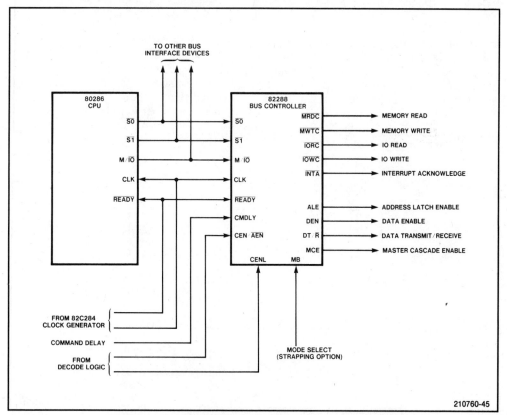

Figure 3-41. 82288 Bus Controller with an 80286 CPU

The 82288 Bus Controller has several control inputs that allow its command timing to be customized for a particular implementation. Other control inputs permit the Bus Controller to be used in systems having more than one local bus, or systems having a local bus and one or more system buses, including the Intel MULTIBUS. The following sections describe each of the functions of the Bus Controller, and discuss some of the alternatives in designing an 80286 system using the 82288.

Systems Having More Than One Bus Controller

The 82288 Bus Controller makes it easy to implement an 80286 system having more than one bus. In a typical multiple-bus system, one 82288 Bus Controller is used to generate commands for each bus. The Bus Controller's CENL (Command Enable Latched) input selects the particular Bus Controller that is to respond to the current bus cycle. A strapping option selects whether the Bus Controller generates signal timing compatible with the 80286 local bus, or follows the MULTIBUS timing specifications.

SELECTING A CONTROLLER

The 82288 CENL (Command Enable Latched) input selects whether the Bus Controller will respond to the current bus cycle. This input is sampled at the start of the first T_c state of each bus cycle. For systems that use only one Bus Controller, this input may be strapped high.

In systems that use multiple Controllers, address-decode logic typically selects the Bus Controller that executes the current bus cycle. CENL set-up time is 20 ns for an 8 MHz system; sampling occurs on the falling edge of CLK between T_s and T_c. If CENL is sampled high, the Controller ignores the current bus cycle (e.g., DEN and commands are not asserted) and waits for the next cycle to begin. It should be noted that in the case of a write cycle, DEN is already active when CENL is sampled. Therefore, when CENL is sampled low during a write, DEN will be driven low to disable the data buffers within 35 ns for an 8 MHz system, as shown in Figure 3-42.

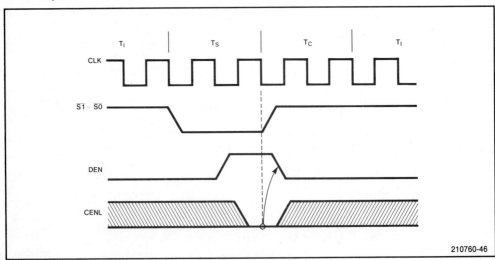

Figure 3-42. CENL Disable of DEN on Write Cycle

SELECTING MULTIBUS® TIMING

The 82288 MB (MULTIBUS) control input is a strapping option that configures bus controller timing for local or MULTIBUS mode. In local bus mode, the bus controller generates commands and control signal timing compatible with the 80286 local bus. In MULTIBUS mode, timing is altered to meet MULTIBUS interface timing requirements for address and data setup times. All MULTIBUS cycles require at least one wait state. Strapping MB high selects MULTIBUS mode; strapping MB low selects local mode. Figure 3-43 shows typical bus command timing for an 82288 operating in both local mode and MULTIBUS mode. Chapter Seven provides detailed guidelines for implementing a MULTIBUS interface for the 80286.

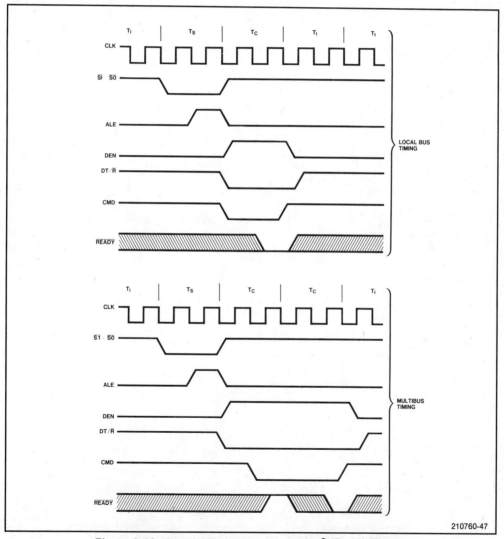

210760-47

Figure 3-43. Local (MB=0) Vs. MULTIBUS® (B=1) Timing

Figure 3-44 shows two 82288 bus controllers being used in an 80286 system. One controller interfaces the 80286 CPU to a local bus and is configured for local bus mode (MB strapped to ground). The second controller is configured in MULTIBUS mode (MB strapped to +5V) and connects the CPU to the MULTIBUS interface. The local bus controller also has CEN strapped to +5V. CMDLY is tied low; commands are not delayed. Address decode logic selects one of the two bus controllers via the CENL inputs. The select signal for the MULTIBUS controller also enables the 82289 Bus Arbiter.

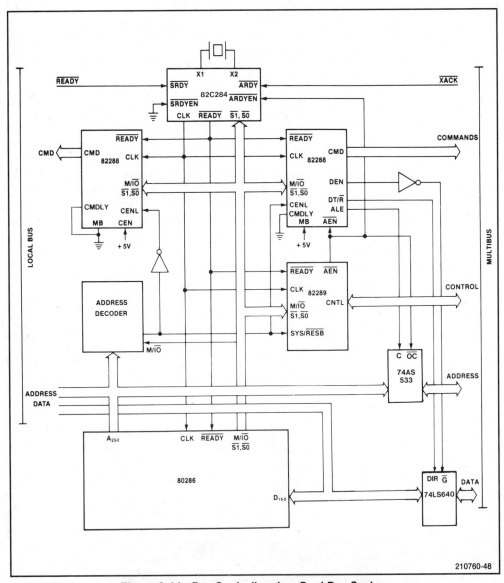

Figure 3-44. Bus Controllers in a Dual Bus System

Access to a multimaster system bus such as the MULTIBUS is controlled by the 82289 Bus Arbiter. The Bus Arbiter decodes the $\overline{S1}$, $\overline{S0}$, M/$\overline{IO}$, and SYSB/$\overline{RESB}$ lines to determine when the 80286 requires access to the multimaster bus. After requesting and gaining control of the bus, the 82289 enables the Bus Controller and address latches to allow the access to take place. Chapter Seven describes the operation and use of the 82289 Bus Arbiter in detail.

Modifying the Bus Control Timing

To accommodate systems with slower memories or timing requirements, bus commands from the 82288 can be delayed using the Bus Controller's CMDLY (Command Delay) and CEN/$\overline{AEN}$ (Command Enable/Address Enable) inputs. Command delays allow increased address and write-data setup times before command active for devices that require lengthy setup times.

CMDLY (COMMAND DELAY)

The 82288 CMDLY input delays command generation by one or more CLK cycles. Each CLK delay allows at least 62.5 ns additional set-up time from address/chip select to command active for an 8 MHz 80286. Command delays may be required, for example, on write operations when write data must be valid before the $\overline{WR}$ command is asserted. When no delays are required, CMDLY can be strapped to ground to always issue the command as soon as possible.

A simple method for generating 0 or 1 command delays is shown in Figure 3-45. The CMDLY input to the Bus Controller is driven by the output of an address-decode PROM gated to the Bus Controller's Address Latch Enable (ALE). CMDLY is driven high while ALE is active, but only when the PROM output is also high. CMDLY falls low after ALE is driven low.

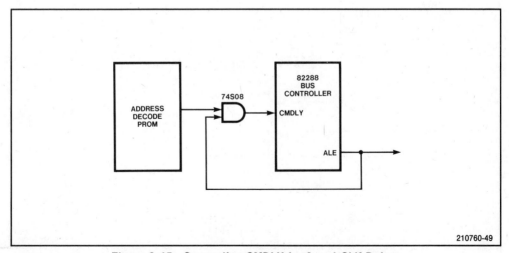

210760-49

Figure 3-45. Generating CMDLY for 0 or 1 CLK Delays

For devices that require more than one command delay, a counter can be used to generate the appropriate number of delays (Figure 3-46). Set-up time for CMDLY is 20 ns before the falling edge of CLK for an 8 MHz system. Note that delaying commands does not lengthen the bus cycle, nor does CMDLY affect the DEN signal controlling the data transceivers. For example, if READY is sampled active low before CMDLY is sampled high, the bus cycle will be terminated, with no command being issued (see Figure 3-47).

When the Bus Controller is configured in MULTIBUS mode, commands are automatically delayed for the proper duration (CMDLY should be strapped low).

CEN/AEN (Command Enable/Address Enable)

The 82288 CEN/AEN input is a dual-function, asynchronous input that disables commands and control signals. The function of the input depends on the mode of the Bus Controller. In local mode (MB=0), the input functions as CEN (Command Enable); in MULTIBUS mode (MB=1), the input functions as AEN (Address Enable).

CEN provides the Bus Controller with an additional command enable signal that can be used for address decoding or delaying commands and control signals asynchronously to the system clock. In contrast to CENL, CEN is not latched internally and, when used as part of an address decoding scheme, requires an external latch.

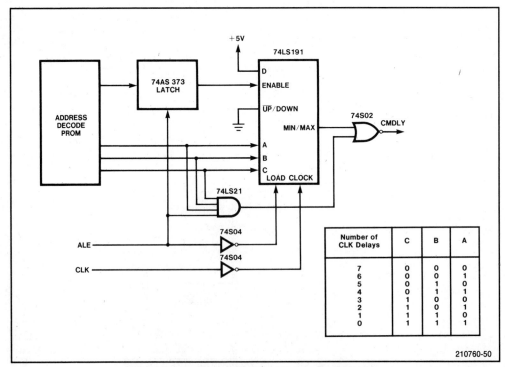

Figure 3-46. Generating 0 to 7 Command Delays

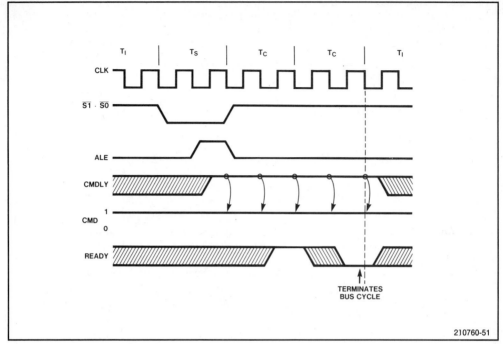

Figure 3-47. Bus Cycle Terminated with No Command Issued

CEN contrasts with CMDLY in its ability to delay both command signals and DEN asynchronously to the system clock. Whereas the minimum CMDLY controlled delay is 62.5 ns for an 8 MHz system (one system clock), no minimum is required for CEN.

As shown in Figure 3-48, when CEN is low, commands and DEN are inactive. When CEN goes high, commands and control signals immediately go active.

$\overline{AEN}$ is a signal typically generated by the 82289 Bus Arbiter to control commands and data during accesses to the MULTIBUS interface. For MULTIBUS bus cycles, address decode logic enables the 82289 Bus Arbiter (SYSB/$\overline{RESB}$) and 82288 Bus Controller (CENL) assigned to the MULTIBUS interface. After requesting and gaining control of the interface, the 82289 Bus Arbiter outputs the active-low $\overline{AEN}$ signal to the Bus Controller to enable the MULTIBUS commands and data transceivers.

$\overline{AEN}$ is asynchronous to the system CLK. When $\overline{AEN}$ goes high, the Bus Controller drives DEN inactive and its command lines enter the tri-state OFF condition. Chapter Seven describes the use of $\overline{AEN}$ in greater detail.

Another operating mode of the 82288 allows tri-stating the Bus Controller's command outputs in non-MULTIBUS mode. To do this, the CEN/$\overline{AEN}$ input is tied HIGH and the MB input is used to control the command outputs. MB must be stable 20 ns before the falling edge of CLK. Changing MB to HIGH will tri-state the command outputs on the falling edge of CLK. Changing MB to LOW will enable the control outputs first, then the command outputs will go active two CLK cycles later if a command is active.

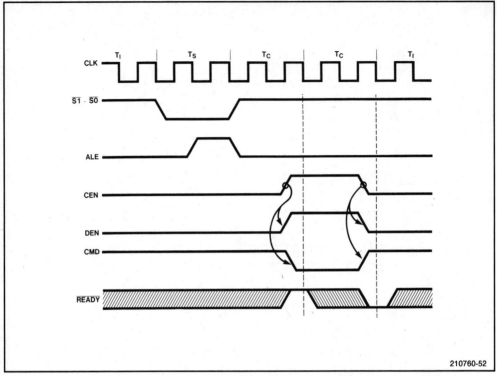

210760-52

Figure 3-48. CEN Characteristics (No Command Delay)

LOCAL BUS DESIGN CONSIDERATIONS

Address Bus Interface

80286 systems operate with a 24-bit address bus, using the pipelined address timing described previously. Since the majority of system memories and peripherals require stable address and chip-select inputs for the duration of the bus cycle, the address bus and/or decoded chip-selects should be latched.

The 82288 Bus Controller provides an ALE signal to capture the address in a transparent latch (see Figure 3-49). The latches propagate the input signals through to the outputs while ALE is high and latch the outputs on the falling edge of ALE (see Figure 3-50). The outputs are enabled by the active-low $\overline{OE}$ input.

Chapter Four discusses other address strobe techniques that do not use the ALE signal from the 82288 Bus Controller. These special address strobes can be used to customize the 80286 bus cycle timing to accommodate particular memory or peripheral devices.

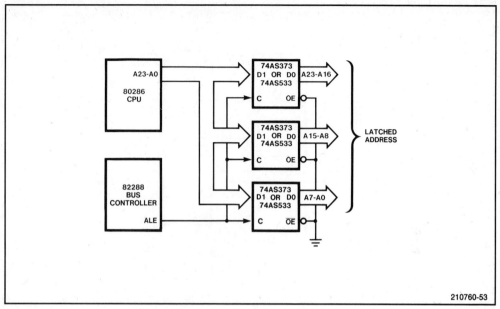

Figure 3-49. Latching the 80286 Address

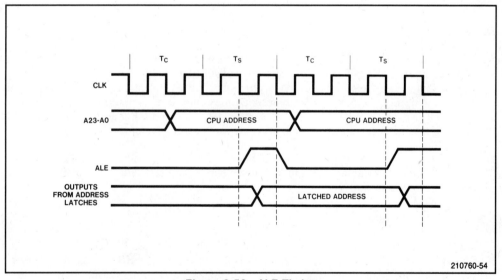

Figure 3-50. ALE Timing

For optimum system performance and compatibility with multi-processor MULTIBUS systems, the address should be latched at the interface to each bus. As shown in Figure 3-51, systems that use both buffered local and public system buses can have separate address buses with separate latches and Controllers for each bus. The 100 pf maximum capacitance drive specification of the 80286 allows at least five sets of address latches to be connected to the address outputs of the 80286.

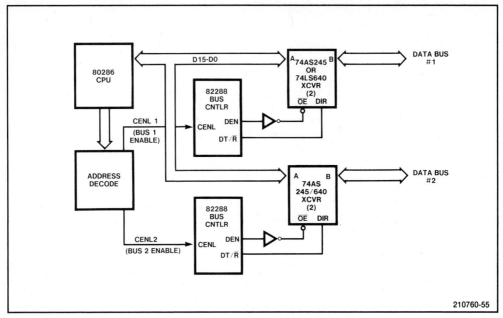

Figure 3-51. Dual Address Bus System

Address Decoding

Address decoding in an 80286 system can be performed between the time that the address is generated at the CPU pins and the rising edge of ALE. At least 68 ns exist for an 8-MHz system for this address decode logic to operate and produce a select output from the latches with the same timing as addresses. Such decode time comes free since it does not delay when a device can respond to an address. Select signals decoded from CPU address pins must be latched to guarantee that they will remain stable for the duration of the bus cycle.

Decoded select signals that drive the CENL input to the Bus Controller or the SYSB/$\overline{\text{RESB}}$ input to the Bus Arbiter do not need to be latched (both the Bus Controller and Bus Arbiter latch these signals internally).

NON-LATCHED CHIP SELECTS

Figure 3-52 shows an example circuit that decodes the address, M/$\overline{\text{IO}}$=0, and COD/$\overline{\text{INTA}}$=0 signals to provide non-latched CENL and SYSB/$\overline{\text{RESB}}$ selects for the Bus Controller and Bus Arbiter and additional non-latched selects to other devices in the system. The example assumes two system buses with all interrupts on bus #1. The M/$\overline{\text{IO}}$ and COD/$\overline{\text{INTA}}$ signals are used to enable bus #1 during interrupt-acknowledge cycles (the address bus floats during interrupt-acknowledge cycles).

Set-up time for the Bus Controller CENL input is 20 ns before the start of T_c (assuming that commands are not delayed and an 8 MHz system). This means that the time from A23-A0, M/$\overline{\text{IO}}$, and COD/$\overline{\text{INTA}}$ active to CENL is 107.5 ns max. To meet the set-up time

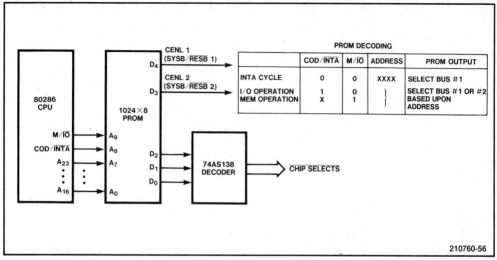

Figure 3-52. Non-Latched Chip Selects

for the Bus Arbiter SYS/$\overline{\text{RESB}}$ input, the time from A23-A0, M/$\overline{\text{IO}}$, and COD/$\overline{\text{INTA}}$ active to SYSB/$\overline{\text{RESB}}$ is 127.5 ns maximum. Since the same PROM output must meet both these requirements, the decoder PROM must have an access time of 107.5 ns or less.

To accommodate the timing requirements for individual devices, the 82288 Bus Controller has a CMDLY input to delay the leading edge of commands from the Bus Controller by one or more CLK cycles. Typical devices require zero or one command delays. This CMDLY (Command Delay) input to the Bus Controller is described in a previous section.

The CMDLY signal is typically generated by address-decode logic, and is not latched either externally or by the 82288. The same address-decoding techniques used for other non-latched selects can be used to generate zero or more command delays for individual devices or ranges of addresses. Figure 3-45 shown previously illustrates a method for generating zero- or one-CLK command delays based on a non-latched output from an address-decode PROM gated with ALE.

LATCHED CHIP SELECTS

Most memory and peripheral devices require a stable device-select signal that can be provided only by latched chip-selects. Latched chip-selects can easily be generated by adding latches to the outputs of decode logic shown in Figure 3-52. Transparent latches such as the 74AS373/533 can latch the selects in response to the ALE signal from the Bus Controller.

Figure 3-53 shows an example of a circuit that latches chip-selects. The timing for latched chip-selects differs from that of non-latched selects. Since ALE goes high only 68 ns after the 80286 address is valid for an 8 MHz system, the address-decode PROM must have an access time of less than 68 ns to prevent the chip-select outputs from changing after being passed through the latches.

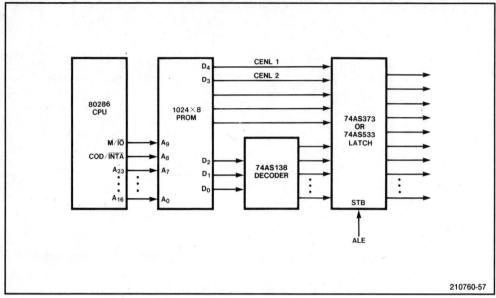

Figure 3-53. Latched Chip Selects

Depending on the required set-up times from chip-select to command-active, the maximum PROM access time can be increased by up to 62.5 ns. To provide sufficient set-up times from chip-select to command-active, however, commands from the Bus Controller may have to be delayed one CLK cycle when using this technique. By delaying commands one CLK cycle, the same circuit can be used with a gain of up to 62.5 ns in additional set-up time from chip-select to command active.

Depending on speed, cost, and available board space, the designer may substitute programmed array logic or discrete TTL logic for the PROM to decode latched and non-latched select signals from 80286 addresses.

Data Bus Interface

Since the 80286 provides separate address and data pins, demultiplexing of the data bus is unnecessary. The design considerations for connecting devices to the 80286 local bus are whether or not to buffer the data bus and whether a single or double level of buffering is required for the intended application.

In general, buffering of the data bus is required for memory devices with $\overline{OE} \uparrow$ to data-bus-float times of 42 ns or more (to avoid contention with the 80286 during back-to-back read-write cycles). Most memory and I/O devices will therefore require buffering of the data bus. Unbuffered devices must not present a load exceeding the CPU's maximum drive capability of 3.0 mA with a capacitive loading of 100 pF.

A major concern in both buffered and non-buffered systems is the contention on the data bus that occurs when one device begins driving the bus before the previously-selected device has disabled its output drivers. Devices that have separate chip-select and output-enable or read inputs provide one solution to this problem. The output-enable signal can be driven by the Read command signal (see Figure 3-54) to assure that the output drivers are not enabled during write cycles and the read command can be delayed one CLK cycle to prevent any overlap between output drivers of two peripheral devices. Delaying commands may already be necessary for some devices to provide the necessary chip-select to command-active set-up time.

Devices without output-enable or Read inputs (chip-select alone) can be dealt with in a similar manner (Figure 3-55). The chip-select in this circuit is gated with Read and Write.

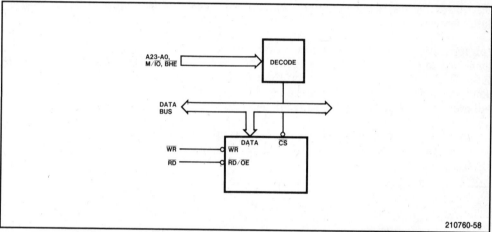

Figure 3-54. Devices with Output Enables on a Non-Buffered Data Bus

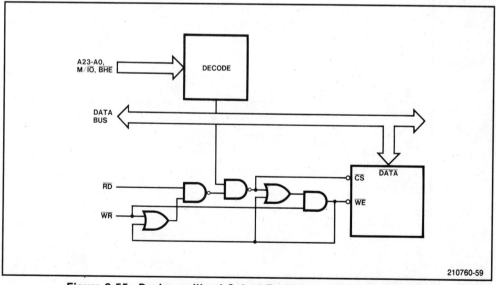

Figure 3-55. Devices without Output Enables on the Local Data Bus

The tradeoffs with this method include (1) chip select time is reduced to the read access time for reads and (2) no time is allowed for chip-select to write-command set-up and (3) no hold time from CS high or WE high for writes. Designers should check the device specifications to verify whether or not these tradeoffs create a problem for a specific case. In general, devices with separate output-enables are preferred.

To satisfy the capacitive loading and drive requirements of larger systems, the data bus must be buffered. As shown in Figure 3-56, the $\overline{OE}$ and DIR inputs to the transceivers are driven by DEN and DT/$\overline{R}$ from the 82288 Bus Controller. DEN enables the devices, while DT/$\overline{R}$ controls the direction of data through the devices. The $\overline{DISABLE}$ term is used if any other device may drive local data bus (i.e., 80287) instead of data transceivers. Chapter Six describes using the 80287 in an 80286/287 system, and describes how to control the local data transceivers.

For applications that require separate system buses, two or more sets of transceivers can be connected to the 80286 data pins. Figure 3-57 shows a configuration having two separate buses. Each bus has its own 82288 Bus Controller to control its own set of data transceivers. Since the address-decode logic selects one bus at a time, only one of the two DEN signals will ever be active at any time during a read cycle.

Another alternative when implementing a data bus is to add a second level of buffering, reducing the load seen by peripheral devices connected to the system bus (Figure 3-58).

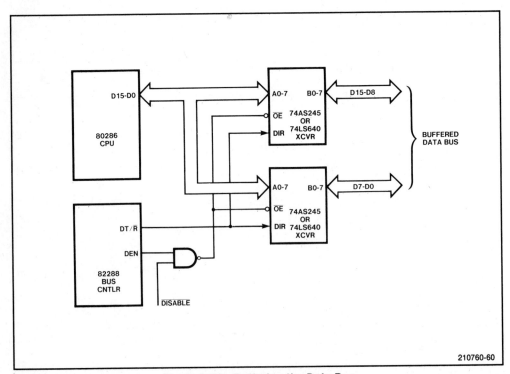

210760-60

Figure 3-56. Buffering the Data Bus

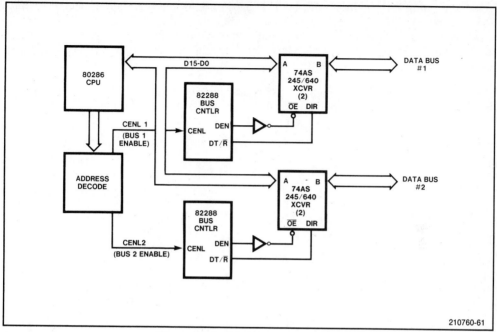

210760-61

Figure 3-57. Dual Data Bus System

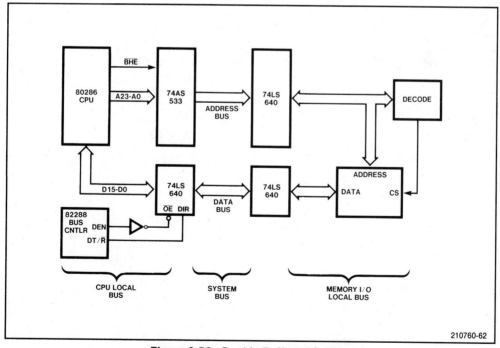

210760-62

Figure 3-58. Double Buffered System

Double-buffering is typically used for multi-board systems and isolation of memory arrays. The concerns with this configuration are the additional delay for access, and more importantly, control of the second level of transceivers in relationship to the system bus and the device being interfaced to the system bus. Several techniques can be used to control these transceivers.

The first technique (shown in Figure 3-59) simply distributed DEN and DT/$\overline{\text{R}}$ throughout the system. The second example (shown in Figure 3-60) provides control for devices with

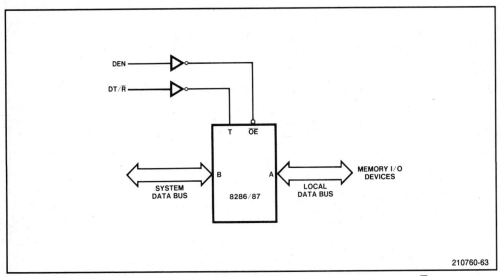

Figure 3-59. Controlling System Transceivers with DEN and DT/$\overline{\text{R}}$

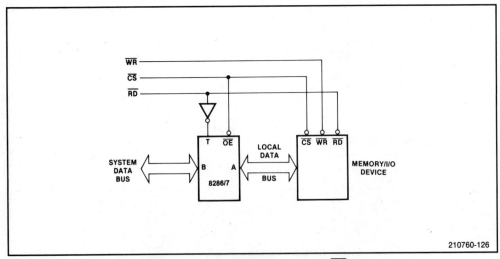

Figure 3-60. Buffering Devices with $\overline{\text{OE}}$/RD

output enables. The buffers are selected whenever the device on the local bus is selected. $\overline{RD}$ directs the data to the local bus device during read cycles.

Bus contention on the local bus is possible during a read as $\overline{RD}$ simultaneously enables the device output and changes the transceiver direction. Contention may also occur when $\overline{RD}$ terminates. If $\overline{OE}$ was active before DIR changes, then the output is the same as the input, with no contention. To eliminate such contention, it is necessary to sequence DIR and $\overline{OE}$.

For devices without output enables, the same technique can be applied if the chip select to the device is conditioned by read or write signals (see Figure 3-61). Controlling the chip select with read/write prevents the device from driving against the transceiver prior to the command being received. This technique limits access time to read/write time and chip select to write set-up and hold times.

One last technique is given for devices with separate inputs and outputs (see Figure 3-62). Separate receivers and drivers are provided, rather than a single transceiver. The receiver is always enabled while the bus driver is controlled by $\overline{RD}$ and chip-select. The only possibility for bus contention in this system occurs as multiple devices on each line of the local read bus are enabled and disabled during chip selection changes.

Other Bus Masters on the 80286 Local Bus

The 80286 provides on-chip arbitration logic that supports a protocol for transferring control of the local bus to other bus masters. This protocol is implemented by a pair of handshake signals called hold (HOLD) and hold acknowledge (HLDA). The sequence of signals shown in Figures 3-63 and 3-64 illustrate this protocol. To gain control of the local bus, the requesting bus master asserts an active high signal on the 80286 HOLD input (Figure 3-63). This HOLD input need not be synchronous to the 80286 CLK.

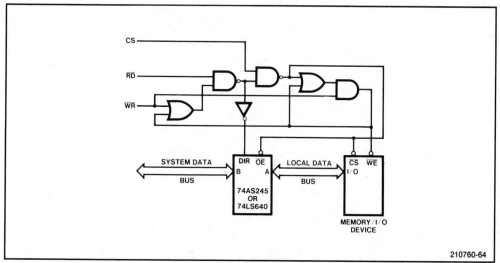

Figure 3-61. Buffering Devices without $\overline{OE}$/RD and with Common or Separate Input/Output

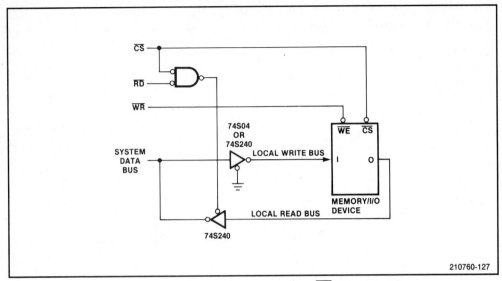

Figure 3-62. Buffering Devices without $\overline{OE}$/RD and with Separate Input/Output

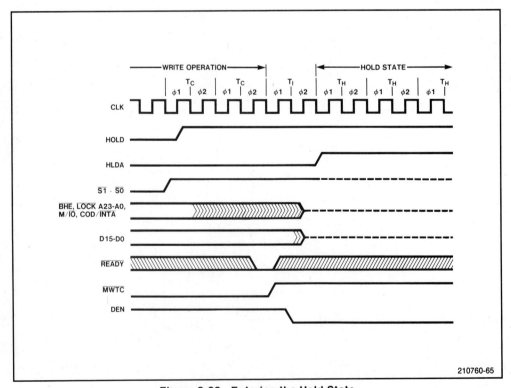

Figure 3-63. Entering the Hold State

When HOLD is asserted, the 80286 completes the current bus sequence and then tri-states all bus outputs (except HLDA) to effectively remove itself from the local bus. The 80286 then drives HLDA high to signal the requesting bus master that it now has control of the bus. The requesting bus master must maintain a high on the HOLD line until it no longer requires the local bus.

The hold request to the CPU affects the 80286 Bus Unit (BU) directly, and only indirectly affects the other units. The Execution Unit continues to execute from the instruction queue until both the instruction queue and the pre-fetch queue are empty, or until an instruction is encountered that requires a bus cycle. When hold request is dropped, the bus unit will not drive the address, data, or status/control lines until a bus cycle is required. Since the CPU may still be executing pre-fetched instructions when HOLD drops, a period of time may pass when the CPU is not driving the bus. Internal pull-up resistors on the 82C284 $\overline{S1}$ and $\overline{S0}$ inputs make this time look like an idle cycle and prevent spurious commands from being issued. Figure 3-64 shows the sequence of signals for exiting the hold state and immediately starting an 80286 bus cycle.

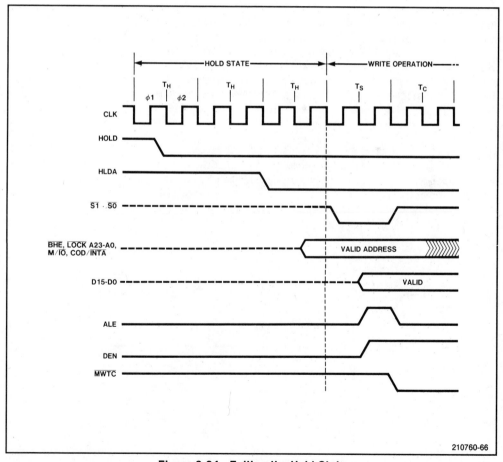

Figure 3-64. Exiting the Hold State

To guarantee valid system operation, the designer must ensure that the requesting device does not assert control of the bus prior to the 80286 relinquishing control (no bus cycles should be performed by the device until HLDA is received). The device must also relinquish control of the bus (tri-state all outputs to the bus) before the 80286 resumes driving the bus.

As shown in Figure 3-65, the HOLD request into the CPU must be stable 20 ns prior to the negative going edge of CLK at the start of a bus state (end of phase 2), and must remain stable for 20 ns after CLK goes low to guarantee recognition on that clock edge. This same set-up time is required when HOLD goes low to exit the hold state.

Since other bus masters such as DMA controllers are typically used in time-critical applications, the amount of time that a bus master must wait for access to the local bus is often a critical design consideration.

Figures 3-63 and 3-64 show the minimum possible latency for the 80286 CPU (2½ processor clocks from HOLD active to HLDA active and 1½ processor clocks from HOLD inactive to HLDA inactive).

The maximum possible HOLD-active to HLDA-active time (HOLD latency) depends on the software being executed. The actual HOLD latency at any time depends on the current bus activity, the state of the $\overline{\text{LOCK}}$ signal (internal to the CPU) activated by the $\overline{\text{LOCK}}$ prefix, and interrupts. The 80286 will not honor a HOLD request until the current bus operation is complete. Table 3-5 shows the types of bus operations that can affect HOLD latency, and indicates the types of delays that these operations may introduce. When considering maximum HOLD latencies, designers must select which of these bus operations are possible, and then select the maximum latency from among them.

As indicated in Table 3-5, wait states affect HOLD latency. The 80286 CPU will not honor a HOLD request until the end of the current bus operation, no matter how many wait states are required. Systems with DMA where data transfer is critical must insure that $\overline{\text{READY}}$ returns sufficiently soon.

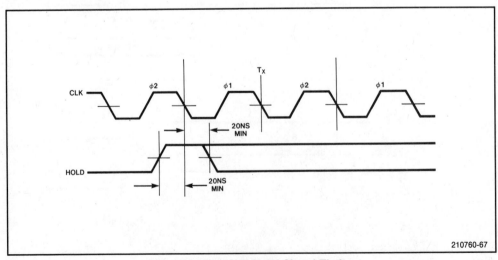

210760-67

Figure 3-65. HOLD Input Signal Timing

Table 3-5. Locked Bus Operations Affecting HOLD Latency in System Clocks

Instructions Using LOCK Prefix	Odd Aligned	Even Aligned
MOVS, INS, OUTS	$6 + 4N(4 + 2W_1)$	$6 + 2N(4 + 2W_1)$
MOV	$6 + 2(4 + 2W_1)$	—
Rotate Memory	$12 + 4(4 + 2W_1) + 2N_R$	$12 + 2(4 + 2W_1) + 2N_R$
Instructions Locked Automatically		
Processor Extension	$6 + 3(4 + 2W_1)$	$6 + 2(4 + 2W_1)$
XCHG	$6 + 4(4 + 2W_1)$	$6 + 2(4 + 2W_1)$
external interrupt (Real Mode)	—	$22 + 3(4 + 2W_1) + 4W_2$
external interrupt (Protected Mode) (TRAP, INTERRUPT, and TASK GATES)	—	$34 + 5(4 + 2W_1) + 4W_2$

NOTES:

N = The number of characters transferred.
N_R = number of rotate operations (31 max).
W_1 = The number of memory wait-states being used in the system.
W_2 = The number of INTRA wait-sates being used in the system. Intel recommends a minimum of one INTRA wait-state to meet 8259A minimum INTA pulse width.

All values are given in system clocks (the double frequency clock). To get processor clocks (PCLK), divide this number by two.

DMA CONFIGURATION

A typical use of the HOLD/HLDA signals in an 80286 system is bus control exchange with DMA controllers or I/O devices that perform DMA. Figure 3-66 shows a block-level inter-connect diagram for a "generic" DMA controller. The DMA controller resides on the local bus. This is probably the simplest DMA configuration possible with the 80286, but it requires that the DMA controller have an interface that functions like the 80286 local bus signals.

DMA controllers that do not have an 80286-like interface may still be configured in an 80286 system at the system bus level. Figure 3-67 shows a general inter-connect diagram for this type of application. The CPU is totally isolated from the system bus when in the T_h state, and the DMA controller must be compatible with the 80286 system bus.

Initializing the 80286 Processor

The 80286 RESET input provides an orderly way to start or restart a system. When the processor detects the positive-going edge of a pulse on RESET, it terminates all activities until the signal goes low, at which time it initializes the CPU to a known internal state; the CPU then begins fetching instructions from absolute address FFFFF0H.

80286 INTERNAL STATES

When an active RESET signal goes low, the 80286 registers are initialized as shown in Table 3-6. The valid fields of the segment and description registers are set on, indicating valid segments. All privilege-level fields are set to zero.

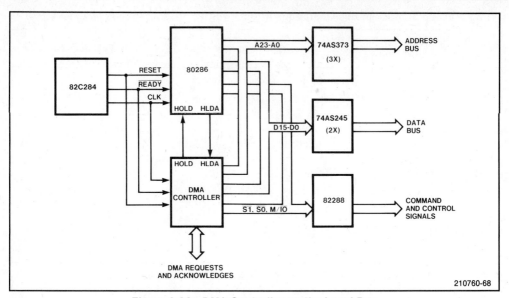

Figure 3-66. DMA Controller on the Local Bus

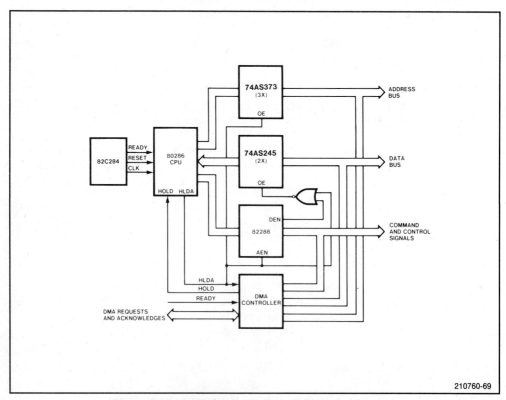

Figure 3-67. DMA Controller on a Private System Bus

Table 3-6. CPU State Following RESET

CPU Component	Content
Flags	0002H
MSW	FFF0H
IP	FFF0H
CS Selector	F000H
DS Selector	0000H
SS Selector	0000H
ES Selector	0000H
CS Base	FF0000H
DS Base	000000H
SS Base	000000H
ES Base	000000H
CS Limit	FFFFH
DS Limit	FFFFH
SS Limit	FFFFH
ES Limit	FFFFH
IDT Base	000000H
IDT Limit	FFFFH

The RESET signal initializes the CPU in Real-Address mode, with the CS base register containing FF0000H and IP containing FFF0H. The first instruction fetch cycle following reset will be from the physical address formed by these two registers, i.e., from address FFFFF0H. This location will normally contain a JMP instruction to the actual beginning of the system bootstrap program.

For 80286 systems to operate in Protected Virtual-Address mode, the 80286 (executing in Real-Address mode) must enter Protected mode as part of the software initialization routine.

To accommodate an 80286 operating in both Real-Address mode and Protected mode, the EPROMs containing the system bootstrap program must answer to both a 20-bit and a 24-bit physical address. In Real-Address mode, the system bootstrap EPROMs must respond to addresses in the available 1-Megabyte address space (ignoring the upper four address bits). In Protected mode, these same EPROMs typically respond to addresses only in the top megabyte of the available 16-Megabyte address space (using the full 24-bit address).

Figure 3-68 shows a circuit that permits this type of operation by generating one of the terms in the address-decode logic selecting the bootstrap EPROMs. This term inhibits the decoding of A23-A20 after RESET, when the system runs in Real-Address mode. After entering Protected mode, the bootstrap program must strobe the $\overline{\text{PROTMODE}}$ signal to allow full use of the available 16-Megabyte address space.

80286 EXTERNAL SIGNALS

At power-up, the 80286 CPU requires 5 milliseconds to allow the capacitor connected to the CAP pin to charge up. RESET should be asserted during this time to prevent spurious outputs. After power-up, the CPU requires a high on the RESET input with a minimum pulse width of 16 processor clocks. The processor is internally active for a minimum of 38 CLK cycles after RESET goes low before performing the first memory cycle. Maskable and non-maskable interrupts (the INT and NMI inputs) are not recognized during the internal reset.

When RESET is driven high, the 80286 signals will enter the states shown in Table 3-7. The timing for the signals during reset is shown in Figure 3-69.

The 80286 data bus lines enter the tri-state OFF condition when RESET is active. If system RESET occurs during a bus cycle, RESET forces the 82C284 Clock Generator to drive READY low to terminate the bus cycle and reinitialize the 82288 Bus Controller.

The 82C284 Clock Generator contains internal pull-up resistors on its $\overline{S1}$ and $\overline{S0}$ status inputs, causing the Bus Controller to interpret the 80286 RESET condition as an idle bus state. The outputs from the Bus Controller during an idle state are shown in Table 3-8.

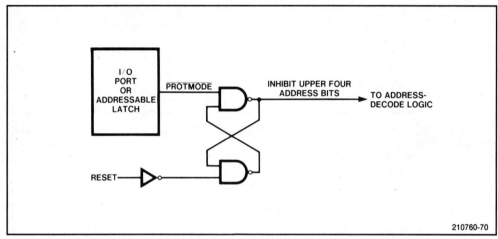

Figure 3-68. Decoding Addresses in Both Real and Protected Modes

Table 3-7. 80286 Bus during RESET

Signals	Condition
A23-A0	Logic 1
D15-D0	Tri-state OFF
$\overline{S1},\overline{S0}$	Logic 1
$\overline{PEACK}$	Logic 1
$\overline{BHE}$	Logic 1
$\overline{LOCK}$	Logic 1
M/$\overline{IO}$	Logic 0
COD/$\overline{INTA}$	Logic 0
HLDA	Logic 0

Table 3-8. 82288 Command States during RESET

Signal	State
ALE	Logic 0
DEN	Logic 0
DT/$\overline{R}$	Logic 1
MCE	Logic 0
Commands	Logic 1

Note that the 82288 Bus Controller does not tri-state its command outputs during idle bus states. In a single CPU system, if the system designer wishes to effectively remove the 80286 CPU from the bus during RESET, the RESET signal can be connected to the 82288's MB input and to the output enable of the address latches (Figure 3-70). This forces the command

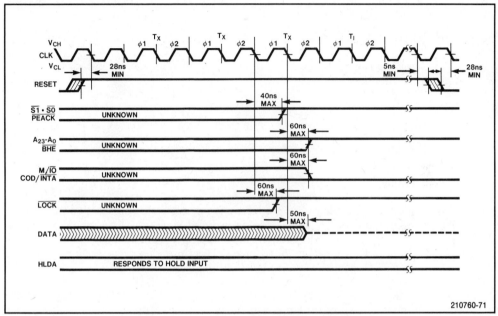

Figure 3-69. Signal States during RESET

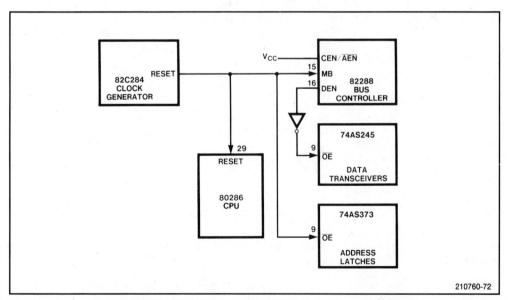

Figure 3-70. Disabling the 80286 Bus Interface on RESET

and address bus interface into the tri-state OFF condition while the 82288 drives DEN inactive, disabling the data bus transceivers. If the 82288 command outputs are tri-stated during RESET, the command lines should be pulled to V_{cc} through 2.2K ohm resistors to keep these signals in the HIGH state.

80286 Bus Timing

Figure 3-71 shows the timing relationships of the major 80286 local bus cycles. Included in this figure are the timing relationships for:

- Address and ALE timing
- Command timing
- $\overline{\text{READY}}$ timing
- Read cycle timing
- Write cycle timing

For most of these signals, timing is controlled by the system CLK signal. For this reason, the timing relationships between signals can be deduced simply by determining the clock cycles between the controlling clock edges, and adding or subtracting the appropriate minimum or maximum timing delays. Additional delays through any transceivers or latches must also be considered when determining signal timing.

One aspect of system timing not compensated for by this method is the worst-case relationship between minimum and maximum parameter values (i.e., tracking relationships). For example, consider a signal that has specified minimum and maximum turn-on and turn-off delays. For MOS devices such as the 80286 components, it is typically not possible for a device to simultaneously demonstrate a maximum turn-on and minimum turn-off delay even though worst-case analysis might imply the possibility. Because of this, worst-case analyses that mix both minimum and maximum delay parameters will typically exceed the worst case obtainable. Therefore, these analyses need not undergo further subjective degradation to obtain reliable worst-case values.

The following sections provide guidelines for analyzing the critical 80286 timing relationships for each of the signal groups described above.

For a more detailed discussion of local bus timing related specifically to interfacing memory and peripheral devices to the 80286, see Chapters Four and Five.

ADDRESS AND ALE TIMING

The address/ALE timing relationship is important to determine the ability to capture an address and local chip-selects during a bus cycle. The following discussion considers the standard bus timing using the ALE signal from the 82288 Bus Controller. Other design techniques having different timing relationships are described in Chapter Four.

The maximum address valid delay ($(13)_{max}$ = 60 ns) from the 8 MHz 80286 guarantees an address set-up time of at least 68 ns before ALE goes active, even assuming a minimum

MAJOR CYCLE TIMING

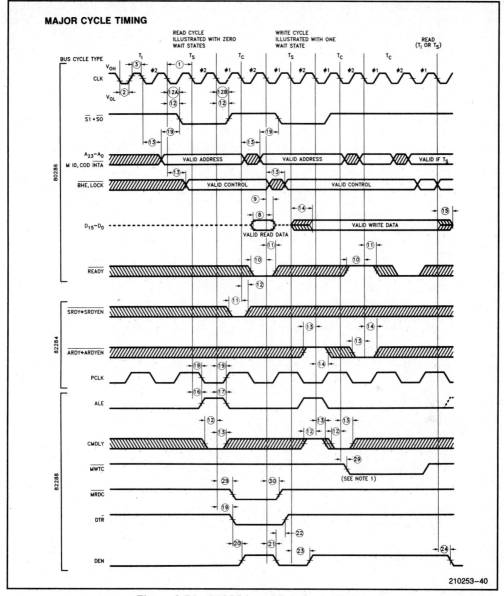

Figure 3-71. 80286 Local Bus Cycle Timing

ALE active delay ((16)$_{min}$ = 3 ns). If we assume a maximum strobe to output delay for the latches (STB-to-Output delay (max) = 11.5 ns for 74AS373 and 9.0 ns for 74AS533), and a maximum ALE active delay ((16)$_{max}$ = 20 ns), then the latest a valid address will be available at the outputs to the latches would be 31.0 ns before the start of T$_c$ for the 74AS373 latch, and 33.5 ns for the 74AS533 latch.

The minimum address hold time from ALE inactive (37.5 ns for an 8 MHz system) guarantees a stable address until well after ALE goes low. The ALE and latched address hold times guarantee a valid address to the system for a minimum of 40.5 ns after command inactive (again for an 8 MHz system).

Note that the maximum valid delay and minimum hold time for $\overline{BHE}$ guarantee that it will be latched by ALE and will be available to the system at the same time and for the same duration as the latched address.

ALE may also be used to capture latched chip-selects for local memory or I/O. To provide valid selects before ALE falls low, address decoding must be performed in the window between address valid and the trailing edge of ALE:

Address Valid to ALE Inactive					
Timing	Symbol	6 MHz	8 MHz	10 MHz	12.5 MHz
3 CLK Cycles − Address Valid Delay (max) + ALE Inactive Delay (min) − Input-To-STB Setup Time (min)	 13 17 	249.9 ns −80.0 ns 0.0 ns 0.0 ns	187.5 ns −60.0 ns 0.0 ns 0.0 ns	150.0 ns −35.0 ns 0.0 ns 0.0 ns	120.0 ns −32.0 ns 0.0 ns 0.0 ns
Maximum Address Decode Time =		169.9 ns	127.5 ns	115.0 ns	88.0 ns

Decoding should be performed sooner if a device select is required before a command signal goes active. Latched chip-selects are described in a previous section.

COMMAND TIMING

Command timing in Figure 3-71 is shown for an $\overline{MRDC}$ command with no delays, and for an $\overline{MWTC}$ command with 1 delay. Commands are typically delayed using the 82288 CMDLY input to provide a longer time from address and chip-select valid to command active. The use of CMDLY was discussed in a previous section. Note that delaying a command does not automatically lengthen the bus cycle.

Commands are enabled on the falling edge of CLK at the start of T_c. Commands are disabled on the falling edge of CLK after the end of T_c. The minimum command pulse width is:

Minimum Command Pulse Width					
Timing	Symbol	6 MHz	8 MHz	10 MHz	12.5 MHz
2 CLK Cycles − Command Active Delay from CLK (max) + Command Inactive Delay from CLK (min)	 29 30	166.6 ns −40.0 ns 5.0 ns	125.0 ns −25.0 ns 5.0 ns	100.0 ns −21.0 ns 5.0 ns	80.0 ns −21.0 ns 5.0 ns
Minimum Command Pulse Width =		131.6 ns	105.0 ns	84.0 ns	64.0 ns

with no delay (42.5 ns with 1 delay for an 8 MHz 80286). These command pulse widths are increased by 2 CLK cycles for each wait state inserted into a bus cycle.

READY TIMING

The detailed requirements of the 80286 $\overline{\text{READY}}$ signal and the Ready inputs for the 82C284 were described in an earlier section. The 82C284 Ready inputs are typically generated from the decoded address for a selected device, or address decode and command signals. Ready timing is shown for 0 wait state execution to illustrate the relationship of the 82C284 $\overline{\text{ARDY}}$ and $\overline{\text{SRDY}}$ input requirements with respect to address decode outputs and command signals.

Outputs from address decode logic can easily meet the $\overline{\text{ARDY}}$ or $\overline{\text{SRDY}}$ input requirements. $\overline{\text{ARDY}}$ obviously cannot be qualified by a command signal even when the command is not delayed. A command with no delay will meet the set-up requirements of $\overline{\text{SRDY}}$. Using an 8 MHz system as an example, once the maximum command active delay of 25 ns and the minimum $\overline{\text{SRDY}}$ set-up time of 17 ns are subtracted from phase 1 of the T_c clock cycle (62.5 ns), 20.5 ns remains for external logic to generate the $\overline{\text{SRDY}}$ signal. Commands with 0 or 1 delays may be used to qualify either ready input if the system is running with one or more wait states. Assuming the maximum command active delays, the external logic times for one wait state operation follows:

82C284 Input	Speed	Setup Time	Hold Time	External Logic Time 0 CMD Delay 1 Wait State	External Logic Time 1 CMD Delay 1 Wait State
$\overline{\text{ARDY}}$	12.5 MHz	0.0 ns	25.0 ns	59.0 ns	19.0 ns
	10 MHz	0.0 ns	30.0 ns	79.0 ns	29.0 ns
	8 MHz	0.0 ns	30.0 ns	100.0 ns	37.5 ns
	6 MHz	5.0 ns	30.0 ns	121.6 ns	38.3 ns
$\overline{\text{SRDY}}$	12.5 MHz	15.0 ns	2.0 ns	84.0 ns	44.0 ns
	10 MHz	15.0 ns	2.0 ns	114.0 ns	64.0 ns
	8 MHz	17.0 ns	0.0 ns	145.5 ns	83.0 ns
	6 MHz	25.0 ns	0.0 ns	184.9 ns	101.6 ns

An additional 2 CLK cycles are added to external logic time for each additional wait state.

READ CYCLE TIMING

Read timing consists of conditioning the bus, activating the read command, and establishing the data transceiver enable and direction controls. Figure 3-71 shows read timing for a CPU running with 0 wait states. During a read, the latched address is available to the system a minimum of 31.0 ns before the start of T_c, or 34.0 ns before command active. The read command is driven active early in T_c to enable the addressed device. DT/$\overline{\text{R}}$ is also driven low to condition the data transceivers to receive data, and DEN then enables the transceivers.

Data from the selected device must be valid at the CPU 10 ns before the end of T_c and must hold valid for 8 ns after T_c for an 8 MHz system. Any propagation delay through data transceivers must also be considered. For example; maximum input to output delay through a 74AS245 is 7.5 ns, and the maximum delay through a 74AS640 is 7 ns. This results in the following minimum address valid to data valid time (using 74AS245 non-inverting transceivers):

ALE Active to Valid Address Delay					
Timing	Symbol	6 MHz	8 MHz	10 MHz	12.5 MHz
3 CLK Cycles		249.9 ns	187.5 ns	150.0 ns	120.0 ns
— ALE Active Delay (max)	16	−25.0 ns	−20.0 ns	−16.0 ns	−16.0 ns
— 74AS373 C-To-Output Delay (max)		−11.5 ns	−11.5 ns	−11.5 ns	−11.5 ns
— 74AS245 Transceiver Delay (max)		−7.5 ns	−7.5 ns	−7.5 ns	−7.5 ns
— Read Data Setup Time (min)	8	−20.0 ns	−10.0 ns	−8.0 ns	−5.0 ns
Minimum Address Access Time =		185.9 ns	138.5 ns	107.0 ns	80.0 ns

Minimum command active to read data valid time is shown below.

Minimum Command Active to Data Valid (unbuffered)					
Timing	Symbol	6 MHz	8 MHz	10 MHz	12.5 MHz
2 CLK Cycles		166.6 ns	125.0 ns	100.0 ns	80.0 ns
— Command Active Delay from CLK (max)	29	−40.0 ns	−25.0 ns	−21.0 ns	−21.0 ns
— Read Data Setup Time (min)	8	−20.0 ns	−10.0 ns	−8.0 ns	−5.0 ns
Command Active to Data Valid =		106.6 ns	90.0 ns	71.0 ns	54.0 ns

These timing relationships increase by 2 CLK cycles for each wait state added to the bus cycle, as follows:

Read Cycle Timing					
Minimum Times	Speed	0 Wait States	1 Wait State	2 Wait State	3 Wait State
Address Valid to	12.5 MHz	80.0 ns	160.0 ns	240.0 ns	320.0 ns
Buffered Data Valid	10 MHz	107.0 ns	207.0 ns	307.0 ns	407.0 ns
(using 74AS245)	8 MHz	138.5 ns	263.5 ns	388.5 ns	513.5 ns
	6 MHz	185.9 ns	352.5 ns	519.1 ns	685.7 ns
Address Valid to	12.5 MHz	87.5 ns	167.5 ns	247.5 ns	327.5 ns
Data Valid	10 MHz	114.5 ns	214.5 ns	314.5 ns	414.5 ns
(unbuffered)	8 MHz	146.0 ns	271.0 ns	396.0 ns	521.0 ns
	6 MHz	193.4 ns	360.0 ns	526.6 ns	693.2 ns
Command Active to	12.5 MHz	54.0 ns	134.0 ns	214.0 ns	294.0 ns
Data Valid	10 MHz	71.0 ns	171.0 ns	271.0 ns	371. 0 ns
	8 MHz	90.0 ns	215.0 ns	340.0 ns	465. 0 ns
	6 MHz	106.6 ns	273.2 ns	439.8 ns	606.4 ns

WRITE CYCLE TIMING

Write timing involves providing write data to the system, generating the write command, and controlling data bus transceivers. Figure 3-71 shows write timing for a CPU running with 0 wait states. The transceiver direction control signal $DT/\overline{R}$ is conditioned to transmit at the end of each read cycle and does not change during a write cycle ($DT/\overline{R}$ is shown going high after a read). Data is placed on the data bus and DEN is driven active early in the bus cycle. Write data is guaranteed to be valid before the start of T_c (12.5 ns min for an 8 MHz system), and before the write command becomes active (15.5 ns min for an 8 MHz system). The write command is enabled early in T_c. Following is minimum time from write data valid until the data is latched into the system device (command inactive):

Minimum Write Data Valid to MWTC Inactive					
Timing	Symbol	6 MHz	8 MHz	10 MHz	12.5 MHz
3 CLK Cycles − Write Data Valid Delay (max) + Command Inactive Delay from CLK (min)	 14 30	249.9 ns −65.0 ns 5.0 ns	187.5 ns −50.0 ns 5.0 ns	150.0 ns −30.0 ns 5.0 ns	120.0 ns −30.0 ns 5.0 ns
Write Data Setup Time =		189.9 ns	142.5 ns	125.0 ns	95.0 ns

Write command pulse width is 105 ns minimum for an 8 MHz system. Data is held valid for a minimum of 37.5 ns after the write command goes inactive. All of these timing relationships increase 2 CLK cycles for each added wait state, as follows:

Write Cycle Timing					
Timing	Speed	0 Wait States	1 Wait State	2 Wait State	3 Wait State
Data Valid to Command Delay	12.5 MHz 10 MHz 8 MHz 6 MHz	95.0 ns 125.0 ns 142.5 ns 189.9 ns	175.0 ns 225.0 ns 267.5 ns 356.5 ns	255.0 ns 325.0 ns 392.5 ns 523.1 ns	335.0 ns 425.0 ns 517.5 ns 689.7 ns
Command Pulse Width	12.5 MHz 10 MHz 8 MHz 6 MHz	64.0 ns 84.0 ns 105.0 ns 131.6 ns	144.0 ns 184.0 ns 230.0 ns 298.2 ns	224.0 ns 284.0 ns 355.0 ns 464.8 ns	304.0 ns 384.0 ns 480.0 ns 631.4 ns

Of course, any propagation delays through data transceivers should be considered when finding the actual data set-up times for the system device being written to.

INTERRUPT-ACKNOWLEDGE TIMING

Timing for an interrupt-acknowledge cycle is identical to a read, with the $\overline{INTA}$ command being issued instead of $\overline{MRDC}$ or $\overline{IORC}$. The MCE signal is also issued during an interrupt-

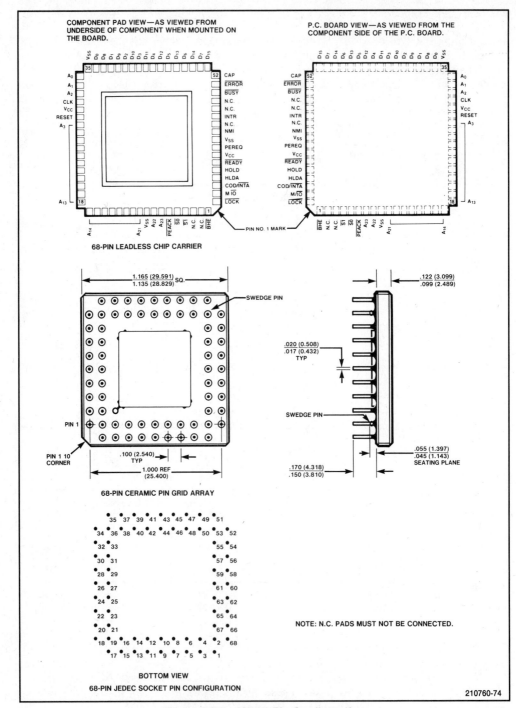

Figure 3-72. 80286 Pin Configuration

acknowledge cycle, going high following the start of Phase 2 of Ts during the first INTA cycle, and falling low during Phase 2 of the final T_c of the cycle. The two back-to-back INTA cycles required to complete an interrupt-acknowledge sequence have been described in an earlier section.

Physical Design Considerations

When designing a system using the 80286 processor, the physical design considerations include the connection and decoupling of power, ground, and the 80286 CAP pin, and physical provisions for debugging with an oscilloscope, logic analyzer, or Intel Integrated In-Circuit Emulator (I²ICE).

The 80286 processor is packaged in either a JEDEC-approved 68-pin leadless chip carrier, or in a Pin Grid Array package. Figure 3-72 shows the pin configurations for both the pad/pin view (the underside of the component when mounted on a PC board) and the top view (the top of the component when mounted on a PC board). The footprint of the Pin Grid Array package is identical to that of the socket for the leadless chip carrier, as shown in the figure.

POWER, GROUND, AND CAP CONNECTIONS

As shown in Figure 3-73, the 80286 processor has two power pins and three ground pin connections. The two power pins must be connected to +5 volts; all three ground pins must be connected to 0 volts. A 0.1 μF low-impedance decoupling capacitor should be connected between power and ground. This capacitor should be located as close as possible to the CPU socket.

The power and ground connections from the power supply to the CPU should be as low impedance and inductance as practically possible. Large surge currents are possible, for example, when all 24 address outputs change at once.

A 0.47μF ± 20% 12V capacitor must be connected between the 80286 CAP pin and ground. This capacitor filters the output of the internal substrate bias generator. A maximum leakage current of 1 μA is allowed through the capacitor.

DEBUGGING CONSIDERATIONS

The 68-pin JEDEC socket does not allow for direct access to the pins of the CPU using an oscilloscope or logic analyzer probe. Most of the CPU signals are accessible on the DIP leads of the latches, transceivers, and the Bus Controller. To allow convenient access to the signals directly at the CPU, however, physical debugging aids should be provided in the PC board layout.

Solder pads located around the CPU package and labelled with the signal name provide the easiest and most inexpensive solution to access by a scope probe. To allow probes to be temporarily attached (clipped) to the signal, terminal posts should be soldered into holes at the solder pad locations (Figure 3-74). These terminal posts allow easy attachment of oscilloscope and logic analyzer probes.

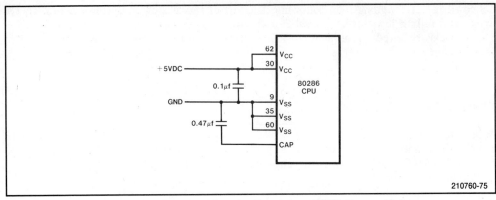

Figure 3-73. Required Power, Ground and CAP Connections

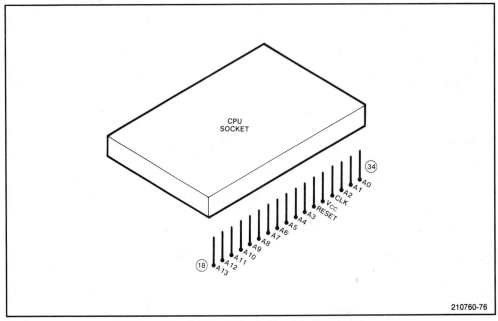

Figure 3-74. Terminal Posts Provide Signal Access

When using Intel's I²ICE as a debugging tool, the designer must also make provisions for connecting the 80286 probe cable to the CPU socket. Figure 3-75 shows the requirements to physically support debugging with I²ICE. The 80286 probe exits the socket on the side corresponding to pins 18-34 of the CPU package (the 80286 component is installed upside down in the socket). A Texttool 268-5400 or similar socket is recommended for ICE access. The texttool lid must allow access to the socket by the ICE cables. At least one inch of space must be provided on that side of the socket to allow the probe cable to fan away from the board. DIP packages soldered to the printed circuit board probably will not interfere with the cable on the 80286 probe. High profile devices or devices installed in socket may interfere with the cable and should not be located near that side of the CPU package.

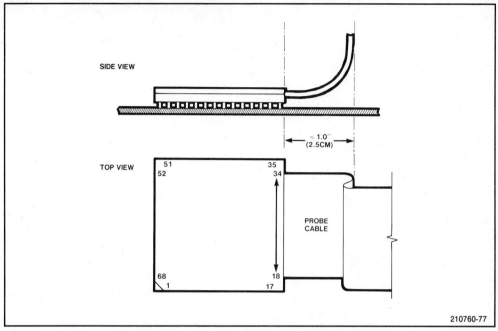

Figure 3-75. I²ICE™ Probe Cabling Requirements

THE iLBX™ BUS—A HIGH-PERFORMANCE LOCAL BUS STANDARD

The iLBX bus is a high-performance bus interface standard that permits the modular expansion of 80286 systems by simply adding additional boards containing memory, I/O subsystems, and other peripheral devices or controllers to the 80286 local bus.

The iLBX Local Bus Expansion standard is described in the *iLBX™ Bus Specification*, Order Number 144456, Rev. B.

Memory Interfacing

4

CHAPTER 4
MEMORY INTERFACING

This chapter provides guidelines for designing memory subsystems for the 80286.

One of the principal considerations in designing memory subsystems for the 80286 is the effect of memory performance on the performance of the overall 80286 system. In this chapter, the performance implications of specific memory designs are examined in detail:

- In the first section of this chapter, the tradeoff between system performance and memory cost is examined in detail. The important relationships to consider are the relationship of system performance to memory performance, memory performance to memory device speed, and, finally, memory device speed to memory cost.

- The second section uses benchmark test results to identify the actual relationship between memory performance (measured by the number of required wait states) and overall system performance. The impact of wait states on overall system performance is not as severe as you might initially expect.

- In the third section, several memory interface techniques are introduced to show that memory system performance is determined as much by the memory system design as it is by the actual speed of the memory devices used. Specifically, two interface techniques can be used to gain increased memory performance while using relatively slow memories.

- The fourth section contains a detailed timing analysis of the three memory interface techniques introduced in the previous section.

- The fifth section of this chapter contains specific details for interfacing common types of memory devices to the 80286. ROMs, static RAMs, and pseudo-static RAMs are described, as well as the use of the 8207 Advanced Dynamic RAM Controller and the 82C08 DRAM Controller to interface to dynamic RAMs.

MEMORY SPEED VS. PERFORMANCE AND COST

In a high-performance microprocessing system, overall system performance is linked very closely with the performance of its memory subsystems. Memory is used for program storage, and for the storage of data and information used in processing. The vast majority of bus operations in a typical microprocessing system are operations to or from memory.

It makes little sense to couple a high-performance CPU with low-performance memory; a high-performance CPU running in a system with a large number of wait states provides no better throughput than a low-performance processor, and is certainly more expensive. To realize the performance potential of the 80286 CPU, it is imperative that the CPU be coupled to relatively fast memory.

At the same time, however, fast memory devices are more expensive than slower memory devices. In a system such as the 80286 supporting up to sixteen megabytes of addressable memory, it is clear that providing a large physical memory space using the fastest available memory devices would result in an exceedingly costly design.

This cost/performance tradeoff can be mediated to some extent by partitioning functions and using a combination of both fast and slow memories. Locating the most frequently-used functions in fast memory and the less-used functions in slower memory will reduce costs over a system that uses fast memory throughout. For example, in a RAM-based system that uses read-only memory devices primarily during initialization, the PROM/EPROM can be very slow (3-4 wait states) with little affect on system performance. RAM memory can also be partitioned into fast local memory and slower system memory.

It is clear, then, that designers must strike a balance between system performance and system costs, and that the choice of memory subsystems is the balancing factor. In order to intelligently tradeoff cost versus performance, however, it is useful to examine the principle relationships that make up this balance.

Three relationships tie together system cost and system performance:

1. System performance as a function of memory performance

2. Memory performance as a function of memory subsystem design and memory device speed

3. Memory device speed as related to memory subsystem cost

System Performance and Memory Performance

System performance measures the speed at which the microprocessing system performs a given task or set of instructions. Memory performance measures the speed at which the microprocessor can access or store a single item of information into memory. To accommodate slower memories, wait states can be inserted into the 80286 bus cycle. A less-common alternative is to use a slower clock frequency for the 80286, thereby lengthening the 80286 bus cycle.

Each wait state that is inserted into a bus operation represents a 50% increase in bus cycle time over zero-wait-state operation. Although at first glance you might expect memory performance and overall system performance to track each other in a one-to-one relationship, this is not actually the case.

As explained in the following section, the increased bus cycle time for each additional wait state results in an average increase of only 25% in overall CPU execution time, rather than the 50% increase that simple hand calculations might predict. Benchmark tests reveal that overall CPU execution time increases by about 25% over zero-wait operation when running with 1 wait state, and an additional 25% over zero-wait operation for each additional wait state. The following section of this chapter explains the architectural and operational characteristics of the 80286 which reduce the effect of wait states on system performance.

The 80286 clock frequency is directly related to system performance; execution time increases in direct proportion to the increase in clock period, or the reduction in clock frequency. A 6-MHz 80286 requires 33 percent more time to execute a program than an 8 MHz 80286 operating with the same number of wait states. Since a slower clock frequency increases the 80286 bus cycle times, however, fewer wait states may be required to accommodate slow memory devices. A slight reduction in clock frequency may actually increase system performance in some instances if the slower clock allows the same memories to be used with fewer wait states.

Memory Speed and Memory Performance

The relationship between memory subsystem performance and the speed of individual memory devices is determined by the design of the memory subsystem. A later section of this chapter describes several design alternatives that permit relatively high-performance memory subsystems to be designed using relatively slower memory devices. These design alternatives include the use of special address strobe logic and the use of interleaved memory banks.

Special address strobe logic can be used in place of the 82288 ALE signal to generate a valid address to the memory subsystem earlier in the 80286 bus cycle. This technique results in an increased memory access time, permitting the use of slower memories without requiring additional wait states.

Interleaving memory access between two or more banks of memory devices can also increase the memory access time for most bus cycles. Using interleaved memory, memory devices are grouped into banks so that each sequential fetch comes from the next memory bank. In a memory system partitioned into four memory banks, for example, a program that fetches four 16-bit words from consecutive addresses actually fetches one word from each bank. The early address generated by the CPU can be latched and made available to the next memory bank while the address for the previous cycle is still valid for the previously-selected memory bank. These memory interface techniques are described in more detail later in this chapter.

80286 SYSTEM PERFORMANCE WITH WAIT STATES

The 80286 system supports wait states in the 80286 bus cycle to allow the use of slower memory and peripheral devices. These wait states extend the time required to perform individual bus operations, however, and so directly influence 80286 system performance.

Wait states extend the 80286 bus cycle by adding an additional T_c state for each wait state desired. For an 8-MHz 80286, each wait state adds an additional 125 ns (an increase of 50%) to the minimum bus cycle time of 250 ns. An 80286 CPU running with one wait state executes a bus cycle in 375 ns, compared with the 250 ns required when operating with zero wait states.

Calculating performance degradation from this figure alone, however, will lead to overly-pessimistic results. On average, benchmark tests show that each wait state adds an additional 25% of the zero-wait execution time to the overall execution time of a task. Simple hand calculations would predict an increase of 50% over the zero-wait execution time for each wait state.

Table 4-1 shows the results of benchmark tests using four Pascal benchmarks and five assembly-language benchmark programs. These benchmarks were executed on an 80286 system operating with from zero to four wait states. The Pascal benchmarks averaged a 23% increase in execution time for each additional wait state, while the assembly-language benchmarks showed an average 20% increase in execution time for each additional wait state.

Explaining the Benchmark Results

As shown in the benchmark results in Table 4-1, the effect of wait states on 80286 performance varies with the nature of the program that is executing and the types of bus cycles being performed. The pipelining within the 80286 CPU sometimes causes idle bus cycles while the CPU is executing prefetched instructions, and no other bus operations are requested. Wait states reduce the number of these idle bus cycles and, on average, do not produce as severe a degradation in performance as simple performance calculations might predict.

The characteristics of an individual program are important in determining processor performance with wait states. For example, when the CPU is executing a program containing many multiplication and division operations, performance is not degraded significantly by wait states. This is because processor performance is limited by processing speed and not by bus throughput.

During program execution, the 80286 Bus Unit will prefetch instructions and fill the instruction and prefetch queues. These prefetch operations occur several clock cycles ahead of execution and occur when the bus would otherwise be idle. Any wait states in these instruction prefetches will not usually delay program execution.

On the other hand, a program that makes extensive use of the bus for manipulating data will show greater degradation in performance when wait states are introduced. Programs that use many data read and write operations are examples of programs that are bus-limited.

Since data read operations are performed in response to an executing instruction, the Execution Unit must wait for the data to be read. Therefore, any delay in reading the data will have a direct impact on system performance. Each wait state will add an additional processor clock cycle to the execution time of the current instruction. Word data read from odd addresses will result in two back-to-back byte read operations, resulting in twice the delay before completion of the read instruction.

Data write operations are performed by the 80286 Bus Unit from information stored in temporary data and address registers. The Execution unit fills these temporary registers and continues executing. Because the Execution unit is not delayed, isolated data write operations with several wait states will not affect system performance.

Wait states in the write operation may delay subsequent data read operations or instruction prefetches, however. If several back-to-back data write operations are performed, the 80286 Execution unit may have to wait for the Bus unit to finish before performing the next data write. Word writes to odd addresses will result in twice the number of delays as for word writes to even addresses.

Table 4-1. 80286 Performance with Wait States (8 MHz)

Intel Pascal Benchmarks (8 MHz)						
Benchmark	Performance	0 Wait States	1 Wait State	2 Wait States	3 Wait States	4 Wait States
Queens	Time (s)	7.19	9.224	11.496	14.43	17.2
	Perform.	1.0	1.28	1.6	2.0	2.4
GCD	Time (s)	12.13	14.665	16.87	20.48	24.23
	Perform.	1.0	1.21	1.39	1.69	2.0
Bubble	Time (s)	5.587	7.586	9.74	11.83	14.64
Sort	Perform.	1.0	1.36	1.74	2.12	2.62
Matrix	Time (s)	6.92	7.607	9.12	11.08	13.33
Mult.	Perform.	1.0	1.1	1.32	1.6	1.93
Average Performance:		1.0	1.23	1.51	1.85	2.23

Intel Assembly-Language Benchmarks (8 MHz)					
Program	Performance	0 Wait States	1 Wait State	2 Wait States	3 Wait States
PCALL	Time (us)	17.0	21.38	27.50	33.25
	Perform.	1.0	1.26	1.62	1.96
BSORT	Time (us)	494.0	633.0	778.0	946.0
	Perform.	1.0	1.28	1.58	1.92
XLAT	Time (us)	415.0	466.0	565.0	698.0
	Perform.	1.0	1.12	1.36	1.68
XFORM	Time (ms)	285.0	317.0	346.0	385.0
	Perform.	1.0	1.12	1.22	1.35
INSPECT	Time (ms)	217.0	254.0	289.0	346.0
	Perform.	1.0	1.17	1.33	1.59
Average Performance:		1.0	1.19	1.42	1.70

Since the nature of the program has a direct impact on the performance of the 80286 with one or more wait states, any estimate of CPU performance must take this information into account. The best estimates can be made by using the results tabulated for a benchmark program with characteristics most closely matching those of the intended application. The only way to obtain a precise figure for a particular application is to run that application and measure its performance.

The Intel Pascal Benchmarks

The Pascal benchmark results shown in Table 4-1 reflect the performance of an 80286 operating in Real-Address mode. These benchmarks were written in Pascal and compiled using Intel's Pascal-86 compiler version 2.0. The benchmarks themselves are described in the *8086 System Benchmark Report*, Order Number 210352. The following paragraphs give a brief description of the Intel Pascal benchmarks.

QUEENS (Chess Simulation)

The Intel Queens benchmark lists all possible combinations of non-attacking queens on a 9 × 9 chessboard. This program tests control structures and boolean evaluations, and evaluates the code generated for certain commonly-used statements (A = A + 1, for example).

GCD (Greatest Common Denominator)

This Intel program computes the greatest common denominator of two integers using a recursive function call. Function overhead and the MOD operator are tested by this benchmark.

BUBBLE SORT

This Intel benchmark sorts 1000 integers into numerically-ascending order using the exchange (bubble) sort algorithm. This benchmark extensively tests control structures, relational expressions, and array references.

MATRIX MULTIPLY

This Intel benchmark uses a simple row/column inner product method to compute the product of two 32 × 32 matrices. The elements of the matrices are integers. The benchmark tests control structure arrays, array references, and integer arithmetic.

The Intel Assembly-Language Benchmarks

The assembly-language benchmark results shown in Table 4-1 reflect the performance of an 80286 operating in Protected mode. These benchmarks are described in the *8086 16-Bit Microprocessor Benchmark Report*. The following paragraphs give a brief description of each of these assembly-language benchmarks.

INSPECT (Automated Parts Inspection)

The automated parts inspection program controls an image-dissection camera having two 8-bit D/A converters (for X and Y axis control) and a 12-bit A/D converter that generates a gray-scale signal. For each of the 16,384 (128 × 128) points, the measured gray-scale signal is compared with a known good gray-scale value (stored in memory) to determine if it is within tolerance. One 16-bit multiply and one 16-bit divide are performed for each of the 16,384 points.

XLAT (Block Translation)

The block translation benchmark translates each EBCDIC character from a memory buffer into an ASCII character to be stored in a second buffer. The translation detects when an EOT character is encountered or when the entire EBCDIC buffer has been translated. For the benchmark tests, the EBCDIC buffer contains 132 EBCDIC characters, none of which is an EOT character.

BSORT (Bubble Sort)

The bubble sort benchmark sorts a one-dimensional array containing 16-bit integer elements into numerically-ascending order using the exchange (bubble) sort algorithm. For the benchmark tests, the array contains 10 integers that are initially arranged in descending order.

XFORM (Graphics X-Y Transformation)

The X-Y transformation benchmark expands or compresses (scales) a selected graphics window containing 16-bit unsigned integer X-Y pairs. Each X data value is offset by X_0 and multiplied by a fractional scale factor, while each Y data value is offset by Y_0 and multiplied by the same scale factor. One 16-bit multiply and one 16-bit divide are performed for each of the X-Y coordinates. For the benchmark test, the selected window contains 16,384 X-Y pairs.

PCALL (Reentrant Procedure)

The reentrant-procedure benchmark exercises processor features that are used to implement a reentrant procedure. Three input parameters are passed by value to the reentrant procedure. Prior to the call, one parameter is in one of the general registers, while the other parameters are stored in memory locations. Upon entry, the reentrant procedure preserves the state of the processor, assuming that it will use all of the general registers. The reentrant procedure then allocates storage for three local variables, adds the three passed parameters, and stores the result in a local variable. Upon exit, the state of the processor is restored.

MEMORY INTERFACE TECHNIQUES

In the previous section, the impact of memory performance and wait states on system performance was examined in detail. In this section, memory performance itself is examined in order to understand how the performance of a memory subsystem is determined as much by the subsystem design as by the speed of the individual memory devices. Three different memory interface techniques are introduced, and the advantages and tradeoffs of each are described. The *Memory Design Handbook* describes still other techniques that may be used.

Standard Address Strobe Logic

Chapter Three describes a straightforward method for interfacing to memory, using the ALE output of the 82288 Bus Controller to strobe the address and chip-select latches. Figure 4-1 shows this memory-interface model, showing the ALE signal from the 82288 Bus Controller being used to control the 74AS373 address latches.

The timing of this straightforward interface technique using the standard ALE address strobe is examined in Chapter Three. Although this technique is simple and requires only a small number of devices to implement, it provides only 138.5 ns of address access time at zero-wait-states for an 8 MHz 80286 system. This limited access time is sufficient only for very fast static RAM devices; slower memory devices will require additional wait states and corresponding reductions in system performance.

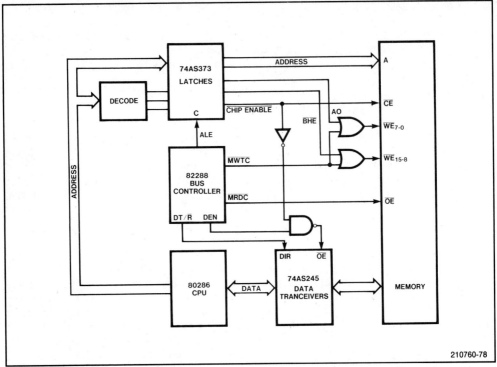

Figure 4-1. Memory Interface Using Standard ALE Signal

Other, more complex, methods of interfacing memory devices to the 80286 can increase address access time to permit high-performance operation with slower memory devices. The following two sections introduce these two techniques.

Special Address Strobe Logic

As an enhancement to the timing characteristics of the standard memory-interface technique described above, special address strobe logic can be used to generate a valid address to the memory devices at an earlier point in the bus cycle. This special address strobe logic is shown in Figure 4-2.

The address strobe logic shown in Figure 4-2 generates an address strobe as early as possible in the memory cycle; that is, as soon as the command from the previous memory operation becomes inactive. This memory-interface technique trades off address hold time following command inactive (few memory devices require a lengthy address hold) in order to gain additional address access time.

The timing of this special address strobe logic is described in detail in a later portion of this chapter. The principle advantages of the special strobe logic depicted in Figure 4-2 is that address access time is increased from 138.5 ns at zero wait states using the standard ALE

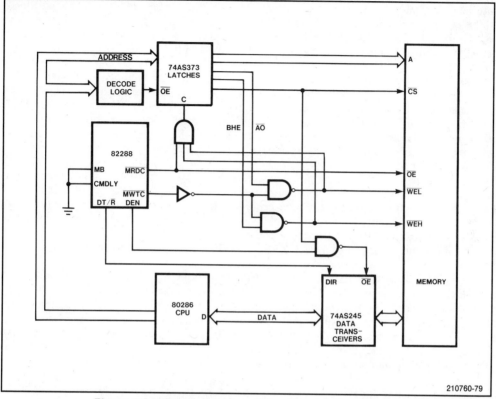

Figure 4-2. Memory Interface Using Special Strobe Logic

strobe to as much as 190.5 ns using the special address strobe on an 8 MHz 80286 system. This increased address access time permits slower memory devices to be used in 80286 systems, while still permitting operation at zero wait states.

The tradeoff made when using this special strobe logic is the increased hardware overhead required to implement the strobe logic. The cost savings of using slower memories to obtain a given level of performance more than offsets the cost of the additional logic required.

Interleaved Memory

For systems that require large amounts of memory, an interleaved memory subsystem can provide even greater economies than using the special strobe logic just described, at the cost of extra address latches and additional control logic.

With an interleaved memory subsystem, memory devices are grouped into banks so that every sequential memory fetch comes from a different memory bank. For example, in a memory system partitioned into four memory banks, a program that fetches four 16-bit words from consecutive addresses actually fetches one word from each bank.

Interleaved memory banks permit designers to take full advantage of the 80286's pipelined address timing. By letting the early address from the 80286 propagate into the next memory bank while the address for the current memory cycle is still valid in another bank, address access times for the individual memory devices can be greatly increased.

Of course, occasional back-to-back memory cycles to the same memory bank may occur, which will require a longer bus cycle than if the access was to a different bank. The interleave control logic must accommodate the longer bus cycle times by inserting an additional wait state into the cycle. On the average, though, these memory "hits" comprise only 7% of all memory cycles using two interleaved memory banks, and 80286 execution time for typical software is increased only 4% on average over execution exclusively at zero wait states.

Figure 4-3 shows an example circuit that uses interleaved addressing and special address strobes to increase the access time for most memory cycles. The memory devices are configured into two banks with successive memory words assigned to alternate banks (address line 1 is used as a bank select). Each bank has its own address latches and strobe signal. A decoder such as the 74F138 decodes the CPU address to generate chip enables for the individual memory devices, and a $\overline{\text{BANKSEL}}$ signal is decoded to enable the address strobes.

Figure 4-4 shows the logic that generates the address strobe signals to the individual banks, and detects consecutive reads to the same bank. Generally, the address strobes will be high until a read to one of the memory banks occurs. The high address strobes maintain the address latches in their transparent state to enable an address generated by the CPU to be transmitted to the memories in the shortest possible time. (With the standard memory model, the address would not be transmitted to memory until just before the start of T_c due to the 82288 ALE timing and strobe to output delays.)

The address strobe to the selected bank is driven low on the falling edge of CLK at the start of the first T_c state to latch the address and chip selects to the respective memory devices. The address strobe to the non-selected bank remains high, maintaining the respective address latches in their transparent state.

The timing of this interleaved memory system is described in a later section of this chapter. The principal advantage of using an interleaved memory system such as this is the increased access time provided at the beginning of most 80286 bus cycles. Access time requirements as long as 223.5 ns for an 8 MHz system can be accommodated using this configuration, while still permitting most 80286 memory operations to occur with zero wait states. With one wait state, access times as long as 348.5 ns can be reliably accommodated, as compared with access times of 263.5 ns for the standard memory configuration at one wait state.

This increased access time results in a direct cost savings without reducing performance. For an example system using EPROMs with one wait state, the savings from interleaving are composed of the savings from using 300 ns EPROMS instead of the more expensive 250 ns EPROMS, multiplied by the number of EPROMS, and subtracting the additional interleave circuitry. For large-memory systems, this cost savings without reducing performance can be well worth the effort.

Table 4-2 compares the various memory interface techniques and provides guidelines on selecting a particular technique for specific applications. The following section analyzes the timing of each of these interface techniques in more detail.

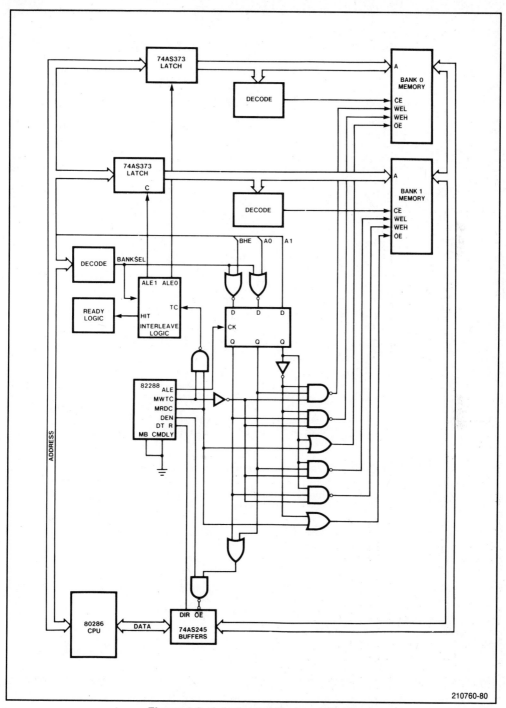

Figure 4-3. Interleaved Memory Circuit

210760-80

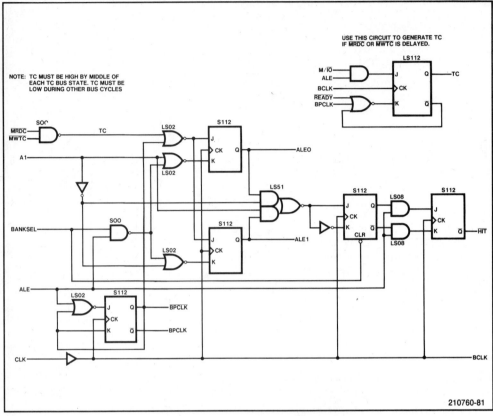

Figure 4-4. Address Strobe Generation

Table 4-2. Comparing Several Memory Interface Techniques

	Address Access Time Provided Memory Interface by Single-Buffered System with Technique 0 Wait States				
	12.5 MHz	10 MHz	8 MHz	6 MHz	Usage Guidelines
Standard ALE Strobe	80.0 ns	107.0 ns	138.5 ns	185.9 ns	Useful for implementing small bootstrap EPROMs.
Special Address Strobe Logic	110.5 ns	147.5 ns	190.5 ns	258.7 ns	Useful for small static RAM systems; Insufficient address hold time for I/O devices.
Interleaved Memories	144.0 ns	188.0 ns	223.5 ns	297.5 ns	Useful for large EPROM or static RAM arrays; 2 sets of address latches with 6 TTL DIPs to control interleaving.

TIMING ANALYSIS FOR MEMORY OPERATIONS

To design a memory subsystem for the 80286, designers must understand the timing of the 80286 memory cycle. In the sections that follow, critical timing values are calculated for each of the memory interface techniques described in the previous section.

Calculations using worst-case timing, rather than typical timing, are used exclusively throughout this manual and are strongly recommended to all designers using these materials. By using worst-case timing values, you will be able to determine critical timing paths, the need for wait states, and compatibility between various memory devices.

Analyses using typical timing parameters make implicit assumptions about the system under study. Typical calculations assume that with 5 to 8 devices in series, the probability of all devices simultaneously exhibiting worst-case timing is acceptably remote. However, since many modern designs use only 2 or 3 devices in series, the probability of all devices showing worst-case timing characteristics becomes unacceptably high.

For this reason, worst-case timing calculations are used to assure reliable operation over all variations in temperature, voltage, and individual device characteristics. Worst-case timing values are determined by assuming the maximum delay in the latched address, chip-select, and command signals, and the longest propagation delays through data buffers and transceivers.

Standard ALE Timing

The 80286 memory cycle using the standard ALE timing from the 82288 Bus Controller is described in Chapter Three. The analysis of timing is largely dependent on the particular memory configuration. Figure 4-1, shown previously, shows the memory model used to analyze timing using the standard ALE signal timing. Address and chip selects are measured from the outputs of latches (strobed by ALE). Data valid is measured at the data pins of the CPU. $\overline{\text{MRDC}}$ is an 82288 output.

A single data buffer is used to prevent the AC loading from the memory subsystem from exceeding the 80286 capacitive limit of 100 pF. For very small systems, the 80286 can be used without data buffers. For large, multi-board systems, two levels of buffering may be used. In any case, the appropriate buffer delays should be considered when performing timing calculations.

READ OPERATIONS

Figure 4-5 shows the timing for zero-wait state memory read cycles using the standard ALE address strobe.

For read operations, data must be valid at the pins of the 80286 10 ns before the falling edge of CLK at the end of the final T_c for an 8 MHz system. The critical timing parameters that determine whether one or more wait states are required for a given memory subsystem design are the required address and command access times before read data will be valid.

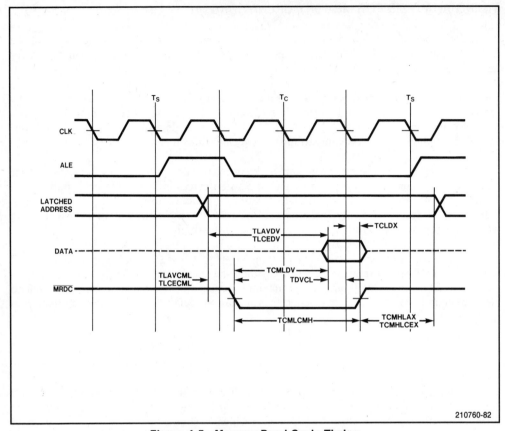

210760-82

Figure 4-5. Memory Read Cycle Timing

The maximum allowable address and chip-enable access times for the memory configuration shown in Figure 4-1, with zero wait states, and incorporating one transceiver delay, can be calculated as follows:

Standard ALE Strobe - ALE Active to Valid Data Delay for a Read					
Timing	Symbol	6 MHz	8 MHz	10 MHz	12.5 MHz
3 CLK Cycles		249.9 ns	187.5 ns	150.0 ns	120.0 ns
— ALE Active Delay (max)	16	−25.0 ns	−20.0 ns	−16.0 ns	−16.0 ns
— 74AS373 C-To-Output Delay (max)		−11.5 ns	−11.5 ns	−11.5 ns	−11.5 ns
— 74AS245 Transceiver Delay (max)		−7.5 ns	−7.5 ns	−7.5 ns	−7.5 ns
— Read Data Setup Time (min)	8	−20.0 ns	−10.0 ns	−8.0 ns	−5.0 ns
Maximum Address Access Time =		185.9 ns	138.5 ns	107.0 ns	80.0 ns

The calculations for maximum allowed command or output-enable access time before data valid are similar:

Standard ALE Strobe - Command Active to Data Valid for a Read					
Timing	Symbol	6 MHz	8 MHz	10 MHz	12.5 MHz
2 CLK Cycles — Command Active Delay from CLK (max) — 74AS245 Transceiver Delay (max) — Read Data Setup Time (min)	 29 8	166.6 ns −40.0 ns −7.5 ns −20.0 ns	125.0 ns −25.0 ns −7.5 ns −10.0 ns	100.0 ns −21.0 ns −7.5 ns −8.0 ns	80.0 ns −21.0 ns −7.5 ns −5.0 ns
Maximum Command Access Time =		99.1 ns	82.5 ns	63.5 ns	46.5 ns

Because of the pipelined address timing of the 80286 CPU, the memory configuration shown in Figure 4-1 provides a significant timing interval after the 80286 address is valid and before the address latch (ALE) strobe becomes active. This interval can be used for address decoding without reducing the chip-enable access times calculated above. The maximum address decode time that this memory configuration can provide without reducing the chip-enable access time is calculated as follows:

Standard ALE Strobe - Address Valid to ALE Active for a Read					
Timing	Symbol	6 MHz	8 MHz	10 MHz	12.5 MHz
2 CLK Cycles — Address Valid Delay (max) + ALE Active Delay (min)	 13 16	166.6 ns −80.0 ns 3.0 ns	125.0 ns −60.0 ns 3.0 ns	100.0 ns −35.0 ns 3.0 ns	80.0 ns −32.0 ns 3.0 ns
Maximum Address Decode Time =		89.6 ns	68.0 ns	68.0 ns	51.0 ns

This maximum decode time is not affected by the use of wait states in the 80286 bus cycle.

If wait states are inserted into the memory cycle, access times for the relevant parameters are increased by 2 CLK cycles for each wait state. Address, chip-enable, and command access times for a single buffered 80286 system running with from zero to three wait states are shown in Table 4-3.

In view of the timing values shown in the table, fast static RAMs and very fast DRAMs can be used in this configuration with zero wait states. An 80286 operating with a single wait state provides sufficient timing for almost all static RAM devices, a large number of dynamic RAM devices, and faster ROM/PROM/EPROM devices. An 80286 operating with two wait states provides sufficient timing for all but the slowest semiconductor memory devices.

Table 4-3. Timing for Read Operations Using Standard ALE Strobe

Maximum Access Times	Speed	0 Wait States	1 Wait State	2 Wait States	3 Wait States
Address Access Time (max)	12.5 MHz	80.0 ns	160.0 ns	240.0 ns	320.0 ns
	10 MHz	107.0 ns	207.0 ns	307.0 ns	407.0 ns
	8 MHz	138.5 ns	263.5 ns	388.5 ns	513.5 ns
	6 MHz	185.9 ns	352.5 ns	519.1 ns	685.7 ns
Chip Select Access Time (max)	12.5 MHz	80.0 ns	160.0 ns	240.0 ns	320.0 ns
	10 MHz	107.0 ns	207.0 ns	307.0 ns	407.0 ns
	8 MHz	138.5 ns	263.5 ns	388.5 ns	513.5 ns
	6 MHz	185.9 ns	352.5 ns	519.1 ns	685.7 ns
Command Access Time (max)	12.5 MHz	46.5 ns	126.5 ns	206.5 ns	286.5 ns
	10 MHz	63.5 ns	163.5 ns	263.5 ns	363.5 ns
	8 MHz	82.5 ns	207.5 ns	332.5 ns	457.5 ns
	6 MHz	99.1 ns	265.7 ns	432.3 ns	598.9 ns

Another critical timing parameter for memory read operations is the output data float time; that is, the time from the memory output-enable inactive until the memory device disables its data drivers following a read operation. This timing value is critical if the 80286 attempts to perform a write operation immediately following a read from the memory device. If this back-to-back read/write sequence occurs, the memory device must disable its data drivers before the 82288 Bus Controller re-enables the data transceivers, or data bus contention will occur.

For the memory configuration shown in Figure 4-1, the maximum data float time afforded a memory device at 8 MHz is 54.5 ns maximum. For certain memory devices, this allowed data float time may be inadequate. If this is the case, then the possibility of bus contention must be specifically prevented.

To accommodate the data float time requirements of slower memory and I/O devices, the output enables of the data bus transceivers must be delayed for the necessary length of time. Figure 4-6 shows an example circuit that delays enabling the data transceivers following a read operation to the selected memory devices. This circuit provides a maximum data float time for memory devices of:

Standard ALE Strobe - Command Inactive to DEN Active for a Read					
Timing	Symbol	6 MHz	8 MHz	10 MHz	12.5 MHz
2 CLK Cycles − Command Inactive Delay from CLK (max) + 74AS245 Transceiver Enable Time (min)	30	166.6 ns −30.0 ns 2.0 ns	125.0 ns −25.0 ns 2.0 ns	100.0 ns −20.0 ns 2.0 ns	80.0 ns −20.0 ns 2.0 ns
Maximum Data Float Time (Fig. 4-6) =		138.6 ns	102.0 ns	82.0 ns	62.0 ns

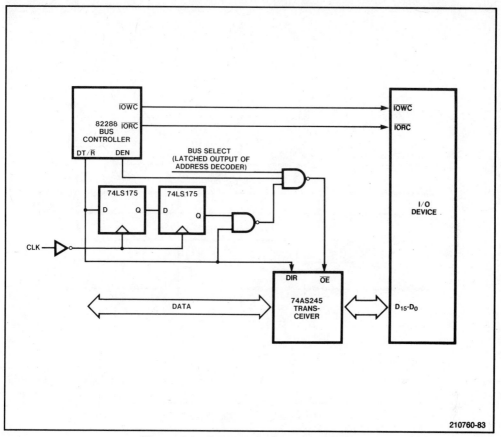

Figure 4-6. Delaying Transceiver Enable

WRITE OPERATIONS

For typical write operations to a memory device, data is latched into the device on the rising edge of the Write command at the end of T_c. The important timing parameters determining whether wait states are required are the address and command access times before command high.

The timing for memory write cycles, shown in Figure 4-7, uses the same model as that for read cycles. Address, chip select/enable, and command generation are the same as for read operations.

Since the latest time that data is active coincides with the latest possible latched address and chip select times (2.5 ns before the falling edge of CLK at the start of T_c), the maximum

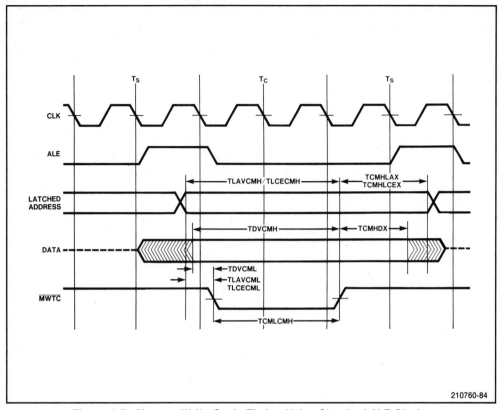

Figure 4-7. Memory Write Cycle Timing Using Standard ALE Strobe

address-valid to command-high access time provided during write operations with zero wait states is:

Standard ALE Strobe - Maximum Address Valid to Command High Access Time for Write					
Timing	Symbol	6 MHz	8 MHz	10 MHz	12.5 MHz
3 CLK Cycles		249.9 ns	187.5 ns	150.0 ns	120.0 ns
− ALE Active Delay (max)	16	−25.0 ns	−20.0 ns	−16.0 ns	−16.0 ns
− 74AS373 C-To-Output Delay (max)		−11.5 ns	−11.5 ns	−11.5 ns	−11.5 ns
+ Command Inactive Delay from CLK (min)	30	5.0 ns	5.0 ns	5.0 ns	5.0 ns
Maximum Address Access Time =		218.4 ns	161.0 ns	127.5 ns	97.5 ns

Worst-case command-active to command-inactive timing is calculated in a similar manner (the command pulse width for write operations is not affected by buffers in the data path):

Standard ALE Strobe - Command-Active to Command-Inactive Timing for a Write					
Timing	Symbol	6 MHz	8 MHz	10 MHz	12.5 MHz
2 CLK Cycles − Command Active Delay from CLK (max) + Command Inactive Delay from CLK (min)	 29 30	166.6 ns −40.0 ns 5.0 ns	125.0 ns −25.0 ns 5.0 ns	100.0 ns −21.0 ns 5.0 ns	80.0 ns −21.0 ns 5.0 ns
Maximum Command Pulse Width =		131.6 ns	105.0 ns	84.0 ns	64.0 ns

The data-valid to command-inactive time for write operations must include data buffer delays. Assuming a 7.5 ns maximum delay through 74AS245 buffers, the data-valid to command-inactive setup time is:

Standard ALE Strobe - Data-Valid to Command-Inactive Setup Time for a Write					
Timing	Symbol	6 MHz	8 MHz	10 MHz	12.5 MHz
3 CLK Cycles − Write Data Valid Delay (max) − 74AS245 Transceiver Delay (max) + Command Inactive Delay from CLK (min)	 14 30	249.9 ns −65.0 ns −7.5 ns 5.0 ns	187.5 ns −50.0 ns −7.5 ns 5.0 ns	150.0 ns −30.0 ns −7.5 ns 5.0 ns	120.0 ns −30.0 ns −7.5 ns 5.0 ns
Maximum Write Data Setup Time =		182.4 ns	135.0 ns	117.5 ns	87.5 ns

If wait states are inserted into the memory cycle, each of the relevant parameters for write operations are increased by 2 CLK cycles for each wait state. Address, chip-enable, command, and data-valid times for a single-buffered 80286 system running with from zero to three wait states are shown in Table 4-4. As for read operations, 80286 operation with zero wait states is possible using only fast static RAMs for a 12.5 MHz system. One or two wait states are required to provide sufficient timing for the majority of static and dynamic RAM devices.

The CMDLY and CEN inputs to the 82288 can significantly alter bus cycle timing. CMDLY can delay commands to produce more address, chip enable, and data setup time before a command is issued. CEN can hold commands and data buffer control signals inactive, also altering bus cycle timing. When used, the effects of these inputs must also be included in any worst-case timing analysis.

Table 4-4. Timing for Write Operations Using Standard ALE Strobe

Maximum Access Times	Speed	0 Wait States	1 Wait State	2 Wait States	3 Wait States
Address Access Time (max)	12.5 MHz	97.5 ns	177.5 ns	257.5 ns	337.5 ns
	10 MHz	127.5 ns	227.5 ns	327.5 ns	427.5 ns
	8 MHz	161.0 ns	286.0 ns	411.0 ns	536.0 ns
	6 MHz	218.4 ns	385.0 ns	551.6 ns	718.2 ns
Chip-Select Access Time (max)	12.5 MHz	87.5 ns	167.5 ns	247.5 ns	327.5 ns
	10 MHz	117.5 ns	217.5 ns	317.5 ns	417.5 ns
	8 MHz	151.0 ns	276.0 ns	401.0 ns	526.0 ns
	6 MHz	208.4 ns	375.0 ns	541.6 ns	708.2 ns
Command Pulse Width (max)	12.5 MHz	64.0 ns	144.0 ns	224.0 ns	304.0 ns
	10 MHz	84.0 ns	184.0 ns	284.0 ns	384.0 ns
	8 MHz	105.0 ns	230.0 ns	355.0 ns	480.0 ns
	6 MHz	131.6 ns	298.2 ns	464.8 ns	631.4 ns
Write Data Setup Time (max)	12.5 MHz	87.5 ns	167.5 ns	247.5 ns	327.5 ns
	10 MHz	117.5 ns	217.5 ns	317.5 ns	417.5 ns
	8 MHz	135.0 ns	260.0 ns	385.0 ns	510.0 ns
	6 MHz	182.4 ns	349.0 ns	515.6 ns	682.2 ns

For some RAM devices, the data setup time before write-command active is a critical parameter. With no command delays, the write command may become active before the write data is valid at the pins of the memory device:

Standard ALE Strobe - Maximum Data Setup Time for a Write					
Timing	Symbol	6 MHz	8 MHz	10 MHz	12.5 MHz
1 CLK Cycle		83.3 ns	62.5 ns	50.0 ns	40.0 ns
− Write Data Valid Delay (max)	14	−65.0 ns	−50.0 ns	−30.0 ns	−30.0 ns
− 74AS245 Transceiver Delay (max)		−7.5 ns	−7.5 ns	−7.5 ns	−7.5 ns
+ Command Active Delay from CLK (min)	29	3.0 ns	3.0 ns	3.0 ns	3.0 ns
Maximum Data Setup Time =		13.8 ns	8.0 ns	15.5 ns	5.5 ns

With one command delay, the write command from the 82288 Bus Controller is delayed by 62.5 ns, producing an acceptable 70.5 ns data setup time for an 8 MHz 80286 before command active. This command delay reduces the command pulse width by 62.5 ns, however, and so additional wait states may be necessary to meet this and other timing requirements.

If the circuit shown in Figure 4-6 is used to delay transceiver enable during write commands, the data setup time is affected again. Using this circuit to accommodate slow output-data-float times by delaying DEN results in a data setup time to end of command of 92 ns minimum for an 8 MHz 80286:

Standard ALE Strobe - Minimum Data Setup Time Using Circuit in Figure 4-6 for a Write					
Timing	Symbol	6 MHz	8 MHz	10 MHz	12.5 MHz
2 CLK Cycles		166.6 ns	125.0 ns	100.0 ns	80.0 ns
− S04 Inverter (CLK) Delay (max)		−4.5 ns	−4.5 ns	−4.5 ns	− 4.5 ns
− S175 Flip-Flop Delay (max)		−17.0 ns	−17.0 ns	−17.0 ns	−17.0 ns
− S00, S30 Gate Delays (max)		−5.0 ns	−5.0 ns	−5.0 ns	−5.0 ns
− 74AS245 Transceiver Output Enable Time (max)		−9.0 ns	−9.0 ns	−9.0 ns	−9.0 ns
+ Command Active Delay from CLK (min)	29	3.0 ns	3.0 ns	3.0 ns	3.0 ns
Minimum Data Setup Time =		134.1 ns	92.5 ns	67.5 ns	47.5 ns

At the end of the write operation, some RAM devices require that the write data remain valid for a short interval following write command inactive. The maximum data hold requirement permitted by the 80286 is:

Standard ALE Strobe - Maximum Address Hold Time for a Write					
Timing	Symbol	6 MHz	8 MHz	10 MHz	12.5 MHz
1 CLK Cycle		83.3 ns	62.5 ns	50.0 ns	40.0 ns
− Command Inactive Delay from CLK (max)	30	−30.0 ns	−25.0 ns	−20.0 ns	−20.0 ns
+ 74AS245 Transceiver Delay (min)		2.0 ns	2.0 ns	2.0 ns	2.0 ns
Maximum Data Hold Time =		55.3 ns	39.5 ns	32.0 ns	22.0 ns

Some memory devices require that the address remain valid following a write operation. For this standard memory configuration, the maximum address hold time following write is:

Standard ALE Strobe - Maximum Address Hold Time for a Write					
Timing	Symbol	6 MHz	8 MHz	10 MHz	12.5 MHz
1 CLK Cycle		83.3 ns	62.5 ns	50.0 ns	40.0 ns
− Command Inactive Delay from CLK (max)	30	−30.0 ns	−25.0 ns	−20.0 ns	−20.0 ns
+ ALE Active Delay (min)	16	3.0 ns	3.0 ns	3.0 ns	3.0 ns
+ 74AS373 C-To-Output Delay (min)		5.0 ns	5.0 ns	5.0 ns	5.0 ns
Maximum Address Hold Time =		61.3 ns	45.5 ns	38.0 ns	28.0 ns

Most memory devices do not require such a lengthy address hold time following a write operation. The following section shows how the special strobe logic introduced previously trades away some of this unused address hold time to gain increased address access time.

Special Address Strobe Timing

As described in a previous section, special address strobe logic can be used to generate an address latch strobe much earlier in the 80286 bus cycle than the 82288 ALE strobe. This special address strobe technique trades off address hold time after command inactive for additional address and chip-enable access time, permitting slow memories to be used with fewer wait states relative to the standard address strobe technique described in the previous section.

Figure 4-2 shown previously shows the memory configuration that will be used in this analysis. Figure 4-8 shows the timing of this special address strobe logic.

The timing of this address strobe logic is relatively straightforward. Maximum address and chip-select access time for an 80286 operating at zero wait states is:

Special Address Strobe Timing - Maximum Address and Chip-Select Access Time for a Read					
Timing	Symbol	6 MHz	8 MHz	10 MHz	12.5 MHz
4 CLK Cycles		333.2 ns	250.0 ns	200.0 ns	160.0 ns
— Command Inactive Delay from CLK (max)	30	−30.0 ns	−25.0 ns	−20.0 ns	−20.0 ns
— AS08 Gate Delay (max)		−5.5 ns	−5.5 ns	−5.5 ns	−5.5 ns
— 74AS373 C-To-Output Delay (max)		−11.5 ns	−11.5 ns	−11.5 ns	−11.5 ns
— 74AS245 Transceiver Delay (max)		−7.5 ns	−7.5 ns	−7.5 ns	−7.5 ns
— Read Data Setup Time (min)	8	−20.0 ns	−10.0 ns	−8.0 ns	−5.0 ns
Maximum Address Access Time =		258.7 ns	190.5 ns	147.5 ns	110.5 ns

Minimum address hold after command inactive is only 6 ns minimum, equal to the minimum 74AS373 C-to-output delay.

Since the memory configuration using the special strobe logic does not alter the command inputs to the memory devices, command access times are the same as for the standard memory interface.

Special Address Strobe Timing - Maximum Command Address Time for a Read					
Timing	Symbol	6 MHz	8 MHz	10 MHz	12.5 MHz
2 CLK Cycles		166.6 ns	125.0 ns	100.0 ns	80.0 ns
— Command Active Delay from CLK (max)	29	−40.0 ns	−25.0 ns	−21.0 ns	−21.0 ns
— 74AS245 Transceiver Delay (max)		−7.5 ns	−7.5 ns	−7.5 ns	−7.5 ns
— Read Data Setup Time (min)	8	−20.0 ns	−10.0 ns	−8.0 ns	−5.0 ns
Maximum Command Access Time =		99.1 ns	82.5 ns	63.5 ns	46.5 ns

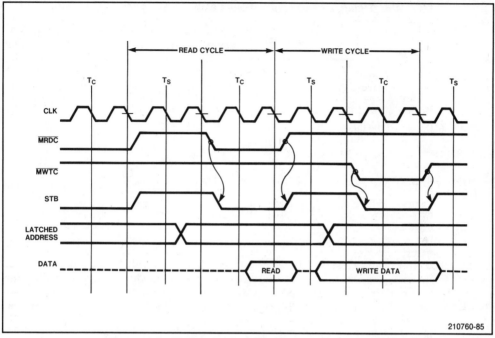

Figure 4-8. Timing for Special Address Strobe Logic

Because the address strobes are generated earlier in the bus cycle, the allowed address decode time before the address strobe goes high is reduced. Maximum decode time without reducing chip-enable access time is:

Special ALE Strobe - Maximum Address Decode Time for a Read					
Timing	Symbol	6 MHz	8 MHz	10 MHz	12.5 MHz
1 CLK Cycle		83.3 ns	62.5 ns	50.0 ns	40.0 ns
− Address Valid Delay (max)	13	−80.0 ns	−60.0 ns	−35.0 ns	−32.0 ns
+ Command Inactive Delay from CLK (max)	30	30.0 ns	25.0 ns	20.0 ns	20.0 ns
+ AS08 Gate Delay (max)		5.5 ns	5.5 ns	5.5 ns	5.5 ns
Maximum Data Hold Time =		38.8 ns	33.0 ns	40.5 ns	33.5 ns

If wait states are inserted into the memory cycle, access times for the relevant parameters are increased by 2 CLK cycles for each wait state. Address, chip-enable, and command access times for a single-buffered 80286 system running with from zero to three wait states are shown in Table 4-5.

For write operations, the data setup and hold times for this memory configuration are not affected by the special address strobe logic. The Write command pulse width using this memory configuration is identical to that for the standard memory interface.

Table 4-5. Timing for Read Operations Using Special Address Strobe

Maximum Access Times	Speed	0 Wait States	1 Wait State	2 Wait States	3 Wait States
Address Access Time (max)	12.5 MHz	110.5 ns	190.5 ns	270.5 ns	350.5 ns
	10 MHz	147.5 ns	247.5 ns	347.5 ns	447.5 ns
	8 MHz	190.5 ns	315.5 ns	440.5 ns	565.5 ns
	6 MHz	258.7 ns	425.3 ns	591.9 ns	758.5 ns
Chip-Select Access Time (max)	12.5 MHz	110.5 ns	190.5 ns	270.5 ns	350.5 ns
	10 MHz	147.5 ns	247.5 ns	347.5 ns	447.5 ns
	8 MHz	190.5 ns	315.5 ns	440.5 ns	565.5 ns
	6 MHz	258.7 ns	425.3 ns	591.9 ns	758.5 ns
Command Pulse Width (max)	12.5 MHz	46.5 ns	126.5 ns	206.5 ns	286.5 ns
	10 MHz	63.5 ns	163.5 ns	263.5 ns	363.5 ns
	8 MHz	82.5 ns	207.5 ns	332.5 ns	457.5 ns
	6 MHz	99.1 ns	265.7 ns	432.3 ns	598.9 ns

As described previously, the special address strobe logic trades off address hold time for additional address access time. Some memory devices specify an address hold time following a write operation. Using the special address strobe logic, the maximum address hold time allowed for a memory device following Write command inactive is 5 ns, the minimum C-to-output delay of the 74AS373 address latch:

Maximum address hold after write = 5 ns max.

This timing value illustrates the essential tradeoff between address access time and address hold time using the special address strobe logic. Still other memory interface techniques are possible which make other allowances in order to optimize the critical address access parameter.

When using the Special Address Strobe Logic to create an early ALE signal CMDLYs must not be inserted into the bus cycles. Because the address is latched on the falling edge of ALE, if a CMDLY is inserted the address will become invalid before ALE can latch the address.

Interleaved Memory Timing

Interleaved memory subsystems have been introduced in a previous section. The interleaving technique, like the special strobe logic, produces increased address access times and allows considerably slower memory devices to be used while still providing performance equal to that of faster memories using the standard memory interface.

An example circuit showing an interleaved RAM system is shown in Figures 4-3 and 4-4. The timing for this circuit is shown in Figure 4-9. This figure shows a sequence of four CPU bus cycles performed in the following order:

1. Write cycle to non-interleaved memory

2. Read cycle from RAM bank 1

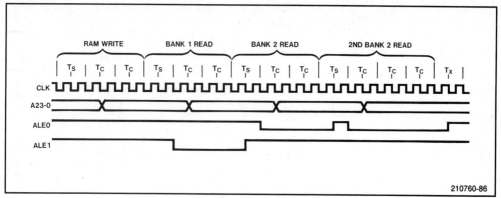

Figure 4-9. Interleaved Memory Timing

3. Read cycle from RAM bank 2

4. Read cycle from RAM bank 2

The sequence of signals required to perform these four bus cycles are as follows:

1. During the write cycle to RAM, both address strobes (ALE0 and ALE1) are high. Since the interleaved memory is not selected, chip enables to the interleaved memories are not generated.

2. At the start of the read cycle from RAM bank 1, the address decode logic generates chip-enable signals to the appropriate devices and $\overline{\text{BANKSEL}}$ activates the interleave logic to generate an appropriate address strobe. ALE1 toggles low on the falling edge of CLK at the end of T_s to latch the address and chip-enable signals to bank 1. $\overline{\text{MRDC}}$ enables the output drivers of the RAMs. Note that ALE0 remains high throughout the bus cycle, maintaining the Bank 2 address latches in their transparent states.

3. At the start of the read cycle from RAM bank 2, the address decode logic generates chip-enable signals to the appropriate devices as before. ALE1 is driven high on the falling edge of CLK halfway through T_s, and remains high throughout the rest of the bus cycle. ALE0 toggles low at the start of T_c to latch the address and chip-enable signals to bank 2. $\overline{\text{MRDC}}$ enables the output drivers of the RAMs in bank 2, while DEN and the latched $\overline{\text{BANKSEL}}$ enable the interleave-memory data transceivers.

4. The second read cycle to EPROM bank 2 begins with ALE0 low. ALE0 is not driven high until CLK goes low halfway through T_s. This delay reduces the data access time in comparison to the previous bus cycles; the delay is accommodated by adding one additional wait state to the bus cycle. Two S112 flip-flops are used to compare the bank-selects for the current and previous memory cycles to detect the occurrence of back-to-back cycles to the same memory bank. The $\overline{\text{HIT}}$ output of this interleave logic is used to drive the system Ready logic to insert the additional wait state.

    The sequence of signals for this second bank 2 read is the same as the first, with the addition of one extra wait state. ALE0 is driven high one CLK cycle after the last T_c state. ALE1 remains high throughout the entire cycle.

The timing analysis for this interleaved memory system is straightforward, merely incorporating the appropriate delays through the latches and buffers.

The maximum address access time for the configuration shown in Figure 4-3 is:

Interleaved Memory Timing - Maximum Address Access Time for a Read					
Timing	Symbol	6 MHz	8 MHz	10 MHz	12.5 MHz
5 CLK Cycles — Address Valid Delay (max) — 74AS373 C-To-Output Delay (max) — 74AS245 Transceiver Delay (max) — Read Data Setup Time (min)	13 8	416.5 ns −80.0 ns −11.5 ns −7.5 ns −20.0 ns	312.5 ns −60.0 ns −11.5 ns −7.5 ns −10.0 ns	250.0 ns −35.0 ns −11.5 ns −7.5 ns −8.0 ns	200.0 ns −32.0 ns −11.5 ns −7.5 ns −5.0 ns
Maximum Address Access Time =		297.5 ns	223.5 ns	188.0 ns	144.0 ns

Maximum chip-enable access time must incorporate the additional 74F138 decoder delay:

Interleaved Memory Timing - Maximum Chip-Enable Access Time for a Read					
Timing	Symbol	6 MHz	8 MHz	10 MHz	12.5 MHz
5 CLK Cycles — Address Valid Delay (max) — 74AS373 C-To-Output Delay (max) — 74AS138 Decoder Delay (max) — 74AS245 Transceiver Delay (max) — Read Data Setup Time (min)	13 8	416.5 ns −80.0 ns −11.5 ns −10.0 ns −7.5 ns −20.0 ns	312.5 ns −60.0 ns −11.5 ns −10.0 ns −7.5 ns −10.0 ns	250.0 ns −35.0 ns −11.5 ns −10.0 ns −7.5 ns −8.0 ns	200.0 ns −32.0 ns −11.5 ns −10.0 ns −7.5 ns −5.0 ns
Maximum Chip-Enable Access Time =		287.5 ns	213.5 ns	178.0 ns	134.0 ns

If a subsequent memory access to the same memory bank occurs, an additional wait state will be inserted into the memory cycle. The maximum address access time with this interleave "hit" is:

Interleaved Memory Timing - Maximum Address Access (W/"hit") for a Read					
Timing	Symbol	6 MHz	8 MHz	10 MHz	12.5 MHz
5 CLK Cycles — Command Inactive Delay from CLK (max) — 74AS373 C-To-Output Delay (max) — 74AS245 Transceiver Delay (max) — Read Data Setup Time (min)	30 8	416.5 ns −30.0 ns −11.5 ns −7.5 ns −20.0 ns	312.5 ns −25.0 ns −11.5 ns −7.5 ns −10.0 ns	250.0 ns −20.0 ns −11.5 ns −7.5 ns −8.0 ns	200.0 ns −20.0 ns −11.5 ns −7.5 ns −5.0 ns
Maximum Address Access Time (w/"hit") =		347.5 ns	258.5 ns	203.0 ns	156.0 ns

Chip-enable access time with an interleave "hit" is the same as the address access time, less the 5.5 ns 74F138 decoder delay:

Maximum chip-enable access (w/ "hit") = 253.0 ns max. for an 8 MHz 80286.

Since memory read and write commands are passed directly to the memory devices as in the standard memory interface, the command access times and command pulse widths calculated for interleaved memory systems will be the same as for non-interleaved memory systems.

If wait states are inserted into the memory cycle, access times for the relevant parameters are increased by 2 CLK cycles for each wait state. Address, chip-enable, and command access times for a single-buffered 80286 system running with from zero to three wait states are shown in Table 4-6.

Interleave "hits," or back-to-back accesses to the same memory bank, typically occur during only about 7% of all bus cycles. Since an interleave hit results in an additional wait state inserted into the bus cycle, this wait state may impact overall execution time and so affect system performance. Generally, instruction prefetches by the 80286 bus unit will not result in any interleave "hits" since the prefetcher accesses sequential addresses. On average, only interleave hits that occur due to data read operations will directly affect 80286 execution time, as described previously; delays in data write operations do not affect the 80286 Execution unit.

Table 4-7 shows the results of several benchmarks run on an 80286 system using an interleaved memory system and one using a memory system having the same number of wait states without interleaving. The values shown in the table are the ratios of execution times with interleaving to those without interleaving. In general, execution times with interleaved memory are typically only 4% more than execution times with memories having a comparable number of wait states.

Table 4-6. Timing for Interleaved Memory Operations

Maximum Access Times	Speed	0 Wait States	1 Wait State	2 Wait States	3 Wait States
Address Access Time (max)	12.5 MHz	144.0 ns	224.0 ns	304.0 ns	384.0 ns
	10 MHz	188.0 ns	288.0 ns	388.0 ns	488.0 ns
	8 MHz	223.5 ns	348.5 ns	473.5 ns	598.5 ns
	6 MHz	297.5 ns	464.1 ns	630.7 ns	797.3 ns
Chip-Select Access Time (max)	12.5 MHz	134.0 ns	214.0 ns	294.0 ns	374.0 ns
	10 MHz	287.5 ns	387.5 ns	487.5 ns	587.5 ns
	8 MHz	213.5 ns	338.5 ns	463.5 ns	588.5 ns
	6 MHz	287.5 ns	454.1 ns	620.7 ns	787.3 ns
Command Access Time (max)	12.5 MHz	46.5 ns	126.5 ns	206.5 ns	286.5 ns
	10 MHz	63.5 ns	163.5 ns	263.5 ns	363.5 ns
	8 MHz	82.5 ns	207.5 ns	332.5 ns	457.5 ns
	6 MHz	99.1 ns	265.7 ns	432.3 ns	598.9 ns

Table 4-7. 80286 Performance with Interleaved Memories

Program Benchmark	Ratio of Execution Time for interleaved to non-interleaved memories when most bus operations occur with:	
	0 Wait States	1 Wait State
DSO Bubble Sort (Pascal)	1.061	1.070
DSO Matrix Mult. (Pascal)	1.003	1.068
Berkeley Puzzle (Pascal)	1.020	1.028
Berkeley Sieve (C)	1.058	1.044
Quicksort (32-bit C)	1.057	1.061
Intel XFORM (ASM86)	1.007	1.007
Intel Bubble Sort (ASM86)	1.032	1.034
Average of 17 Programs	1.036	1.046

MEMORY INTERFACE EXAMPLES

The following sections describe specific examples using common types of memory devices with the 80286. These interface examples include read-only memories, static and pseudo-static RAM devices, and dynamic RAM devices using the 8207 Advanced Dynamic RAM Controller and 82C08 DRAM controller.

Read-Only Memory

The easiest memory devices to interface to any system are read-only memory devices (ROMs, PROMs, and EPROMs). Their byte-wide format provides a simple bus interface, and since they are read-only devices, A0 and $\overline{BHE}$ need not be included in their chip-select/enable decoding (chip-enable is similar to chip-select, but chip-enable typically determines if the device is in the active or standby power mode as well).

For a standard memory model, the address lines connected to the devices start with A1 and continue up to the maximum number the device can accept, leaving the remaining address lines for chip-enable/select decoding. To connect the devices directly to the local bus, the read-only memories must have output-enables. The output-enable is also required to avoid bus contention in some memory configurations.

Figure 4-10 shows the bus connections for read-only memories. Read-only memories require latched chip-selects. Each valid decode selects one device on the upper and lower halves of the bus to allow byte and word access. Byte access is achieved by reading the full word onto the bus; the 80286 accepts only the appropriate byte. The output-enable is controlled by the memory read command from the Bus Controller.

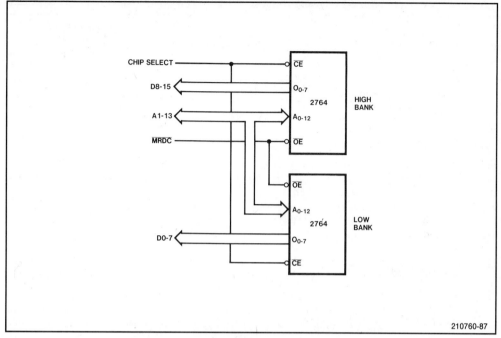

Figure 4-10. ROM/PROM/EPROM Bus Interface

TIMING ANALYSIS FOR ROMS

Read-only memories have four critical timing parameters that must be considered when interfacing these devices to an 80286. These parameters are:

1. Address to Output Delay (Address Access Time)

2. Chip-Enable to Output Delay (Chip-Enable Access Time)

3. Output Enable to Output Delay (Command Access Time)

4. Output Enable High to Output Float (Data Float Time)

By comparing these memory timing requirements to the 80286 timing values, the required number of wait states can be determined to guarantee a reliable memory interface.

As an example, consider a standard memory interface using 2764-20 EPROMs buffered by a single level of 74AS245 transceivers. Table 4-8 shows the requirements of the 2764-20 and the times allowed by an 80286 running with 1 wait state, using the standard ALE memory configuration described previously. By comparing the timing values shown in the table, it is clear that a 2764-20 EPROM is compatible with the 80286 system operating with one wait state.

Table 4-8. Timing Analysis for the 2764-20 EPROM

Timing Parameter	2764-20 EPROM (Max. Required)	10-MHz 80286 1 Wait State (Min. Provided)
Address Access Time	200.0 ns	207.0 ns
Chip-Enable Access Time	200.0 ns	207.0 ns
Command Access Time	75.0 ns	163.5 ns
Data Float Time	55.0 ns	182.0 ns

Timing for an interleaved memory configuration or for systems using special Strobe logic can be determined in a similar manner. It should also be noted that the timing of memory operations using any of the three memory interface techniques can be further modified by slowing the processor clock. An 8-MHz 80286 operating with a 15-MHz clock rather than the usual 16-MHz clock can support 200 ns memories such as the 2764-20 EPROM at zero wait states.

Table 4-9 shows the wait-state requirements for a variety of different Intel EPROMs for several different memory configurations. In each configuration, a single level of data transceivers is assumed.

Table 4-9. Wait-State Requirements for Intel EPROMs

EPROM	Speed	Standard ALE Strobe	Special Strobe Logic	Interleaved Memory System
2732A-20	12.5 MHz	2	2	1
	10 MHz	1	1	1
	8 MHz	1	1	0
	6 MHz	1	0	0
2732A-25	12.5 MHz	2	2	2
	10 MHz	2	2	1
	8 MHz	1	1	1
	6 MHz	1	1	1
2764A-1	12.5 MHz	2	1	1
	10 MHz	1	1	1
	8 MHz	1	0	0
	6 MHz	0	0	0
2764A-20	12.5 MHz	2	2	1
	10 MHz	1	1	1
	8 MHz	1	1	0
	6 MHz	1	0	0
2764A-25	12.5 MHz	2	2	2
	10 MHz	2	2	1
	8 MHz	1	1	1
	6 MHz	1	1	1

Table 4-9. Wait-State Requirements for Intel EPROMs (Cont'd.)

EPROM	Speed	Standard ALE Strobe	Special Strobe Logic	Interleaved Memory System
2764A-30	12.5 MHz	2	2	2
	10 MHz	2	2	2
	8 MHz	2	1	1
	6 MHz	1	1	1
27128A-11	12.5 MHz	1	1	1
	10 MHz	1	0	0
	8 MHz	0	0	0
	6 MHz	0	0	0
27128A-1	12.5 MHz	1	1	1
	10 MHz	1	1	1
	8 MHz	1	0	0
	6 MHz	0	0	0
27128A-20	12.5 MHz	2	2	1
	10 MHz	1	1	1
	8 MHz	1	1	0
	6 MHZ	1	0	0
27128A-25	12.5 MHz	2	2	2
	10 MHz	2	2	1
	8 MHz	1	1	1
	6 MHz	1	1	1
27128A-30	12.5 MHz	2	2	2
	10 MHz	2	2	2
	8 MHz	2	1	1
	6 MHz	1	1	1
27256-1	12.5 MHz	2	1	1
	10 MHz	1	1	1
	8 MHz	1	0	0
	6 MHz	0	0	0
27256-20	12.5 MHz	2	2	1
	10 MHz	1	1	1
	8 MHz	1	1	0
	6 MHz	1	0	0
27256-25	12.5 MHz	2	2	2
	10 MHz	2	2	1
	8 MHz	1	1	1
	6 MHz	1	1	1
27256-30	12.5 MHz	2	2	2
	10 MHz	2	2	2
	8 MHz	2	1	1
	6 MHz	1	1	1
27512-20	12.5 MHz	2	2	1
	10 MHz	1	1	1
	8 MHz	1	1	0
	6 MHz	1	0	0

Table 4-9. Wait-State Requirements for Intel EPROMs (Cont'd.)

EPROM	Speed	Standard ALE Strobe	Special Strobe Logic	Interleaved Memory System
27512-25	12.5 MHz	2	2	2
	10 MHz	2	2	1
	8 MHz	1	1	1
	6 MHz	1	1	1
27512-30	12.5 MHz	2	2	2
	10 MHz	2	2	2
	8 MHz	2	1	1
	6 MHz	1	1	1

Static RAM Devices

Interfacing static RAM to an 80286 CPU introduces several new requirements into the memory design. The address lines A0 and $\overline{BHE}$ must be included in the chip-select/enable decoding for the devices, and write timing must be considered in the timing analysis.

Data bus connections for each device must be restricted to either the upper- or lower-half of the data bus to allow byte transfers to only one half of the data bus. Devices like the 2114 or 2142 must not be configured to straddle both the upper and lower halves of the data bus.

To allow selection of either the upper byte, lower byte, or full 16-bit word for write operation, $\overline{BHE}$ must condition selection of the upper byte and A0 must condition selection of the lower byte. Figure 4-11 shows several techniques for selecting devices with single chip-selects and no output-enables (2114, 2141, 2147A, 2148H/49H). Figure 4-12 shows selection techniques for devices with both chip-selects and output-enables (2128, 2167A).

Devices without output-enables require inclusion of A0 and $\overline{BHE}$ to decode or enable chip selects. The $\overline{MRDC}$ and $\overline{MWRC}$ commands are used to qualify chip-select generation to prevent bus contention. Devices with common input/output pins (2114, 2142) and no output-enable require special care to strobe chip-enable low only after write-enable is valid. Write-enable and write data must be held valid until after chip-enable goes high.

For devices with separate input and output pins (2141, 2147, 2167A), the outputs can be tied together and used as described in Chapter Three.

For devices with output-enables (Figure 4-12), the write command may be gated with $\overline{BHE}$ and A0 to provide upper- and lower-bank write strobes. This simplifies chip-select decoding by eliminating $\overline{BHE}$ and A0 as a condition of decode. Although both devices are enabled during a byte write, only the appropriate high or low byte device will receive a write strobe. No bus contention exists during reads because the read command must be issued to enable the memory output drivers.

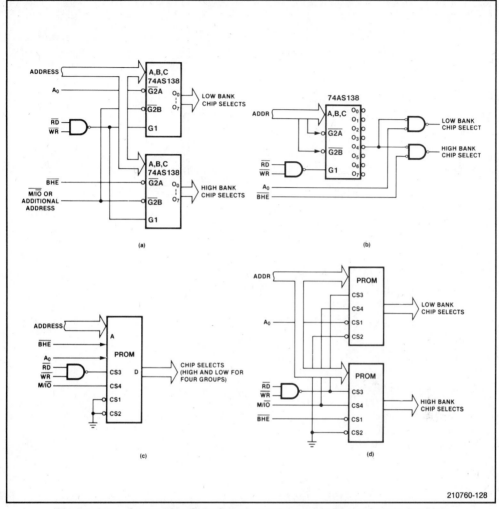

Figure 4-11. Generating Chip Selects for Devices without Output Enables

If multiple chip selects are available at the device, $\overline{BHE}$ and A0 may directly control device selection. This allows normal chip-select decoding of the address space and direct connection of the memory read and write commands to the memory devices. Another alternative is to use the multiple chip select inputs of the device to directly decode the address space (linear selects) and use the separate write-strobe technique to minimize the control circuitry needed to generate chip selects. As with the EPROMs and ROMs, the address lines connected to the memory devices must start with A1 rather than A0 for a standard memory interface.

For an interleaved memory subsystem, the low-order address lines beginning with A1 are used as bank selects. Address lines that connect to the memory devices start with the lowest address bit after the bank select address lines.

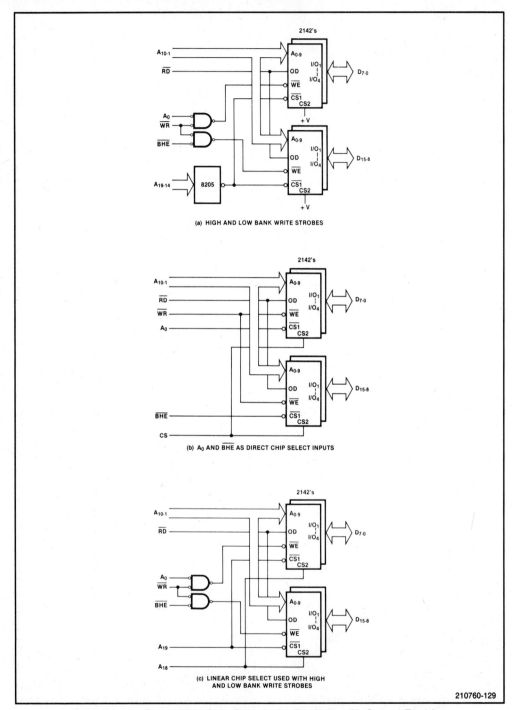

(a) HIGH AND LOW BANK WRITE STROBES

(b) A_0 AND $\overline{BHE}$ AS DIRECT CHIP SELECT INPUTS

(c) LINEAR CHIP SELECT USED WITH HIGH AND LOW BANK WRITE STROBES

210760-129

Figure 4-12. Generating Chip Selects for Devices with Output Enables

TIMING ANALYSIS FOR STATIC RAMS

When interfacing static RAM devices to an 80286, write timing parameters must be considered in addition to read parameters. These additional timing parameters are:

- Address Valid to End of Write (Address Access Time)

- Chip Select to End of Write (Chip-Enable Access Time)

- Write Pulse Width (Command Access Time)

- Write Release (Address Hold From End of Write)

- Data Valid to End of Write (Write Data Access Time)

- Data Hold From End of Write (Write Data Hold Time)

By comparing these memory timing requirements to the 80286 timing values, the required number of wait states can be determined to guarantee a reliable memory interface.

As an example, consider a standard memory interface using 2147H-1 RAM's buffered by a single level of 74AS245 transceivers on both inputs and outputs. Figure 4-13 shows the memory configuration used in the analysis. Table 4-10 shows the timing requirements of the 2147H-1 RAM and the times allowed by the 80286 running with zero wait states.

The Read command access time (Data valid from read) is not applicable in this configuration since WE is high throughout the cycle. $\overline{\text{MRDC}}$ merely enables the output data buffers to transfer data to the CPU. As demonstrated by the times shown in the table, the 2147H-1 static RAM is compatible with a zero-wait-state 80286 CPU.

For slower RAM devices, special address Strobe logic or an interleaved memory configuration can be used to increase the address and chip-select access times to permit operation at zero wait states.

Pseudo-Static RAM Devices

Integrated dynamic RAM devices have many of the same characteristics as static RAM devices, including a simple two-line control interface with output-enable and write-enable, and a simple chip-enable and address inputs. All of the complexities of typical dynamic RAM devices, such as row- and column-addressing, and refresh timing and arbitration, are integrated into the devices themselves. From the system designer's perspective, devices such as the 2186 and 2187 iRAMs can be treated in the same manner as simple static RAM devices.

There are several considerations when designing systems using iRAMS which differ from designs using static RAM devices. First, the iRAM must see a single edge ("glitchless") transition of chip-enable ($\overline{\text{CE}}$) at the beginning of the memory cycle to allow the iRAM to latch addresses and to initialize several internal clocks.

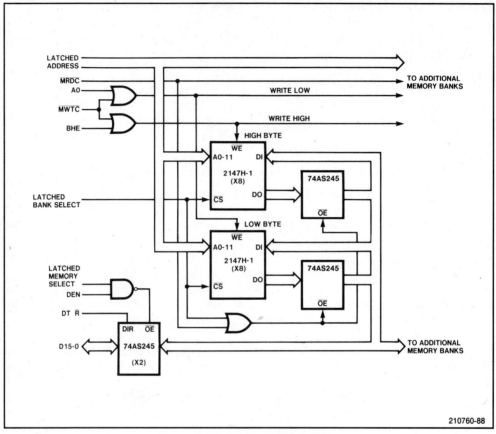

Figure 4-13. Static RAM Interface

Table 4-10. Timing Analysis for the 2147H-1 SRAM

Timing	2147H-1 RAM (Max. Required)	8-MHz 80286 0 Wait States (Min. Provided)
Read Address Access Time	35.0	131.0
Chip-Enable Access Time	35.0	109.0
Read Command Access Time	N/A	N/A
Write Address Access Time	35.0	162.0
Chip-Enable Access Time	35.0	145.0
Command Access Time	20.0	105.0
Write Data Access Time	20.0	145.0
Address Hold Time	0.0	34.7
Write Data Hold Time	10.0	31.7

Second, since the iRAM accepts write data on the falling edge of write-enable ($\overline{\text{WE}}$), the write data must be valid before write-enable is activated.

The timing analysis of iRAM systems is similar to that of static RAM systems, with the exception that command delays may be needed in order to ensure write-data valid before write-command active. Specific details on designing memory systems using the iRAM are described in *Application Note AP-132* "Designing Memory Systems with the 8K × 8 iRAM."

Dynamic RAM Devices

The task of designing a dynamic RAM memory for an 80286 system is made more complex by the requirements for address multiplexing and memory-refresh logic. Fortunately, devices like the 8207 Advanced Dynamic RAM Controller and 82C08 CHMOS DRAM Controller simplify this task considerably.

The 8207 Advanced Dynamic RAM Controller (ADRC) is a programmable, high-performance, systems-oriented controller designed to easily interface 16K, 64K, and 256K dynamic RAMs to a wide range of microprocessors, including the 80286 CPU. Dual-port configurations are supported by two independent ports that operate in both synchronous- and asynchronous-processor environments. The 8207 also supports error detection and correction using the 8206 Error Detection and Correction Unit (EDCU).

The 8207 Controller timing is optimized for maximum performance. With fast dynamic RAMs the 8207 can run at 0 wait states for most bus operations.

As shown in Figure 4-14, the 8207 can be controlled directly by the 80286 status lines or by 82288 command outputs, and can operate synchronously or asynchronously to the system clock. Figure 4-15 provides a block diagram for a single-port 8207 memory subsystem using the command interface. PCTL is tied low to configure the 8207 in command mode for compatibility with the 80286 signals. CPU status signals directly drive the read and write inputs to the controller while the 82C284 CLK signal provides the synchronous clock. Address lines connect directly to the controller, while data transfer is controlled by two sets of latches between the memory banks and the CPU. A byte mark latch decodes A0 and $\overline{\text{BHE}}$ to condition the write enable signals for the high- and low-byte memory banks.

The 8207 is capable of addressing 16K, 64K, and 256K dynamic RAMs, using an interleaved memory arrangement. Memory can be divided into four banks, with each bank having its own $\overline{\text{RAS}}$ and $\overline{\text{CAS}}$ signal pair. Low-order address lines serve as bank selects to allow interleaved memory cycles. (Figure 4-16 shows the address connections to the ADRC for all three types of RAM devices.)

Interleaving memory cycles between different banks of RAM devices result in the access time for a current cycle overlapping with the RAM precharge period for the previous cycle. When back-to-back transfers to the same memory bank occur (about 6% of the time), the 8207 automatically inserts a wait state into the current cycle, adding about 6% to the overall execution time. Slower memory devices can be used with the 8207 at zero wait states than would be possible with RAM controllers that do not support interleaved memory access.

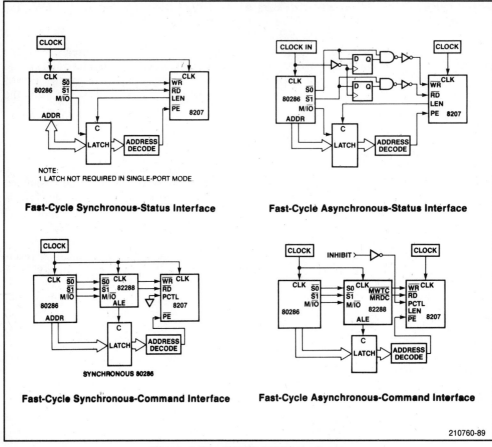

Figure 4-14. 80286-8207 Interfaces

TIMING ANALYSIS FOR THE 8207 RAM CONTROLLER

The analysis of timing for dynamic RAMs is more extensive than for a static RAM or EPROM. The analysis must include RAS, CAS, and refresh timing as well as standard bus interface timing. Figure 4-17 shows the memory subsystem that serves as the model for the timing analysis in this section.

The subsystem shown in Figure 4-17 is a single-port configuration designed with an 8207 ADRC and four banks of 2118-10 16K x 1 bit dynamic RAMs. Each bank is sixteen bits wide and is divided into a high byte (D15-8) and a low byte (D7-0). Most 8207 signals connect directly to 80286, 82288, and 82C284 inputs and outputs. No address buffering is required. The RAM data inputs and outputs are buffered, with the 82288 DEN and DT/R̄ signals controlling the output data buffers. The PEA (Port Enable A) input to the ADRC is a non-latched chip-select driven by address-decode logic.

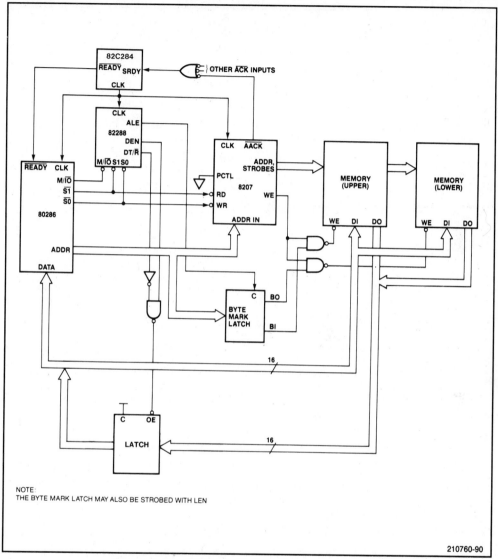

Figure 4-15. 8207 Single-Port Memory Subsystem

The 8207 is programmed at reset through strapping options and a 16-bit program word. PCTLA, $\overline{\text{PCTLB}}$, and RFRQ are strapped high or low to program port and refresh options. PCTLA is tied low to select command mode. ($\overline{\text{PCTLB}}$ is not shown; $\overline{\text{PEB}}$ should be strapped high to ignore the port B interface.) RFRQ is tied high to program the 8207 for self-refresh mode. PDI (Program Data Input) accepts a 16-bit serial bit stream containing the program word. By strapping PDI high or low, one of two sets of default parameters are selected. The example circuit in Figure 4-17 is programmed with the non-ECC mode default parameters shown in Table 4-11.

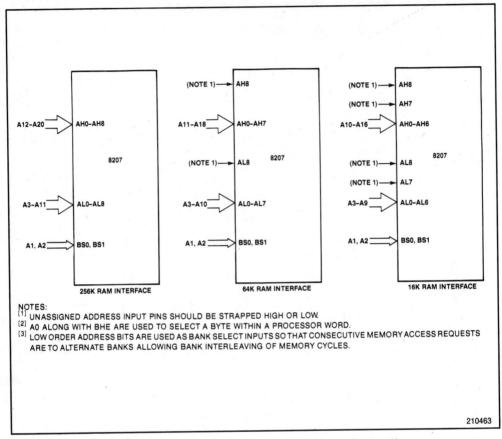

Figure 4-16. 256K, 64K, and 16K RAM Address Connections

As shown in Figure 4-18, PDI can be driven by a 16-bit serial shift register to program the 8207 for non-default operation. Sixteen bits are loaded into the register in parallel during reset and are shifted out in serial by the 8207 program clock (PCLK).

Figure 4-19 shows the timing for three back-to-back memory cycles: a read from bank 1, a write to bank 2, and a read from bank 2. Since the first two cycles are to different memory banks, the $\overline{\text{RAS}}$ for the second cycle is overlapped with the $\overline{\text{RAS}}$ precharge period for the first cycle to allow the subsystem to respond with no wait states.

In the case of back-to-back cycles to the same bank (cycles 2 and 3), the controller automatically waits for the $\overline{\text{RAS}}$ precharge period between cycles before asserting $\overline{\text{RAS}}$. AACKA from the 8207, which must be connected to the 82C284 $\overline{\text{SRDY}}$ input, is delayed long enough to guarantee an additional wait state to compensate for the slower subsystem response time. The 82C284 $\overline{\text{SRDY}}$ input is used rather than the $\overline{\text{ARDY}}$ input to accommodate the critical $\overline{\text{AACKA}}$ signal timing.

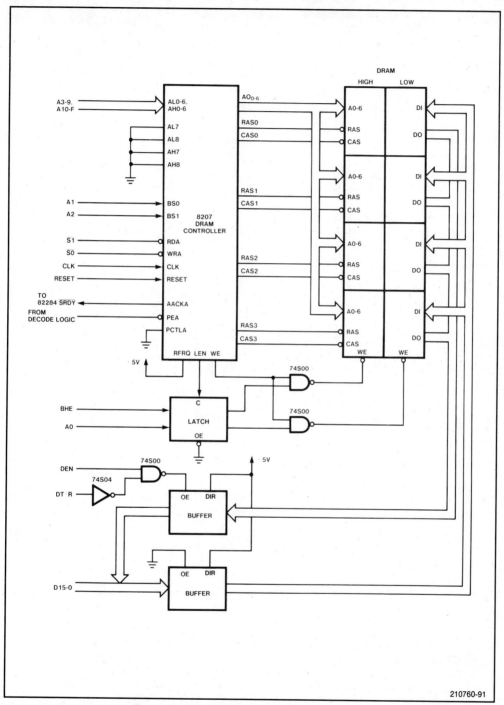

Figure 4-17. 128K-Byte Memory Subsystem

210760-91

Table 4-11. Non-ECC Mode Programming, PDI Pin (57) Tied to Ground

Port A is Synchronous

Port B is Asynchronous

Fast-cycle Processor Interface (80286)

Fast RAM (2118-10 compatible)

Refresh Interval uses 236 clocks

128 Row refresh in 2 ms; 256 Row refresh in 4 ms.

Fast Processor Clock Frequency (16 MHz)

"Most Recently Used" Priority Scheme

4 RAM Banks Occupied

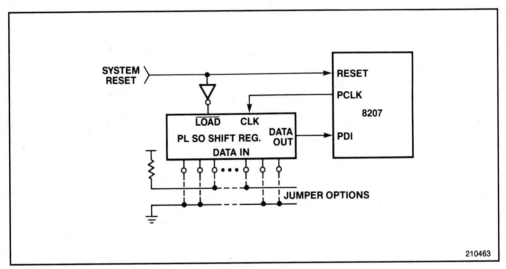

Figure 4-18. External Shift Register Interface

RAM timing to determine device compatibility is measured from $\overline{\text{RAS}}$ going low to data valid at the CPU pins. Maximum allowed $\overline{\text{RAS}}$ access time is:

Timing		Maximum RAS Access Time (8207)		
	Symbol	6 MHz	8 MHz
3 CLK Cycles — RAS active delay (max) — 74LS640 Transceiver Delay (max) — Read Data Setup Time (min)	26 8	249.9 ns −35.0 ns −15.0 ns −20.0 ns	187.5 ns −35.0 ns −15.0 ns −10.0 ns
Maximum Allowed RAS Access Time =		187.9 ns	135.5 ns

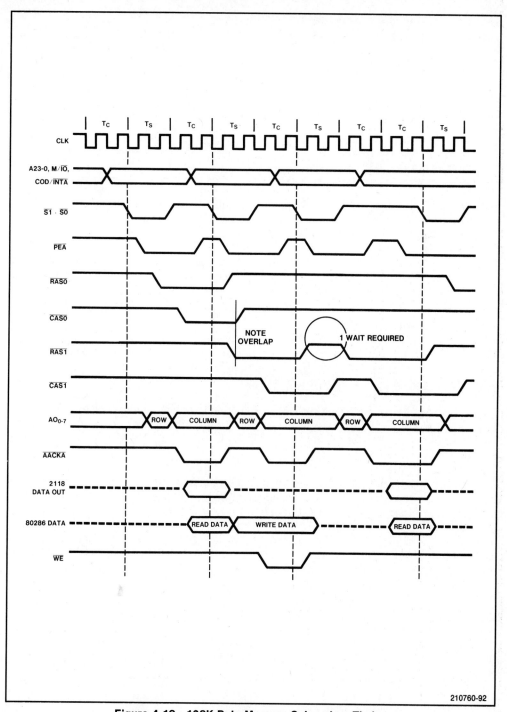

Figure 4-19. 128K-Byte Memory Subsystem Timing

The corresponding $\overline{\text{CAS}}$ access time is:

Timing	Maximum CAS Access Time (8207)		
	Symbol	6 MHz	8 MHz
2 CLK Cycles — RAS active delay (max) — 74LS640 Transceiver Delay (max) — Read Data Setup Time (min)	34 8	166.6 ns −35.0 ns −15.0 ns −20.0 ns	125.0 ns −35.0 ns −15.0 ns −10.0 ns
Maximum Allowed CAS Access Time =		104.6 ns	73.0 ns

For typical DRAM devices, the $\overline{\text{CAS}}$ access time will be the limiting parameter. Table 4-12 shows the timing requirements of a typical 100 ns DRAM and the times allowed by the 80286 and 8207 operating with zero wait states.

The circuit shown in Figure 4-17 will run at 0 wait states for most memory cycles; the subsystem will run with 1 wait state only when back-to-back accesses occur to the same memory bank.

ERROR CORRECTION USING THE 8206 EDCU

The 8207 DRAM Controller supports error detection and correction using the 8206 Error Detection and Correction Unit (EDCU). Figure 4-20 shows a memory subsystem using the 8206 EDCU with the 8207 DRAM Controller.

The 8207 interface to the RAM devices in ECC mode is almost identical to that in non-ECC mode. RAM is divided into four banks with twenty-two devices in each bank. Sixteen RAM devices store data for use by the CPU; the remaining six RAM devices store check bits for use by the 8206 (EDCU).

During data writes, the EDCU computes a check code and writes the code into the check RAM. During data reads, the EDCU compares the read data to the check code to detect errors. Single-bit errors are corrected and double-bit or multiple-bit errors are flagged. The 8206 $\overline{\text{ERROR}}$ and CE (Correctable Error) signals inform the 8207 of error status. $\text{R}/\overline{\text{W}}$ (Read/$\overline{\text{Write}}$) and WZ (Write Zero) from the 8207 control write/read and initialization modes of the 8206. Byte marks determine whether a byte or word write is performed by the 8206.

Table 4-12. 8-MHz Timing Analysis for the 100 ns DRAMs

Timing Parameter	100 ns DRAM (Max. Required)	8-MHz 80286 with 8207 0 Wait States (Min. Provided)
RAS Access Time CAS Access Time	100 ns 50 ns	135.5 73.0

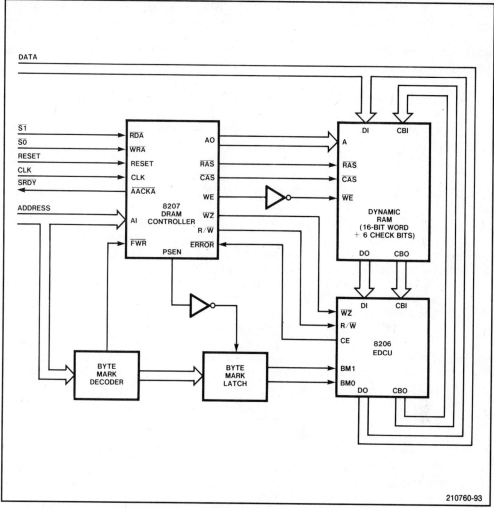

Figure 4-20. 8207 Memory Subsystem with ECC

It is important to note that the 8206 EDCU introduces a propagation delay of 67 ns (max) into memory cycles. The ADRC automatically compensates for the delay by inserting an additional wait state into all bus cycles to ECC-protected memory.

DUAL-PORT MEMORY SUBSYSTEMS USING THE 8207 ADRC

The 8207 DRAM Controller contains on-chip arbitration logic to control dual-port memory subsystems. The concept of a dual-port memory subsystem, permitting access by an 80286 over the 80286 local bus and also access by other processors over a system bus, was introduced in Chapter Two.

In dual-port mode, the 8207 must arbitrate memory requests between port A, port B, and port C—the internal refresh port. Two port priority options can be programmed to select which port has priority over the others in gaining access to the RAM memory array. In addition, the 8207 supports a $\overline{LOCK}$ input to prevent a second port from gaining access to the memory array until the port asserting the $\overline{LOCK}$ request has released the memory.

Chapter Seven contains a detailed explanation of how to configure a dual-port subsystem between the 80286 local bus and the Multibus system bus. Specific examples are given for a dual-port memory subsystem with error checking and correction, and specific guidelines are given for implementing the $\overline{LOCK}$ input to the 8207 to prevent deadlock situations.

The 82C08 Advanced Dynamic RAM Controller

An alternative to using the 8207 Advanced Dynamic Ram Controller for designing DRAM interfaces, is the 82C08 Dynamic RAM Controller. The 82C08 CHMOS DRAM controller provides a highly integrated solution: in addition to performing refreshes, address multiplexing, and control timings, it supports memory bank interleaving and can drive up to two banks of 64K or 256K dynamic RAMs. The 82C08 CHMOS DRAM controller can interface 100 ns DRAMs to a 10 MHz 80286 processor without introducing wait states. In addition, the 82C08 supports both power down and battery back up modes, making it useful for low power or portable systems.

Figure 4-21 shows a memory design using the 82C08 CHMOS DRAM controller to interface 100 ns DRAMs to a 10 MHz 80286 system which can run at zero wait states. In this example, the 82C08 interfaces synchronously to the processor, which results in the best overall performance.

The 82C284 clock generator provides the clocking for both the 82C08 and the 80286. The status lines of the 80286 are connected to the $\overline{RD}$ and $\overline{WR}$ inputs of the 82C08.

The address lines of the 80286 connect directly to the AL0-AH8 address input pins of the 82C08. In the fast cycle (80286) mode, the 82C08 generates an internal strobe to latch the addresses. In addition an external Latch is used to latch the A0 and $\overline{BHE}$ signals, which are then decoded to derive the gating signals for upper and lower (byte) memory.

The least significant address line, A1, is tied directly to the bank select, BS, input. This allows memory interleaving; Multiple bus accesses to consecutive memory addresses causes each access to occur in alternate banks of memory. This allows overlapping the $\overline{RAS}$ precharge of the first access behind the memory access of the next cycle.

The 82C08 performs early write memory cycles, which allows data-in and data-out pins of the DRAMs to be tied together. Data buffers are required between the 80286 Data pins and the DRAM data in/out pins to prevent bus contention which can occur during a read cycle because the 82C08 $\overline{CAS}$ line drivers drive data onto the bus up to 50 ns past the end of the bus cycle. If another bus cycle were to start immediately after a read cycle, there could be bus contention between the processor and the DRAM controller.

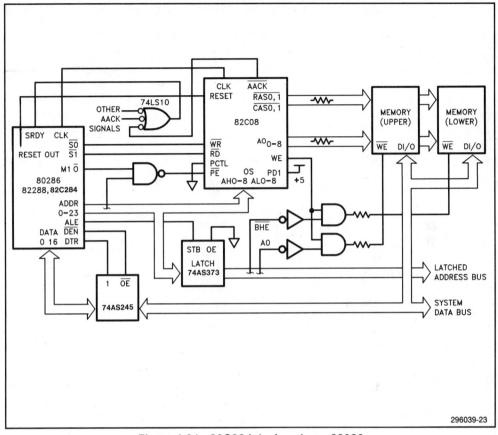

296039-23

Figure 4-21. 82C08 Interface to an 80286

Timing Analysis for the 82C08 DRAM Controller

RAM timing to determine device compatibility is measured from RAS going low to data valid at the CPU pins (see Figure 4-22). Maximum allowed RAS access time is:

Timing	Maximum RAS Access Time (82C08)	
	Symbol	10 MHz
3 CLK Cycles — RAS active delay (max) — 74AS245 Transceiver Delay (max) — Read Data Setup Time (min)	25 8	150.0 ns −25.0 ns −7.5 ns −8.0 ns
Maximum Allowed RAS Access Time =		109.5 ns

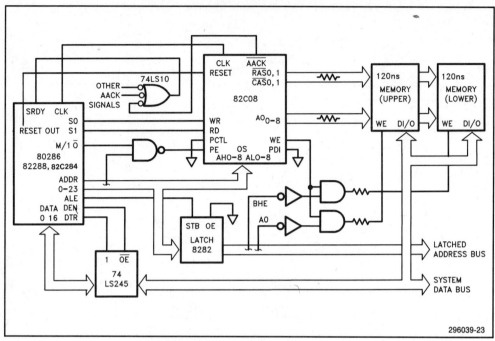

Figure 4-22. Read Data Setup and Hold Time Waveform (C0 Configuration - 100 ns DRAMs)

The corresponding CAS access time is:

Timing	Maximum CAS Access Time (82C08)	
	Symbol	10 MHz
2 CLK Cycles — CAS active delay (max) — 74AS245 Transceiver Delay (max) — Read Data Setup Time (min)	32 8	100.0 ns −35.0 ns −7.5 ns −8.0 ns
Maximum Allowed CAS Access Time =		49.5 ns

For typical DRAM devices, the CAS access time will be the limiting parameter. Table 4-13 shows the timing requirements of a typical 100 ns DRAM and the 82C08 operating with zero wait states.

The circuit shown in Figure 4-21 will run at 0 wait states for most memory cycles; the subsystem will run with 1 wait state only when back-to-back accesses occur to the same memory bank.

For more information refer to the *82C08 User's Manual*, order number 296039-001, and the *82C08 CHMOS Dynamic RAM Controller Data Sheet* which can be found in the *Intel Microprocessor and Perpheral Handbook*, *Vol. II*, order number 230843-004.

Table 4-13. 10 MHz Timing Analysis for the 100 ns DRAMs

Timing Parameter	100 ns DRAM (Max. Required)	10-MHz 80286 with 82C08-20 0 Wait States (Min. Provided)
RAS Access Time	100 ns	109.5
CAS Access Time	25 ns	49.5

I/O Interfacing

5

CHAPTER 5
I/O INTERFACING

The 80286 supports both 8-bit and 16-bit input/output devices that can be mapped into either a special I/O-address space or the 80286 memory-address space.

- I/O-mapping permits I/O devices to reside in a separate 64K I/O address space. Four special I/O instructions are available for device communications, and the I/O Privilege level offers I/O device protection.

- Memory-mapping permits I/O devices to reside anywhere in the 80286 memory space. The full 80286 instruction set can be used for I/O operations, and the full memory-management and protection features of the 80286 can be used for device protection.

This chapter describes how to design I/O devices into an 80286 system:

- The first section of this chapter establishes the tradeoffs between I/O-mapped and memory-mapped I/O.

- The second section describes several techniques for connecting data buses and generating chip-selects for both 8-bit and 16-bit I/O devices. Various alternatives are described for both I/O-mapped and memory-mapped devices.

- The third section discusses the timing considerations for I/O operations, and contains examples of worst-case timing analyses.

- The fourth section contains specific I/O interface examples, including interfaces for the 8274 Multi-Protocol Serial Controller, the 8255A Programmable Peripheral Interface, and the 8259A Programmable Interrupt Controller.

- The last section of this chapter introduces the iSBX™ bus interface; the iSBX bus allows single-board computer systems to be modularly expanded simply by plugging in I/O-mapped iSBX Multimodule Boards.

I/O-MAPPING VS. MEMORY-MAPPING

The 80286 CPU is capable of supporting either I/O-mapped or memory-mapped I/O devices. As outlined in the introduction, these two alternatives differ in three key respects. Although a decision to use one alternative or another will depend on the particular requirements of the design, the tradeoffs between these alternatives should be considered.

Address-Decoding

I/O-mapped devices reside in a separate 64K I/O address space, whereas memory-mapped devices reside in the full 16 Mbyte physical memory space. For this reason, the address-decoding required to generate chip-selects for I/O-mapped devices may be simpler than that required for memory-mapped devices.

80286 Instruction Set

I/O-mapped devices are accessible to programmers using the IN, OUT, INS, and OUTS instructions of the 80286. IN and OUT instructions transfer data between I/O addresses and the AX (16-bit transfers) or AL (8-bit transfers) registers. The first 256 bytes of I/O space are directly-addressable by the I/O instructions, whereas the entire I/O space (64K bytes) can be indirectly-addressed through the DX register. INS and OUTS are string instructions used to transfer blocks of data between memory and I/O devices. For more information on these I/O instructions, see the 80286 Programmer's Reference Manual.

Memory-mapped devices are accessible using the full 80286 instruction set, allowing efficient coding of such tasks as I/O-to-memory, memory-to-I/O, and I/O-to-I/O transfers, as well as compare and test operations.

Figure 5-1 illustrates the advantages of using memory-mapped I/O over I/O-mapped I/O in performing a simple bit-manipulation task. After setting up pointers to the I/O device, the memory-mapped I/O example accomplishes the task in a single instruction; the I/O-mapped example requires three.

```
                     BIT-MANIPULATION FOR
                     I/O-MAPPED I/O DEVICE

    SETBIT: MOV   DX,STAT_REG ; point to status

            IN    AL,DX           ; read status word
            OR    AL,10H          ; set bit 4
            OUT   DX,AL           ; output status word



                     BIT-MANIPULATION FOR
                   MEMORY-MAPPED I/O DEVICE

    SETBIT: MOV   AX,IO_SET_BASE ; I/O base addr
            MOV   ES,AX           ; load seg base

            OR    ES:BYTE PTR STAT_REG,10H
                  ; set bit 4 of status word
```

Figure 5-1. Comparing Memory-Mapped and I/O-Mapped I/O

Device Protection

I/O-mapped devices are offered protection by the 80286 I/O Privilege level. This privilege level can be used either to prevent a task from accessing any I/O devices, or to permit the task access to all of the I/O-mapped devices.

Memory-mapped devices fall under the protection of the 80286 memory-management and protection features. Depending on how devices are mapped into the memory space, individual tasks may be given access to particular I/O devices, while other devices are either visible-but-protected, or else mapped entirely out of the task's visible address space. Memory-mapping of devices thus permits more flexibility in offering protection of individual system resources than I/O-mapping does.

INTERFACING TO 8-BIT AND 16-BIT I/O

Although the 80286 can address I/O devices as either byte (8-bit) or word (16-bit) devices, several considerations must be observed when connecting these devices to the 80286 bus. The following sections describe data bus connections and chip-select techniques for both I/O-mapped and memory-mapped I/O devices.

Address Decoding

As mentioned in the previous section, the address-decoding for I/O-mapped devices is somewhat simpler than that for memory-mapped devices. One simple technique for decoding memory-mapped I/O addresses is to map the entire 80286 I/O space into a 64-Kilobyte region of the 80286 memory space. If desired, the address decoder can be configured so that the I/O devices respond to *both* a memory address and an I/O address. This configuration allows system compatibility with software using the 80286-family I/O instructions, while also permitting the use of software that takes advantage of memory-mapped I/O and the 80286 memory-management and protection features.

Another factor affecting decoder complexity is the particular choice of addresses for either I/O-mapped or memory-mapped devices. Before selecting addresses for various I/O devices, however, designers must be aware of several restricted address spaces imposed by the 80286 architecture. Figure 5-2 shows these restricted address regions for both memory-mapped and I/O-mapped devices.

A third factor worth considering when decoding addresses is that an address decoder can be made less complex by decoding fewer of the lower address lines, resulting in larger granularity in the addresses corresponding to an individual I/O device. The 64-K I/O address space of the 80286 leaves plenty of freedom for allocating addresses to individual I/O devices.

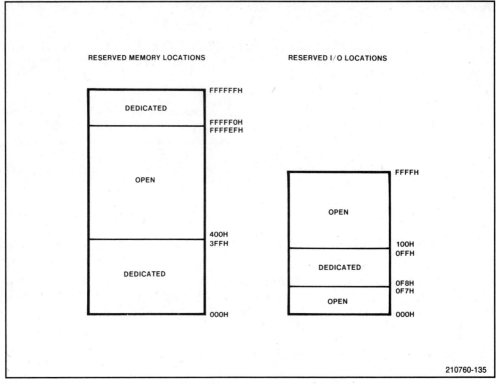

Figure 5-2. Restricted Address Regions

Memory-Mapped I/O

Figure 5-3 shows a simple decoding circuit for mapping the 80286 I/O space into a 64K region of the 80286 memory space. This technique, described above, allows individual I/O devices to respond to both a memory address and an I/O address. This particular circuit maps the I/O space into the region of the 80286 memory space which corresponds to addresses FE 0000H through FE FFFFH (this region is the second 64K region from the top of the physical address space; the top 64K region typically contains the code for 80286 system-reset processing).

When this memory-mapping technique is used, the low sixteen address bits must still be decoded to generate chip selects (in the same manner as for I/O-mapped devices). The $\overline{\text{IORC}}$ and $\overline{\text{IOWC}}$ commands, rather than $\overline{\text{MRDC}}$ and $\overline{\text{MWTC}}$, are generated by the Bus Controller whenever a bus operation accesses addresses in the specified region. For this reason, subsequent sections of this chapter will not distinguish between memory-mapped and I/O-mapped devices.

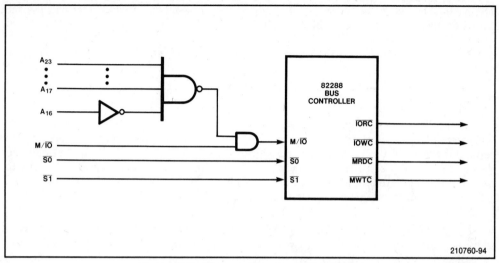

Figure 5-3. Memory-Mapping I/O Devices

The maximum decode time for the simple gating arrangement shown in Figure 5-3 is:

Maximum Decode Time for Circuit in Figure 5-3					
Timing	Symbol	6 MHz	8 MHz	10 MHz	12.5 MHz
2 CLK Cycles − Address Valid Delay (max) − M/IO Setup Time (min)	 13 6	166.6 ns −80.0 ns −28.0 ns	125.0 ns −60.0 ns −22.0 ns	100.0 ns −35.0 ns −18.0 ns	80.0 ns −32.0 ns −15.0 ns
Maximum Decode Time =		58.6 ns	43.0 ns	47.0 ns	33.0 ns

or 43.0 ns from address valid to allow sufficient setup time for $M/\overline{IO}$ to be sampled by the 82288 Bus Controller for an 8 MHz system.

The same circuit technique shown in Figure 5-3 may be used to memory-map I/O devices that reside on the MULTIBUS. The Bus Controller shown in the circuit would then be used to control the MULTIBUS signals; this technique is discussed further in Chapter Seven in conjunction with MULTIBUS I/O.

8-Bit I/O

Although 8-bit I/O devices may be connected to either the upper- or lower-half of the data bus, it is recommended that designers use the lower half of the data bus for 8-bit devices.

The particular address assigned to a device determines whether byte transfers will use the upper- or lower-half of the data bus.

- If a device is connected to the upper half of the data bus, all I/O addresses assigned to the device must be odd (A0 = 1).

- If the device is on the lower half of the bus, its addresses must be even (A0 = 0).

Since A0 will always be high or low for a specific device, this address line cannot be used as an address input to select registers within a device. If a device on the upper half and a device on the lower half of the bus are assigned addresses that differ only in A0 (adjacent odd and even addresses), A0 and BHE must be conditions of chip select decode to prevent a write to one device from erroneously performing a write to the other. Figure 5-4 shows several techniques for generating chip selects for I/O-mapped devices.

The first technique (a) uses separate 74AS138's to generate chip selects for odd- and even-addressed byte peripheral devices. If a word transfer is performed to an even-addressed device, the adjacent odd-addressed I/O device is also selected. This allows accessing the devices individually for byte transfers or simultaneously as a 16-bit device for word transfers. The second technique (b) restricts the chip selects to byte transfers. Word transfers to odd addresses, since they are performed as two byte transfers, are also permitted. The last technique (c) uses a single 74AS138 to generate odd and even device selects for byte transfers. Even device selects are generated for both byte and word transfers to even addresses.

If greater than 256 bytes of I/O space are required, additional decoding beyond what is shown in the examples may be necessary. This can be done with additional TTL, 74AS138's, or PROMs. Figure 5-5 shows a PROM used as an I/O address decoder generating latched chip-selects. The bipolar PROM is slightly slower than multiple levels of TTL (50 ns for PROM vs. 30 to 40 ns for TTL), but provides full decoding in a single package, and allows easy reconfiguration of the system I/O map by inserting a new PROM; no circuit board or wiring modifications are required. By using ALE to latch the decoded chip selects, up to 62 ns are available for decoding without affecting address access timing for an 8 MHz system:

Maximum Address Decode Time					
Timing	Symbol	6 MHz	8 MHz	10 MHz	12.5 MHz
2 CLK Cycles − Address Valid Delay (max) + ALE Active Delay (min)	 13 16	166.6 ns −80.0 ns 3.0 ns	125.0 ns −60.0 ns 3.0 ns	100.0 ns −35.0 ns 3.0 ns	80.0 ns −32.0 ns 3.0 ns
Maximum Address Decode Time =		83.6 ns	62.0 ns	62.0 ns	45.0 ns

One last technique for interfacing with 8-bit peripherals is considered in Figure 5-6. The 16-bit data bus is multiplexed onto an 8-bit bus to accommodate byte-oriented DMA or block transfers to memory-mapped 8-bit I/O. Devices connected to this interface may be assigned a sequence of odd and even addresses rather than all odd or all even.

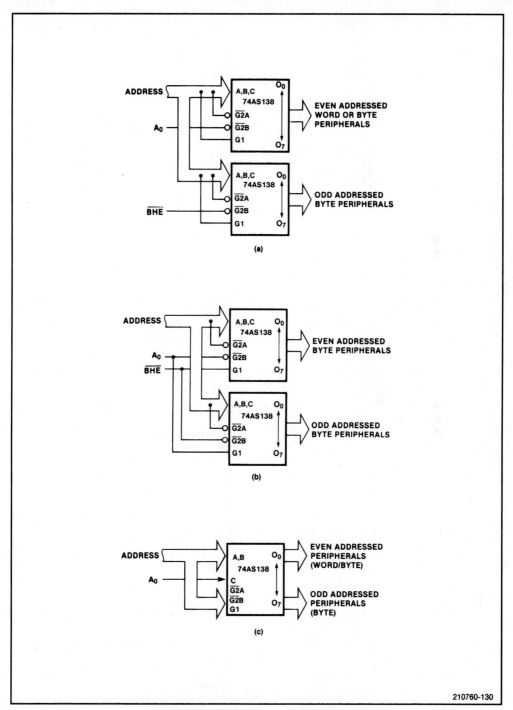

Figure 5-4. Generating I/O Chip Selects

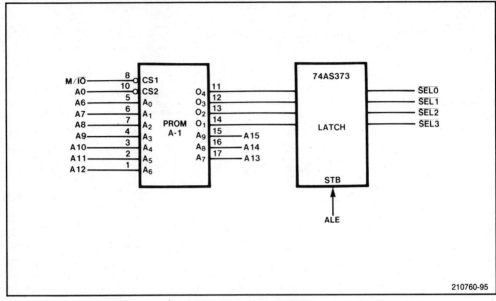

Figure 5-5. Bipolar PROM Decoder for 8-Bit or 16-Bit I/O Devices

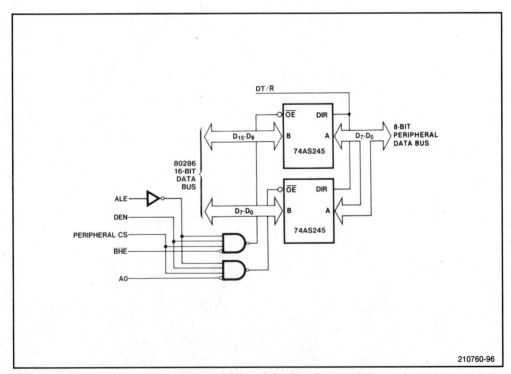

Figure 5-6. 16-Bit to 8-Bit Bus Conversion

16-Bit I/O

For efficient bus utilization and simplicity of device selection, 16-bit I/O devices should be assigned to even addresses. As shown in Figure 5-7, both A0 and $\overline{\text{BHE}}$ should be conditions of chip-select decode to guarantee that a device is selected *only* for word operations.

Linear Chip Selects

Systems with 15 or fewer I/O ports that reside only in I/O space, or that require more than one active select (at least one low active and one high active) can use linear chip selects to access the I/O devices. Latched address lines A1 through A15 connect directly to I/O device selects as shown in Figure 5-8.

TIMING ANALYSIS FOR I/O OPERATIONS

By analyzing the worst-case timing for 80286 I/O cycles, designers can determine the timing requirements for various I/O devices and the need for wait states in the 80286 bus cycle. This section explains how to perform a worst-case timing analysis for I/O operations.

Timing for 80286 I/O cycles is identical to memory cycle timing in most respects and, like memory timing, is dependent on a particular model. Figure 5-9 shows the model used here to discuss worst-case timing analysis. Address and chip selects are measured from the outputs of latches (strobed by ALE). Data valid for reads is measured at the data pins of the CPU. Data valid for writes is measured at the data inputs to the I/O device. IORC and IOWC are 82288 outputs. Figures 5-10 and 5-11 show I/O read and write timing for no-wait-state operation.

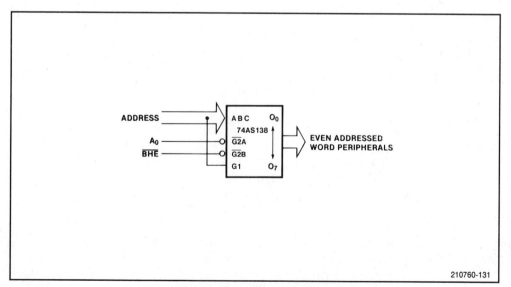

210760-131

Figure 5-7. 16-Bit I/O Decode

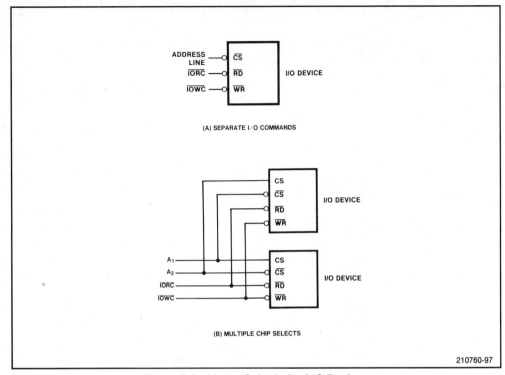

Figure 5-8. Linear Selects for I/O Devices

The timing parameters used in the analysis are defined as follows:

TLAVCML   = Latched address valid to command active
TCMHLAX = Latched address hold from command inactive
TCMLCMH = Command pulse width
TCMLDV   = Command active to data valid
TLAVDV   = Latched address valid to data valid
TDVCMH   = Data valid to command inactive
TCMHDX   = Data hold from command inactive
TCMHDF   = Data float from command inactive
TLCECML   = Latched chip enable to command active
TCMHLCEX = Latched chip enable hold from command inactive
TLCEDV   = Latched chip enable to data valid
TCMLCML   = Interval from one operation to the next
TCMHCML = Interval between commands (not shown)

The worst-case timing values can be calculated by assuming the maximum delay in the latched address, chip select, and command signals, and the longest propagation delay through the data buffers (if present). These calculations provide the minimum possible access time and can be used to determine the compatibility of I/O devices.

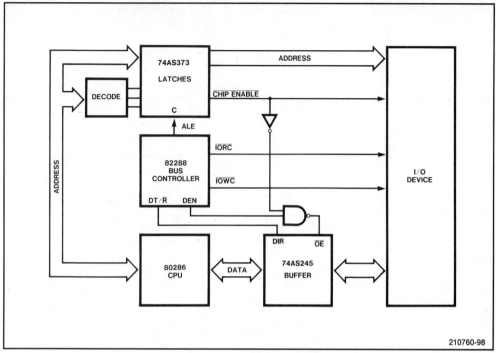

210760-98

Figure 5-9. I/O Cycle Model

Read Operations

For read operations, data must be valid at the pins of the 80286 t_8 ns before the falling edge of CLK at the end of T_c. The important timing parameters that determine whether I/O devices require one or more wait states are the address and command access times required by the device before read data will be valid.

Taking into consideration the maximum propagation delay through the 74AS245 data transceivers, the worst-case address access time provided during read operations with zero wait states is:

Minimum Address Access Time					
Timing	Symbol	6 MHz	8 MHz	10 MHz	12.5 MHz
3 CLK Cycles		249.9 ns	187.5 ns	150.0 ns	120. ns
– ALE Active Delay (max)	16	−25.0 ns	−20.0 ns	−16.0 ns	−16.0 ns
– Address Valid Delay (max)	13	−80.0 ns	−60.0 ns	−35.0 ns	−32.0 ns
– 74AS373 C-To-Ouput Delay (max)		−11.5 ns	−11.5 ns	−11.5 ns	−11.5 ns
– 74AS245 Transceiver Delay (max)		−7.5 ns	−7.5 ns	−7.5 ns	−7.5 ns
– Read Data Setup Time (min)	8	−20.0 ns	−10.0 ns	−8.0 ns	−5.0 ns
Minimum Address Access Time =		184.9 ns	137.5 ns	106.0 ns	79.0 ns

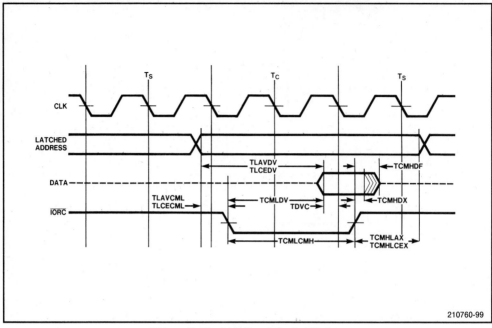

210760-99

Figure 5-10. I/O Read Cycle Timing

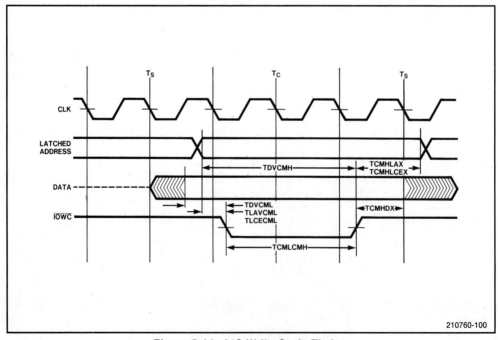

210760-100

Figure 5-11. I/O Write Cycle Timing

210760-002

The calculations for the worst-case command access times provided during read cycles are similar:

Minimum Command Access Time						
Timing	Symbol	6 MHz	8 MHz	10 MHz	12.5 MHz
2 CLK Cycles — Command Active Delay from CLK (max) — 74AS245 Transceiver Delay (max) — Read Data Setup Time (min)	29 8	166.6 ns −40.0 ns −7.5 ns −20.0 ns	125.0 ns −25.0 ns −7.5 ns −10.0 ns	100.0 ns −21.0 ns −7.5 ns −8.0 ns	80.0 ns −21.0 ns −7.5 ns −5.0 ns
Minimum Command Access Time =		99.1 ns	82.5 ns	63.5 ns	46.5 ns

If wait states are inserted into every I/O cycle, access times for the relevant parameters are increased by 2 CLK cycles for each wait state. Address, chip enable, and command times for a single buffered system running with from zero to two wait states are shown in Table 5-1.

Another critical timing parameter for I/O read operations is data float time. Data float time measures the time required by the I/O device to disable its data drivers following a read operation. If the 80286 attempts to perform a write operation immediately following a read from an I/O device, the I/O device must disable its data drivers before the DEN signal from the Bus Controller re-enables the 74AS245 data transceivers, or data bus contention will occur.

For the I/O configuration shown in Figure 5-9, the maximum data float time afforded an I/O device is 57.5 ns. For a typical I/O device, this allowed data float time is inadequate. However, if a buffered local bus contains only I/O devices, the 80286 cannot perform

Table 5-1. Timing Analysis for I/O Read Operations

Worst-Case Access Time	Speed	0 Wait States	1 Wait State	2 Wait States	3 Wait States
Address Access Time (min)	12.5 MHz	79.0 ns	159.0 ns	239.0 ns	319.0 ns
	10 MHz	106.0 ns	206.0 ns	306.0 ns	406.0 ns
	8 MHz	137.5 ns	262.5 ns	387.5 ns	512.5 ns
	6 MHz	184.9 ns	351.5 ns	518.1 ns	684.7 ns
Chip Select Access Time (min)	12.5 MHz	79.0 ns	159.0 ns	239.0 ns	319.0 ns
	10 MHz	106.0 ns	206.0 ns	306.0 ns	406.0 ns
	8 MHz	137.5 ns	262.5 ns	387.5 ns	512.5 ns
	6 MHz	184.9 ns	351.5 ns	518.1 ns	684.7 ns
Command Access Time (min)	12.5 MHz	46.5 ns	126.5 ns	206.5 ns	286.5 ns
	10 MHz	63.5 ns	163.5 ns	263.5 ns	363.5 ns
	8 MHz	82.5 ns	207.5 ns	332.5 ns	457.5 ns
	6 MHz	99.1 ns	265.7 ns	432.3 ns	598.9 ns

back-to-back read-write operations to that bus, and so the circumstances producing bus contention will not occur. If the I/O devices share the bus with memory such as static RAMs, then back-to-back read-write operations are possible and bus contention must be specifically prevented.

To accommodate the data float time requirements of typical I/O devices, and thereby avoid bus contention, the output enables of the data bus tranceivers can be delayed for the necessary length of time. Figure 5-12 shows an example circuit that delays enabling the data transceivers following a read operation to the selected I/O devices. This same circuit, described in the previous chapter for use with memory devices, provides a maximum data float time for a peripheral of:

Minimum Data Float Time					
Timing	Symbol	6 MHz	8 MHz	10 MHz	12.5 MHz
2 CLK Cycles − Command Inactive Delay from CLK (max) + 74AS245 Transceiver Enable Time (min)	30	166.6 ns −30.0 ns 2.0 ns	125.0 ns −25.0 ns 2.0 ns	100.0 ns −20.0 ns 2.0 ns	80.0 ns −20.0 ns 2.0 ns
Maximum Data Float Time =		138.6 ns	102.0 ns	82.0 ns	62.0 ns

Write Operations

For typical write operations to an I/O device, data is latched into the device on the rising edge of the Write command at the end of T_c. The important timing parameters that determine whether wait states are required are the address and command access times before command high.

The worst-case address-valid to command-high access time provided during write operations with zero wait states is:

Maximum Address Access Time					
Timing	Symbol	6 MHz	8 MHz	10 MHz	12.5 MHz
3 CLK Cycles − ALE Active Delay (max) − 74AS373 C-To-Output Delay (max) + Command Inactive Delay from CLK (min)	16 30	249.9 ns −25.0 ns −11.5 ns 5.0 ns	187.5 ns −20.0 ns −11.5 ns 5.0 ns	150.0 ns −16.0 ns −11.5 ns 5.0 ns	120.0 ns −16.0 ns −11.5 ns 5.0 ns
Maximum Address Access Time =		218.4 ns	161.0 ns	127.5 ns	97.5 ns

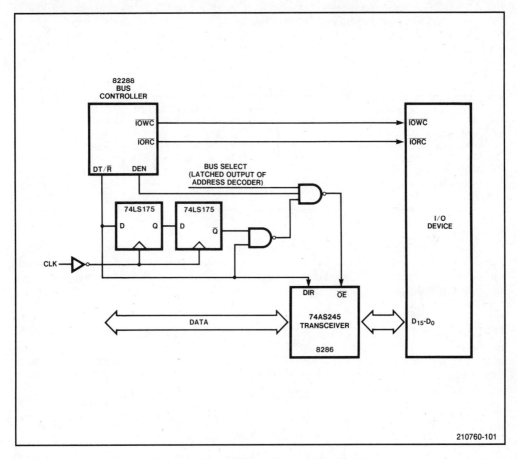

Figure 5-12. Delaying Transceiver Enable

Worst-case command-active to command-inactive timing is calculated in a similar manner (command timing for write opertions in not affected by buffers in the data path):

Minimum Command Pulse Width					
Timing	Symbol	6 MHz	8 MHz	10 MHz	12.5 MHz
2 CLK Cycles − Command Active Delay from CLK (max) + Command Inactive Delay from CLK (min)	 29 30	166.6 ns −40.0 ns 5.0 ns	125.0 ns −25.0 ns 5.0 ns	100.0 ns −21.0 ns 5.0 ns	80.0 ns −21.0 ns 5.0 ns
Minimum Command Pulse Width =		131.6 ns	105.0 ns	84.0 ns	64.0 ns

The data-valid to command-inactive time for write operations must include data buffer delays. The data-valid to command-inactive setup time is:

Maximum Data Setup Time					
Timing	Symbol	6 MHz	8 MHz	10 MHz	12.5 MHz
3 CLK Cycles − Write Data Valid Delay (max) − 74AS245 Transceiver Delay (max) + Command Inactive Delay from CLK (min)	 14 30	249.9 ns −65.0 ns −7.5 ns 5.0 ns	187.5 ns −50.0 ns −7.5 ns 5.0 ns	150.0 ns −30.0 ns −7.5 ns 5.0 ns	120.0 ns −30.0 ns −7.5 ns 5.0 ns
Maximum Data Setup Time =		182.4 ns	135.0 ns	117.5 ns	87.5 ns

If wait states are inserted into every I/O cycle, each of the relevant parameters for write operations are increased by 2 CLK cycles for each wait state. Address, chip-enable, command, and data-valid times for a single buffered system running with from zero to two wait states are shown in Table 5-2.

The CMDLY and CEN inputs to the 82288 can significantly alter bus cycle timing. CMDLY can delay commands to produce more address, chip enable, and (for write operations) data setup time before a command is issued. CEN can hold commands and data buffer control signals inactive, also altering bus cycle timing. When used, the effects of these inputs must also be included in any worst-case timing analysis.

Table 5-2. Timing for Write Operations Using Standard ALE Strobe

Maximum Access Times	Speed	0 Wait States	1 Wait State	2 Wait States	3 Wait States
Address Access Time (min)	12.5 MHz	97.5 ns	177.5 ns	257.5 ns	337.5 ns
	10 MHz	127.5 ns	227.5 ns	327.5 ns	427.5 ns
	8 MHz	161.0 ns	286.0 ns	411.0 ns	536.0 ns
	6 MHz	218.4 ns	385.0 ns	551.6 ns	718.2 ns
Chip-Select Access Time (min)	12.5 MHz	97.5 ns	177.5 ns	257.5 ns	337.5 ns
	10 MHz	127.5 ns	227.5 ns	327.5 ns	427.5 ns
	8 MHz	161.0 ns	286.0 ns	411.0 ns	536.0 ns
	6 MHz	218.4 ns	385.0 ns	551.6 ns	718.2 ns
Command Pulse Width (min)	12.5 MHz	64.0 ns	144.0 ns	224.0 ns	304.0 ns
	10 MHz	84.0 ns	184.0 ns	284.0 ns	384.0 ns
	8 MHz	105.0 ns	230.0 ns	355.0 ns	480.0 ns
	6 MHz	131.6 ns	298.2 ns	464.8 ns	631.4 ns
Write Data Setup Time (min)	12.5 MHz	87.5 ns	167.5 ns	247.5 ns	327.5 ns
	10 MHz	117.5 ns	217.5 ns	317.5 ns	417.5 ns
	8 MHz	135.0 ns	260.0 ns	385.0 ns	510.0 ns
	6 MHz	182.4 ns	349.0 ns	515.6 ns	682.2 ns

Matching I/O Device Requirements

The timing requirements of various I/O devices can be determined by comparing the timing specifications for a device with the worst-case values for 80286 I/O cycles already discussed. From this comparison, the required number of wait states and/or command delays for both read and write cycles can easily be determined.

Table 5-3 shows the correspondence between important 80286 timing parameters and the timing requirements for Intel peripherals.

For an 80286 system operating at 8 MHz, two wait states are required to produce adequate timing for typical I/O devices. One or more command delays may be required to ensure valid chip-select and address inputs before the command becomes active. Table 5-4 shows the wait-state and command-delay requirements of a variety of common peripherals.

I/O INTERFACE EXAMPLES

This section shows I/O interfaces to the 8274 Multi-Protocol Serial Controller, the 8255A-5 Programmable Peripheral Interface, and the 8259A-2 Programmable Interrupt Controller.

8274 Interface

The 8274 Multi-Protocol Serial Controller (MPSC) is designed to interface high-speed serial communications lines using a variety of communications protocols, including asynchronous, IBM bi-synchronous, and HDLC/SDLC protocols. The 8274 contains two independent full-duplex channels, and can serve as a high-performance replacement for two 8251A Universal Synchronous/Asynchronous Receiver Transmitters (USARTs).

Table 5-3. 80286/Peripheral Timing Parameters

80286 Cycle	Peripheral Read	Peripheral Write
TLAVCML	TAR	TAW
TCMHLAX	TRA	TWA
TCMLCMH	TRR	TWW
TCMLDV	TRD	—
TCMHCML	TDF	TRV
TLAVDV	TAD	—
TCMLCML	TRCYC	—
TDVCMH	—	TDW
TCMHDX	—	TWD
TLCECML	TAR	TAW
TCMHLCEX	TRA	TWA
TLCEDV	TRD	—

Table 5-4. Timing Requirements for Selected Peripherals

Intel Peripheral	Required Wait States	Required Command Delays
8251A	2	1
8254-2	2	1
8255-5	2	0
8259A	2	0
8272	2	0
8274	2	0
8291	2	0

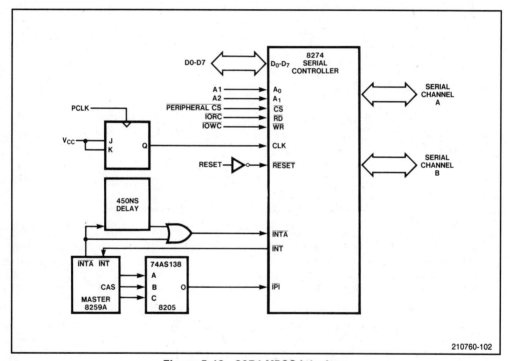

210760-102

Figure 5-13. 8274 MPSC Interface

Figure 5-13 shows the signals required to interface an 8274 MPSC to an 80286. The 8274 MPSC is accessed by the 80286 as a sequence of four 8-bit I/O-address or memory-address locations. For interrupt operation, the 8274 can respond to 80286 interrupt-acknowledge sequences in the same manner as an 8259A Interrupt Controller, and can be used in conjunction with a master 8259A Interrupt Controller in a cascaded configuration.

The chip-select and address inputs (CS, A0, and A1) to the 8274 must all be latched. Typically, address input A0 and A1 would be connected to the latched address lines A1 and A2, respectively, of the local address bus. A single level of buffering is typically used on the 8 data lines between the CPU and the 8274 MPSC.

The 8274 $\overline{RD}$ and $\overline{WR}$ commands are connected to the $\overline{IORC}$ and $\overline{IOWC}$ outputs of the 82288 Bus Controller. To provide an acceptable CLK input for the 8274 MPSC, the 82C284 PCLK clock frequency can be divided by two and used to drive the 8274 CLK input.

For Interrupt operation, the $\overline{INTA}$ signal from the Bus Controller is also connected to the 8274 MPSC. When using the 8274 in a cascaded interrupt configuration, the $\overline{IPI}$ input from the cascade address decoder must be valid before the falling edge of the $\overline{INTA}$ signal. A 450 ns delay circuit is used to delay $\overline{INTA}$ until this decoded CAS address becomes valid.

Further details on interfacing the 8274 MPSC to a microprocessor system can be found in the appropriate data books. The following discussion looks at the bus timing requirements for accessing the 8724 MPSC on a buffered 80286 local bus.

READ TIMING

The Read timing requirements for the 8274 MPSC are as follows:

TARmin = 0 ns
TRAmin = 0 ns
TRRmin = 250 ns
TRDmax = 200 ns
TDFmax = 120 ns

A comparison of TAR (0 ns min. required) with 80286 timing (5.5 ns min. provided) shows that no command delays are required. The command pulse width requirement (TRRmin) of 250 ns minimum indicates that at least two wait states must be inserted into the 80286 bus cycle (command pulse width with two wait states is 310 ns). With these two wait states, read operations to the 8274 result in a data access time of at least 315.5 ns, easily meeting the 8274 requirement for at least 200 ns.

Data float time for the 8274 MPSC is 120 ns maximum, and may necessitate the delayed-transceiver-enable circuit shown in Figure 5-12. The circumstances requiring a delayed transceiver-enable to accommodate lengthy data float times have been described in the previous section on Read Operations.

WRITE TIMING

Write timing requirements for the 8274 MPSC are as follows:

TAWmin = 0 ns
TWAmin = 0 ns
TWWmin = 250 ns
TDWmin = 150 ns
TWDmin = 0 ns
TRVmin = 300 ns

The first three timing requirements (TAWmin, TWAmin, and TWWmin) are identical to their equivalent read parameters, and require identical timing. Like Read operations, write operations to the 8274 must have two wait states inserted into the 80286 bus cycle.

The remaining three parameters are specific to write cycles. With two wait states, the 80286 easily exceeds the minimum 8274 data setup time (TDWmin = 150 ns) by providing at least 255.5 ns. The 8274 requires no data hold time.

TRVmin is the recovery time between write cycles to the USART. Recovery time is required following any mode changes or control accesses. The circuit shown, however, guarantees only 62.5 ns between successive Write commands. The proper recovery time between successive write cycles can be obtained easily through software delays, or can be implemented in hardware by delaying commands by an appropriate four CLK cycles.

8255A-5 Interface

Figure 5-14 shows the interface between an 8255A-5 Programmable Peripheral Interface and an 80286. Timing parameters are as follows:

Read Timing	Write Timing
TARmin = 0 ns	TAWmin = 0 ns
TRAmin = 0 ns	TWAmin = 20 ns
TRRmin = 300 ns	TWWmin = 300 ns
TRDmax = 200 ns	TDWmin = 100 ns
TDFmax = 100 ns	TWDmin = 30 ns

TCYCmin (Reads and Writes) = 850 ns

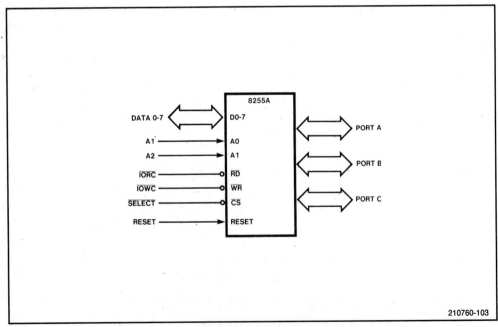

Figure 5-14. 8255A-5 Parallel Port Interface

A bus cycle with two wait states and no command delay, and using the additional delayed-transceiver-enable logic to delay enabling the data transceivers following a read operation, meets all of the timing requirements except for the time between cycles (TCYCmin). This remaining parameter can be met through an appropriate software delay or in hardware by delaying commands the required number of CLK cycles (and inserting wait states to meet the other requirements).

8259A-2 Interface

The 8259A-2 Programmable Interrupt Controller is designed for use in interrupt-driven microcomputer systems, where it manages up to eight independent interrupt sources. The 8259A-2 handles interrupt priority-resolution and individual interrupt masking, and directly supports the 80286 manner of acknowledging interrupts. During 80286 interrupt-acknowledge sequences, the 8259A resolves the highest-priority interrupt that is currently active, and returns a pre-programmed interrupt vector to the 80286 to identify the source of the interrupt.

A single 8259A-2 Interrupt Controller can handle up to eight external interrupts. Multiple 8259A-2 Interrupt Controllers can be cascaded to accommodate up to 64 interrupt requests. A technique for handling more than 64 external interrupts is discussed at the end of this section.

Intel Application Note AP-59 contains much more detailed information on configuring an 8259A in a variety of different ways. The remainder of this section contains specific details for interfacing an 8259A Interrupt Controller to the 80286.

SINGLE INTERRUPT CONTROLLER

Figure 5-15 shows the interface between the 80286 CPU and a single 8259A-2 Interrupt Controller. Timing parameters for the 8259A-2 are as follows (note that symbols used in the 8259A data sheet differ from those used for most of the other Intel peripherals):

Symbol	Parameter	ns
TAHRLmin	A0/CS Setup to RD/INTA Active	0
TRHAXmin	A0/CE Hold from RD/INTA Inactive	0
TRLRHmin	RD/INTA Pulse Width	160
TRLDVmax	Data Valid from RD/INTA Active	120
TRHDZmax	Data Float from RD/INTA Inactive	100
TRHRLmin	End of RD to next RD or End of INTA to next INTA within an INTA sequence only	160
TAHWLmin	A0/CS Setup to WR Active	0
TWHAXmin	A0/CS Hold from WR Inactive	0
TWLWHmin	WR Pulse Width	190
TDVWHmin	Data Valid to WR Inactive	160
TWHDXmin	Data Hold from WR Inactive	0
TWHWLmin	End of WR to Next WR	190
TCHCLmin	End of Command to Next Command (not same type) or End of INTA Sequence to Next INTA Sequence	500

To ensure proper operation, bus operations accessing the 8259A require one wait state. No CMDLYs are necessary. Because the 8259A requires a minimum of 500 ns (typically, two bus cycles) between successive reads or writes, software accessing the 8259A should be suitably written to avoid violating this requirement.

When an interrupt occurs, the 80286 CPU automatically executes two back-to-back interrupt-acknowledge bus cycles. The timing of these interrupt-acknowledge (INTA) cycles is described in Chapter Three. The external Ready logic must insert at least one wait state into each INTA cycle to ensure proper 8259A timing. No CMDLYs are necessary. Between INTA cycles, the 80286 automatically inserts three idle (T_i) cycles in order to meet 8259A timing requirements.

CASCADED INTERRUPT CONTROLLERS

Figure 5-16 shows the interface between the 80286 CPU and multiple 8259A-2 interrupt controllers. The master Interrupt Controller resides on the local bus, while up to eight slave controllers can be interfaced to the system bus. Slave controllers resolve priority between up to eight interrupt requests and transmit single interrupt requests to the master controller. The master controller, in turn, resolves interrupt priority between up to eight slave controllers and transmits a single interrupt request to the 80286 CPU. Up to 64 interrupt requests can be accommodated by the configuration shown.

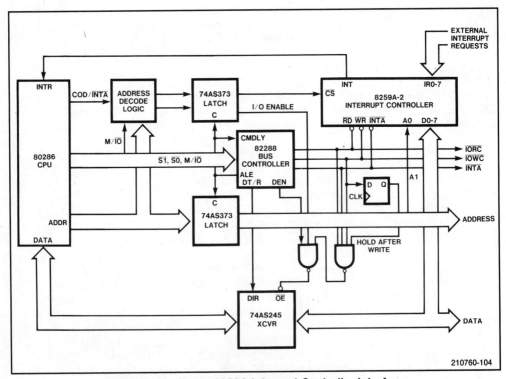

Figure 5-15. Single 8259A Interrupt Controller Interface

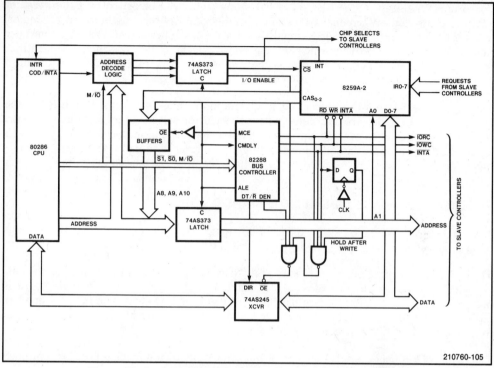

Figure 5-16. Cascaded 8259A Interrupt Controller Interface

The basic read/write timing for cascaded interrupt controllers is the same as for a single interrupt controller. The timing for interrupt-acknowledge sequences, however, involves additional signals over those required for a single interrupt subsystem.

During the first interrupt-acknowledge cycle, the master controller and all slave controllers freeze the state of their interrupt request inputs. The master controller outputs a cascade address that is enabled by MCE (Master Cascade Enable) from the 82288 and latched by ALE; the cascade address is typically gated onto address lines A8-A10 (IEEE 796 MULTI-BUS standard). This cascade address selects the slave controller that is generating the highest-priority interrupt request. During the second interrupt-acknowledge bus cycle, the slave controller responding to the cascade address outputs an interrupt vector that points to an appropriate interrupt service routine.

Chapter Seven includes details for designing systems using cascaded Interrupt Controllers when slave controllers may reside on a system bus such as the MULTIBUS.

HANDLING MORE THAN 64 INTERRUPTS

Cascaded 8259A Interrupt Controllers can accommodate up to 64 independent interrupt requests. 80286 systems that require more than 64 interrupts can use additional 8259A-2 devices in a polled mode.

For example, interrupt request inputs to a slave controller can be driven by a third level of 8259A-2 controllers. When one of these additional controllers receives an interrupt request, it drives one of the interrupt request inputs to the slave controller active. The slave controller signals the master controller, which in turn interrupts the CPU. The interrupt identifier received from the slave controller directs the CPU to a service routine that polls the third level of interrupt controllers to determine the source of the request.

The only additional hardware required to handle more than 64 interrupt sources are the additional 8259A-2 devices and address-decode logic for selecting the additional devices. Polling is performed by writing the poll command to the appropriate 8259A-2, followed immediately by a read command. For maximum performance, use of a third level of interrupt controllers should be restricted to less-critical, less frequently-used interrupts.

THE iSBX™ BUS—A MODULAR I/O EXPANSION BUS

The iSBX Bus is a modular I/O expansion bus that allows single-board computer systems to be expanded simply by plugging in specialized iSBX Multimodule boards.

The iSBX Multimodule boards respond to fully-decoded chip select lines defined on the bus. An $\overline{\text{MPST}}$ control signal indicates to the computer system that a Multimodule board is present. Once a Multimodule board has been installed, the I/O devices on the Multimodule board appear as an integral part of the single-board computer, and can be accessed in software using the standard I/O instruction set.

The timing of bus operations between an 80286 and an iSBX Multimodule Board is controlled by the iSBX $\overline{\text{MWAIT}}$ signal. This signal is asserted to insert wait states with the 80286 bus cycle, and can simply be inverted and used to drive the 82C284 $\overline{\text{ARDY}}$ input.

The iSBX Bus is described in the *iSBX Bus Specification*, Order Number 142686-002. This document contains complete details for designing Multimodule boards compatible with the iSBX bus standard.

Using the 80287 Numeric Processor Extension

6

CHAPTER 6
USING THE 80287 NUMERIC PROCESSOR EXTENSION

The Intel 80287 is a high-performance numeric processor extension that extends the 80286 system by adding floating-point, extended-integer, and BCD data types. The system, comprising an 80286 processor with an 80287 processor extension, contains over fifty additional instructions over those of an 80286 system, and fully conforms to the proposed IEEE 754 Floating Point Standard. The additional instructions added by the Numeric Processor Extension are described in the 8086 Numeric Supplement as well as in the 80287 Data Sheet.

This chapter details how to design an 80286/287 system.

- The first section of this chapter describes the electrical connections of the 80287 to an 80286 system.
- The second section describes the local bus activity you may observe using the 80287 with the 80286. This bus activity includes:

  A. Interactions between the 80286 and 80287 under program control (executing ESC instructions).

  B. Interactions that occur asynchronous to the program, where the 80287 Numeric Processor requests the transfer of operands between itself and system memory using the 80286 Processor Extension Data Channel.

- The final section of this chapter describes how to design an upgradable 80286 system with an empty 80287 socket. This system may be upgraded to an 80286/287 system simply by inserting an 80287 into the empty socket. This section includes an example software routine to recognize the presence of an 80287.

THE 80287 PROCESSOR EXTENSION INTERFACE

The 80287 can be connected to an 80286 system as shown in Figure 6-1.

Four important points should be observed when connecting the 80287 to an 80286 system:

1. The 80287 operates as an extension of the 80286. The 80286 executes programs in the normal manner; the 80287 automatically executes any numeric instructions when they are encountered.

2. The 80287 responds to particular I/O addresses (00F8H, 00FAH, and 00FCH) automatically generated by the 80286.

3. The 80287 can be driven by a separate clock signal, independent of the 80286 clock. This allows a higher-performance 80287 to be used if system performance requirements warrant it.

4. Because the 80287 data lines are connected directly to those of the 80286, the buffer/ drivers driving the local data bus must be disabled when the 80286 reads from the 80287.

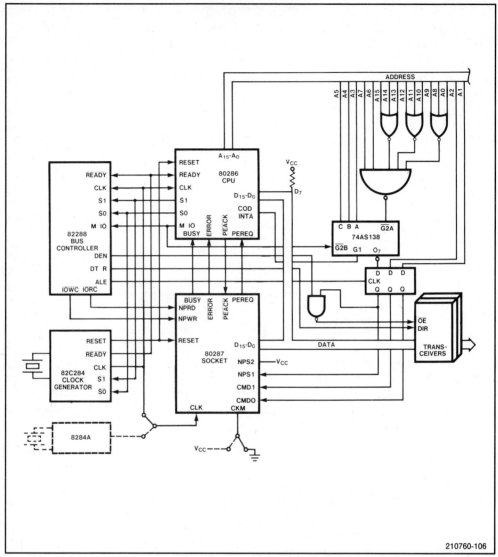

Figure 6-1. 80286/20 System Configuration

The 80287

The 80287 has a number of inputs that are connected directly to the 80286. The $\overline{\text{BUSY}}$ signal from the 80287 is connected directly to the 80286; it signals that the Processor Extension is currently executing a numeric instruction. The 80286 will not execute most ESC instructions until this $\overline{\text{BUSY}}$ signal becomes inactive. The 80286 WAIT instruction and most ESC instructions cause the 80286 to wait specifically until this signal becomes inactive.

The $\overline{\text{ERROR}}$ signal from the 80287 is also connected directly to the 80286; it signals that the previous numeric instruction caused an unmasked exception condition. The 80287 Data Sheet describes these exception conditions and explains how these exceptions may be masked under program control. If an exception occurs, this $\overline{\text{ERROR}}$ signal becomes active before the $\overline{\text{BUSY}}$ signal goes inactive, signalling the end of the numeric instruction.

Addressing the 80287

When the 80286 executes an ESC instruction, the 80286 automatically generates one or more I/O operations to the 80287's reserved I/O addresses. These I/O operations take place independent of the 80286's current I/O privilege level.

Table 6-1 shows the particular I/O addresses reserved for the 80287 and shows how the four processor-select and command inputs of the 80287 must be activated when these I/O addresses are asserted. The CMD0 and CMD1 signals of the 80287 may be connected to the latched A1 and A2 address lines, and, in addition, the $\overline{\text{NPRD}}$ and $\overline{\text{NPWR}}$ signals of the 80287 should be connected to the $\overline{\text{IORC}}$ and $\overline{\text{IOWC}}$ signals from the 82288 Bus controller, respectively.

The 80287 Clock Input

The 80287 can operate either directly from the CPU clock or with a dedicated clock. To operate the 80287 from the CPU clock, the CKM pin of the 80287 is tied to ground. In this mode, the 80287 internally divides the system clock frequency to operate at one-third the frequency of the system clock (i.e., for an 8 MHz 80286, the 16 MHz system clock is internally divided down to 5.3 MHz).

To use a higher-performance (10 MHz) 80287, the CKM pin of the 80287 must be tied high, and an 8284A clock driver and appropriate crystal may be used to drive the 80287 with a 10 MHz, 33% duty-cycle, MOS-level clock signal on the CLK input. In this mode, the 80287 does not internally divide the clock frequency; the 80287 operates directly from the external clock.

Table 6-1. I/O Address Decoding for the 80287

I/O Address (Hexadecimal)	80287 Select and Command Inputs			
	NPS2	$\overline{\text{NPS1}}$	CMD1	CMD0
00F8	1	0	0	0
00FA	1	0	0	1
00FC	1	0	1	0
00FE	* Reserved For Future Use			

NOTE: These addresses are generated automatically by the 80286. Users should not attempt to reference these I/O addresses explicitly, at the risk of corrupting data within the 80287.

LOCAL BUS ACTIVITY WITH THE 80287

The 80287 operates as a parallel processor independent of the 80286, and interacts with the 80286 in two distinct ways:

1. The 80286 initiates 80287 operations during the execution of an ESC instruction. These interactions occur under program control; thus, they are easily recognized as part of the instruction stream.

2. The 80287 requests the 80286 to initiate operand transfers using the Processor Extension Data Channel of the 80286. These operand transfers between the 80287 and system memory occur when the 80287 requests them; thus, they are asynchronous to the regular instruction stream of the 80286.

Execution of ESC Instructions

When the 80286 encounters an ESC instruction, the 80286 first checks for the presence of the Processor Extension and verifies that the Processor Extension is in the proper context. If the BUSY status line from the 80287 is active, the 80286 waits for this signal to become inactive before proceeding to execute the ESC instruction.

When the 80286 executes an ESC instruction, the 80286 automatically generates one or more I/O operations to the 80287's reserved I/O addresses. These I/O operations take place independent of the 80286's current I/O Privilege level or Current Privilege level. The timing of these I/O operations is similar to the timing of any other I/O operation, with no (zero) wait states required for successful transfers.

Figure 6-2 illustrates the timing of data transfers with the 80287.

The Processor Extension Data Channel

All transfers of operands between the 80287 and system memory are performed by the 80286's internal Processor Extension Data Channel. This independent, DMA-like data channel permits all operand transfers of the 80287 to fall under the supervision of the 80286 memory-management and protection model.

DATA CHANNEL REQUESTS

When the 80286 executes an ESC instruction that requires transfers of operands either to or from the 80287, the 80286 automatically initializes the Processor Extension Data Channel, setting the memory address base and memory address limit registers, and setting the direction flag to indicate the direction of the transfer. Once the 80826 has initialized the Processor Extension Data Channel, the Processor Extension can request operand transfers through the Data Channel by raising PEREQ active. This request line remains high until the 80286 acknowledges the request by lowering its $\overline{\text{PEACK}}$ signal.

Figure 6-3 illustrates the timing of PEREQ and $\overline{\text{PEACK}}$ in controlling the operation of a Data Channel transfer. $\overline{\text{PEACK}}$ always goes active during the first bus operation of a Data Channel transfer.

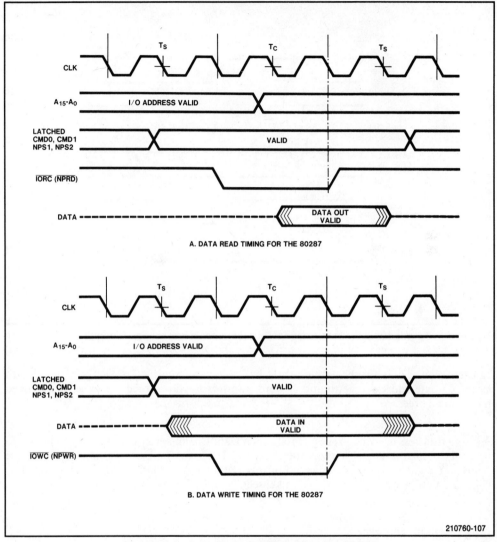

Figure 6-2. Data Transfer Timing for the 80287

DATA CHANNEL TRANSFERS

Numeric data transfers performed by the Processor Extension Data Channel use the same timing as any other 80286 bus cycle. Figure 6-2 illustrates operand transfers between the 80287 and system memory, placing the 16-bit operands at even-aligned word boundaries.

For each operand transfer over the Processor Extension Data Channel, two or three bus operations are performed: one (I/O) bus operation to the 80287, and one or two bus operations to transfer the operand between the 80286 and system memory. Normally, Data Channel

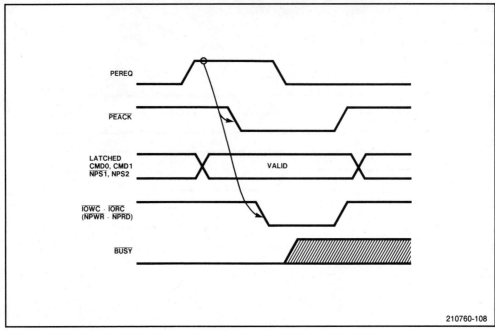

Figure 6-3. Data Channel Request and Acknowledge Timing

transfers require only two bus cycles; three bus cycles are required for each operand aligned on an odd byte address. The timing of word transfers to odd-aligned addresses is described in Chapter Three.

Operand transfers over the Processor Extension Data Channel may occur at any time following an ESC instruction as long as the Processor Extension's $\overline{\text{BUSY}}$ signal is active. Once this $\overline{\text{BUSY}}$ signal becomes inactive, no further requests by the 80287 for the Data Channel will occur until after the execution of a subsequent ESC instruction.

DATA CHANNEL PRIORITY

Data transfers over the Processor Extension Data Channel have a higher priority than either programmed data transfers performed by the 80286 Execution Unit, or instruction prefetch cycles performed by the 80286 Bus Unit.

If the 80286 is currently performing a $\overline{\text{LOCK}}$ed instruction, or is performing a two-byte bus operation required for an odd-aligned word operand, these higher-priority operations will be completed before the Processor Extension Data Channel takes control of the bus. The Processor Extension Data Channel also has a lower priority than external bus requests to the 80286 via the HOLD input.

Performance Using 80287 Parallel Processing

Because the 80287 Numeric Processor executes instructions in parallel with the 80286, the performance of the 80286/287 system is fairly insensitive to memory speed and the number of wait states encountered by the 80286.

Table 6-2 illustrates how the performance of an 80286/287 system is only slightly degraded as the number of wait states is increased. The figures shown are for an 8 MHz 80286-A1 with a 5 MHz 80287-A1 operating in Real mode. For an explanation of the Double-Precision Whetstone Benchmark used in this test, see "A Synthetic Benchmark," H. J. Curnow and B. A. Wichmann; *Computer Journal*, Volume 19, No. 1.

DESIGNING AN UPGRADABLE 80286 SYSTEM

When designing an 80286 system, it is relatively easy to design a socket for the 80287 Numeric Processor Extension that permits the system to be upgraded later to an 80286/287 system. Upgrading the system at a later date is accomplished simply by installing the 80287 Numeric Processor in its socket—no switches or strapping options are required. Using an appropriate initialization sequence, the 80286 system can determine whether an 80287 is present in the system, and respond accordingly. This capability allows a single design to address two different levels of system price vs. performance.

Designing the 80287 Socket

Figure 6-1 shown previously illustrates one way to design an 80287 socket to allow upgradability. All N/C pins on the 80287 socket should be connected as shown in Table 6-3.

Recognizing the 80287

During initialization, the 80286 can be programmed to recognize the presence of the 80287 Numeric Processor Extension. Figure 6-4 shows an example of such a recognition routine.

Table 6-2. Whetstone Performance with Multiple Wait States

Number of Wait States	Performance	
	dWhets*	Relative to 0-Wait States
0	147.9	1.00
1	142.5	0.96
2	138.5	0.94
3	135.4	0.92

*Performance shown in thousands of double-precision Whetstone instructions per second.

Table 6-3. 80287 N/C Pin Connections for Future Product Compatibilities

Previous Pin Value	Connection
Pin 1 (N/C)	Vss
Pin 2 (N/C)	(N/C)
Pin 3 (N/C)	Vcc
Pin 4 (N/C)	Vss
Pin 13 (N/C)	Vcc
Pin 37 (N/C)	Vcc
Pin 38 (N/C)	Vss
Pin 40 (N/C)	Vcc

```
DOS 3.20 (033-N) 8086/87/88/186 MACRO ASSEMBLER V2.0 ASSEMBLY OF MODULE TEST_NPX
OBJECT MODULE PLACED IN FINDNPX.OBJ
ASSEMBLER INVOKED BY:  A:\ASM86.EXE FINDNPX.BAK

LOC  OBJ           LINE    SOURCE


                    1 +1   $title('Test for presence of a Numerics Chip, Revision 1.0')
                    2
                    3            name    Test_NPX
                    4            extrn   dqopen:near,dqcreate:near,dqwrite:near,dqexit:near
                    5
  000D              6    CR      EQU     0DH
  000A              7    LF      EQU     0AH
                    8
  ----              9    stack   segment stack 'stack'
  0000 (100         10           dw      100 dup (?)
     ????
       )
  00C8 ????         11   sst     dw      ?                      ; Top of stack label
  ----              12   stack   ends
                    13
  ----              14   data    segment public 'data'
  0000 0000         15   status  dw      0
  0002 0000         16   co      dw      0
  0004 0000         17   temp    dw      0
  0006 04           18   co_name db      4,':CO:'
  0007 3A434F3A
  000B 21           19   n_npx   db      33,'No 8087, 80287, 80387 found.',CR,LF
  000C 4E6F2038303837
    2C203830323837
    2C203830333837
    20666F756E642E
  0028 0D
  0029 0A
  002A 11           20   f_387   db      17,'Found an 80387.',CR,LF
  002B 466F756E642061
    6E203830333837
    2E
  003A 0D
  003B 0A
  003C 19           21   f_npx   db      25,'Found an 8087 or 80287.',CR,LF
```

Figure 6-4. Software Routine to Recognize the 80287

```
LOC  OBJ                LINE    SOURCE
003D 466F756E642061
     6E203830383720
     6F722038303238
     372E
0054 0D
0055 0A
----                    22      data    ends
                        23 +1   $eject
                        24      dgroup  group   data,stack
                        25      cgroup  group   code
                        26
----                    27      code    segment public 'code'
                        28              assume  cs:cgroup,ds:dgroup
                        29
0000                    30      start:
0000 B8----     R       31              mov     ax,dgroup
0003 8ED8               32              mov     ds,ax
0005 8ED0               33              mov     ss,ax
0007 BCC800     R       34              mov     sp,offset dgroup:sst
000A BB0600     R       35              mov     ax,offset dgroup:co_name
000D 50                 36              push    ax
000E B80000     R       37              mov     ax,offset dgroup:status
0011 50                 38              push    ax
0012 E80000     E       39              call    dqcreate        ; Setup file connection
0015 A30200     R       40              mov     co,ax           ; Save file token
0018 50                 41              push    ax
0019 BB0200             42              mov     ax,2            ; Signal write open
001C 50                 43              push    ax
001D 33C0               44              xor     ax,ax           ; No buffers needed
001F 50                 45              push    ax
0020 B80000     R       46              mov     ax,offset dgroup:status
0023 50                 47              push    ax
0024 E80000     E       48              call    dqopen          ; Open file for writing
0027 FF360200   R       49              push    co              ; Setup for call
002B BB0B00     R       50              mov     bx,offset dgroup:n_npx
002E EB18               51              jmp     short test_npx  ; Enter test code on next page
                        52      ;
                        53      ;       Print message at [BX] then exit
                        54      ;
0030                    55      found_87_287:
0030 BB3C00     R       56              mov     bx,offset dgroup:f_npx
0033                    57      no_npx:
0033                    58      found_387:
0033 43                 59              inc     bx              ; Point at character string
0034 53                 60              push    bx
0035 8A47FF             61              mov     al,[bx-1]       ; Get count
0038 98                 62              cbw
0039 50                 63              push    ax
003A B80000     R       64              mov     ax,offset dgroup:status
003D 50                 65              push    ax
003E E80000     E       66              call    dqwrite         ; Print message
0041 33C0               67              xor     ax,ax
0043 50                 68              push    ax
0044 E80000     E       69              call    dqexit          ; End the program, go back to DOS
0047 CC                 70              int     3               ; Just in case
                        71 +1   $eject
```

Figure 6-4. Software Routine to Recognize the 80287 (Cont'd.)

```
LOC  OBJ                  LINE    SOURCE

                          72      ;
                          73      ;       Look for an 8087, 80287, or 80387 NPX.
                          74      ;       Note that we cannot execute WAIT on 8086/88 if no 8087 is present.
                          75      ;
0048                      76      test_npx:
0048 90DBE3               77              fninit                  ; Must use non-wait form
004B BE0400          R    78              mov     si,offset dgroup:temp
004E C7045A5A             79              mov     word ptr [si],5A5AH ; Initialize temp to non-zero value
0052 90DD3C               80              fnstsw  [si]            ; Must use non-wait form of fstsw
                          81                                      ; It is not necessary to use a WAIT instruction
                          82                                      ;   after fnstsw or fnstcw. Do not use one here.
0055 803C00               83              cmp     byte ptr [si],0 ; See if correct status with zeroes was read
0058 75D9                 84              jne     no_npx          ; Jump if not a valid status word, meaning no NPX
                          85      ;
                          86      ;       Now see if ones can be correctly written from the control word.
                          87      ;
005A 90D93C               88              fnstcw  [si]            ; Look at the control word do not use WAIT form
                          89                                      ; Do not use a WAIT instruction here!
005D 8B04                 90              mov     ax,[si]         ; See if ones can be written by NPX
005F 253F10               91              and     ax,103fh        ; See if selected parts of control word look OK
0062 3D3F00               92              cmp     ax,3fh          ; Check that ones and zeroes were correctly read
0065 75CC                 93              jne     no_npx          ; Jump if no npx is installed
                          94      ;
                          95      ;       Some numerics chip is installed. NPX instructions and WAIT are now safe.
                          96      ;       See if the NPX is an 8087, 80287, or 80387.
                          97      ;       This code is necessary if a denormal exception handler is used or the
                          98      ;       new 80387 instructions will be used.
                          99      ;
0067 9BD9E8               100             fld1                    ; Must use default control word from FNINIT
006A 9BD9EE               101             fldz                    ; Form infinity
006D 9BDEF9               102             fdiv                    ; 8087/287 says +inf = -inf
0070 9BD9C0               103             fld     st              ; Form negative infinity
0073 9BD9E0               104             fchs                    ; 80387 says +inf <> -inf
0076 9BDED9               105             fcompp                  ; See if they are the same and remove them
0079 9BDD3C               106             fstsw   [si]            ; Look at status from FCOMPP
007C 8B04                 107             mov     ax,[si]
007E 9E                   108             sahf                    ; See if the infinities matched
007F 74AF                 109             je      found_87_287    ; Jump if 8087/287 is present
                          110     ;
                          111     ;       An 80387 is present. If denormal exceptions are used for an 8087/287,
                          112     ;       they must be masked. The 80387 will automatically normalize denormal
                          113     ;       operands faster than an exception handler can.
                          114     ;
0081 BB2A00          R    115             mov     bx,offset dgroup:f_387
0084 EBAD                 116             jmp     found_387
                          117
----                      118     code    ends
                          119             end     start,ds:dgroup,ss:dgroup:sst


ASSEMBLY COMPLETE, NO ERRORS FOUND
```

Figure 6-4. Software Routine to Recognize the 80287 (Cont'd.)

The System Bus 7

CHAPTER 7
THE SYSTEM BUS

The concept of a system bus has already been introduced in Chapter Two. A system bus connects one or more processing elements, each of which shares access to the same system resources. One or all of the processing elements in such a system may be 80286 subsystems. Chapter Two outlines how the 80286 system architecture supports a system bus, and details some of the considerations for interfacing an 80286 system to a multiprocessor system bus.

This chapter expands on the description given in Chapter Two and describes how to interface an 80286 subsystem to a multimaster system bus, using the IEEE 796 MULTIBUS protocols.

- The first section of this chapter discusses some of the reasons for using a system bus, and describes the tradeoffs between placing particular system resources on a local bus or the system bus.

- The second section describes a particular implementation of a multiprocessor system bus, the IEEE 796 (Intel MULTIBUS) system bus. This section also details how specific Intel components can make the design and implementation of a MULTIBUS interface easy and efficient.

- The third section describes three of the four principal considerations that must be taken into account when designing an 80286 interface to the MULTIBUS. This section describes:

  A. The decoding of memory and I/O references onto either the 80286 local bus or the MULTIBUS. A technique for mapping MULTIBUS I/O into the 80286 memory space is explained, and a byte-swapping circuit is introduced to comply with the MULTIBUS requirements for byte transfers.

  B. The decoding of interrupts and interrupt acknowledge sequences onto either the local bus or the MULTIBUS.

- The fourth section describes the use of the 82289 Bus Arbiter in implementing a MULTIBUS interface. The Bus Arbiter coordinates the contention of the 80286 system for the MULTIBUS, and controls the release of the MULTIBUS to other MULTIBUS processors following 80286 usage.

- The fifth section contains a timing analysis of the MULTIBUS interface, and summarizes the key MULTIBUS parameters, describing how the 80286 system must be configured to meet these requirements.

- The sixth section discusses using dual-port memories with the MULTIBUS system bus interface, and describes the handling of LOCK signals.

THE SYSTEM-BUS CONCEPT

Previous chapters considered single-bus systems in which a single 80286 processor connects to memory, I/O, and processor extensions. This chapter introduces the system bus concept, which allows several single-bus systems to be connected into a more-powerful multi-processing system.

In a single-bus system, a local bus connects processing elements with memory and I/O subsystems where each processing element can access any resource on the local bus. However, since only one processing element at a time can use the local bus, system throughput cannot be improved by adding more processing elements. For this reason, a local bus typically contains only one general-purpose processing element and perhaps one or more dedicated processors, along with memory and other resources required by the processors.

A system bus can connect several processing subsystems, each of which may have their own local bus and private resources. The system bus may also connect system resources such as memory and I/O, which are shared equally between processing subsystems. In this way, the system bus supports multi-processing. Since each of the processing subsystems can perform simultaneous data transfers on their respective local buses, total system throughput can be increased greatly over that of a single-bus system.

The system bus also establishes a standard interface, allowing computer systems to be expanded modularly using components from different vendors. The Intel MULTIBUS, for example, has over 100 vendors supplying over 800 board-level products that are compatible with the MULTIBUS interface. Using the standard MULTIBUS protocols, a wide variety of I/O devices and memory subsystems are available to expand the capabilities of 80286 systems.

Although the bulk of this chapter describes the MULTIBUS system bus, the concepts discussed here are applicable to any system bus.

The Division of Resources

The heart of the system-bus concept is the division of resources between a processing element's local bus and the system bus. Typically, an 80286 subsystem that interfaces to a system bus will have some amount of memory and perhaps other resources connected to its local bus. An important point to consider in designing a multiprocessing system is how resources will be divided between local buses and the system bus. An 80286 subsystem must communicate with resources on both its local bus and the system bus. There are a number of tradeoffs between placing a particular system resource such as memory on a single processor's local bus, or placing the resource on the system bus.

LOCAL RESOURCES

Resources on a local bus are accessible only by the processor controlling that local bus. This may increase reliability, for such resources are isolated from the effects of failures occurring in other parts of a system. System throughput can also be increased by using local resources, since the local processor does not have to contend with other processors for the use of these resources. In systems where several processors each have their own local memory, multiple tasks can execute in parallel because each processor is fetching instructions from a separate path. In an 80286 system, local memory allows the 80286 to use its capability for overlapped memory cycles to the best effect: 80286 bus cycles can be performed in the least possible time.

Of course, the cost of implementing a separate memory subsystem for each processor must be considered. In addition, some memory will have to be connected to the system bus, to allow different processing elements to communicate with each other. Occasionally-used processor resources may be more cost-effective if they are connected to the system bus, where their use can be shared among several processors.

SYSTEM RESOURCES

Resources directly connected to the system bus are accessible to all processing elements on the system bus; therefore, they can be shared efficiently among different processors. Memory resources connected to the system bus allow processors to pass blocks of data between each other efficiently and thus communicate asynchronously.

A disadvantage of placing resources on the system bus is that a single processor may have to contend with other processors for access to the bus, resulting in slower access times and reduced system throughput. Using system memory also involves a risk of memory corruption because it is conceivable that one processing element may overwrite data being used by another.

In view of these tradeoffs, designers must carefully consider which resources (or how much memory) they will place on a subsystem's local bus, and which or how much to place on the system bus. These choices affect system reliability, integrity, throughput and performance, and often depend on the requirements of the particular target system.

THE IEEE 796 MULTIBUS®—A MULTIMASTER SYSTEM BUS

The Intel MULTIBUS (IEEE 796 Standard) is an example of a proven, industry-standard multiprocessing system bus that is well-tailored for 80286 systems. A wide variety of MULTIBUS-compatible I/O subsystems, memory boards, general-purpose processing boards, and dedicated-function boards are available from Intel to speed product development while ensuring bus-level compatibility. Designers who choose the MULTIBUS protocols in their system bus have a ready supply of system components available for use in their products.

The MULTIBUS protocols are completely described in the Intel MULTIBUS Specification, Order Number 9800683-04.

The job of interfacing an 80286 subsystem to the MULTIBUS is made relatively simple by using several components specifically adapted to handling the MULTIBUS protocols. These interface components include:

- The 82288 Bus Controller, to generate MULTIBUS-compatible memory and I/O read/ write commands, and interrupt-acknowledge commands, as well as appropriate data and address buffer control signals. The 82288 has a strapping option to select the MULTI-BUS mode of operation.

- The 82289 Bus Arbiter, to handle MULTIBUS arbitration logic and to generate appropriate control information.

- Data Transceivers such as the 74LS640 to buffer MULTIBUS data lines (inverting transceivers are required to conform to MULTIBUS convention).

- Latches such as the 74AS533 to buffer MULTIBUS address lines (inverting latches are required to conform to MULTIBUS convention).

- The 8259A Programmable Interrupt Controller, to handle hardware interrupts in conformance with the MULTIBUS bus-vectored interrupt conventions.

These devices are functionally and electrically compatible with the MULTIBUS protocols, and form a simple and cost-effective means of generating signals for a MULTIBUS interface. Figure 7-1 shows how these components interconnect to interface an 80286 subsystem to the MULTIBUS system bus.

MULTIBUS® DESIGN CONSIDERATIONS

One of the important decisions confronting a designer who is considering an implementation of a MULTIBUS interface is the question of how to divide system resources between resources that reside on the MULTIBUS and resources that reside on the 80286 local bus.

Typically, system resources will be split between the local bus and the system bus (MULTIBUS). System designers must allocate the 80286 system's physical address space between the two buses, and use this information to select either the 80286 local bus or the system bus for each bus cycle.

Figure 7-2 illustrates this requirement.

Three different types of bus operations must be considered when designing this decoding function:

1. Memory operations

2. I/O operations

3. Interrupt-acknowledge sequences

For memory and I/O operations, several additional features of the MULTIBUS must be considered. The following paragraphs describe each of these types in detail.

Memory Operations

The decoding of memory operations to select either the local bus or the system bus is relatively straightforward. Typically, memory resources that reside on the system bus can be allocated to particular address windows, or ranges. An address decoder can be used to decode the ranges of addresses for memory that resides on the system bus, and the output of this decoder then selects either the system bus or the local bus for the current bus cycle.

Figure 7-3 illustrates how the output of the address decoder drives the 82288 Bus Controller and 82289 Bus Arbiter circuits to selectively activate either the local bus or the system bus. Since both the CENL input of the Bus Controller and the SYSB/$\overline{\text{RESB}}$ input of the Bus Arbiter are internally-latched, no additional latches are required to maintain selection of the bus for the remainder of the current bus cycle.

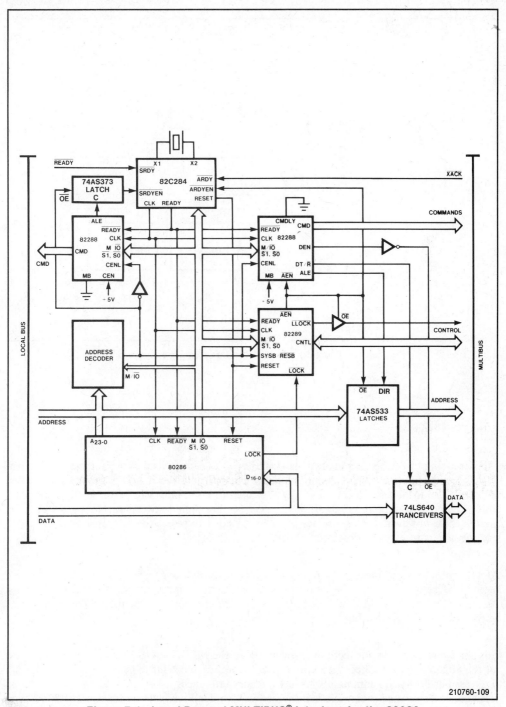

Figure 7-1. Local Bus and MULTIBUS® Interface for the 80286

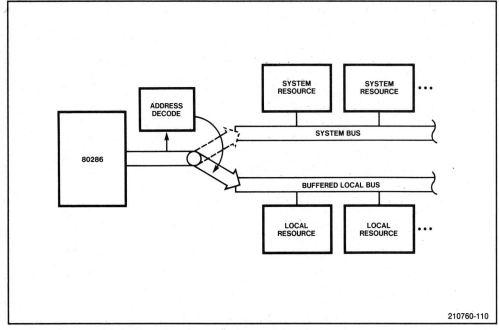

Figure 7-2. Decoders Select the Local vs. the System Bus

I/O Operations

The decoding of 80286 I/O operations is similar to that described above for memory operations. In the simplest case, decoding may not even be required if I/O resources are located solely on the local bus. In this case any I/O operations simply can be directed to the local bus with no decoding required. If I/O resources are split between the local bus and the system bus, however, I/O addresses must be decoded to select the appropriate bus, just as for memory addresses as described above.

If I/O resources are located on the system bus, a second, concurrent issue may be considered. I/O resources on the system bus may be memory-mapped into the 80286 memory space, or I/O-mapped into the I/O address space, independent of how the I/O devices appear physically on the system bus.

Figure 7-4 shows a circuit technique for mapping the MULTIBUS I/O space into a portion of the 80286 memory space. This circuit uses an address-decoder to generate the appropriate I/O-read or I/O-write commands for any memory references falling into the memory-mapped I/O block. This same technique is discussed in Chapter Five, which also contains a detailed discussion of the merits and tradeoffs between memory-mapped and I/O-mapped devices.

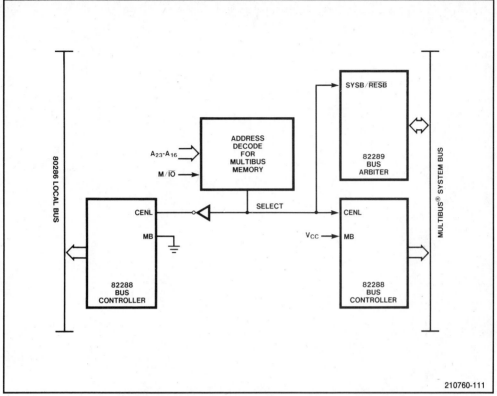

210760-111

Figure 7-3. Selecting the MULTIBUS® for Memory Operations

Interrupt-Acknowledge to Cascaded Interrupt Controllers

A third issue related to the division of system resources between the system bus (MULTI-BUS) and the local bus is that of mapping interrupts between the MULTIBUS and the local data bus. (You may recall that when an interrupt is received by the 80286, the 80286 interrupt-acknowledge sequence uses the data bus to fetch an 8-bit interrupt vector from the interrupting 8259A Programmable Interrupt Controller.)

Designers may encounter three possible configurations:

1. All of the subsystem's Interrupt Controllers (one master and perhaps one or more slaves) reside on the local bus, and, therefore, all interrupt-acknowledge cycles are routed to the local bus.

2. All "terminal" Interrupt Controllers reside on the MULTIBUS system bus (either all 8259A Interrupt Controllers reside on the MULTIBUS bus, or a master 8259A resides on the local bus but services interrupts *only* from slave 8259A Interrupt Controllers that themselves reside on the MULTIBUS), and so all interrupt-acknowledge cycles are automatically routed to the MULTIBUS.

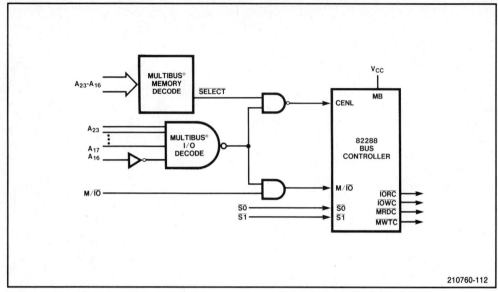

Figure 7-4. Memory-Mapping the MULTIBUS® I/O

3. Some slave Interrupt Controllers reside on the subsystem's local bus, and others reside on the MULTIBUS. In this case, the subsystem's hardware must decode the Master Interrupt Controller's cascade address and select the appropriate bus for the interrupt-acknowledge cycles.

In the first two cases, the implementation is relatively straightforward; all interrupt-acknowledge bus operations can be automatically directed onto the appropriate bus. If one of these two configurations is envisioned for the system you are designing, you can skip this section and continue on. If, however, your 80286 subsystem will have a master 8259A Interrupt Controller on the local bus and *at least one* slave 8259A Interrupt Controller connected to the MULTIBUS, you should read this section to discover how to handle the direction of interrupt-acknowledge bus cycles onto either the MULTIBUS or the local bus.

First, a review of the operation of the 80286 processor and the master and slave 8259A Interrupt Controllers during an interrupt-acknowledge sequence.

The 80286 responds to an INTR (interrupt) input by performing two INTA bus operations. During the first INTA operation, the master 8259A Interrupt Controller determines which, if any, of its slaves should return the interrupt vector, and drives the cascade address pins to select the appropriate slave Interrupt Controller. During the second INTA cycle, the 80286 reads an eight-bit interrupt vector from the selected Interrupt Controller and uses this vector to respond to the interrupt.

In 80286 systems where slave Interrupt Controllers may reside on the MULTIBUS, the three cascade address lines from the master 8259A Interrupt Controller must be decoded to select whether the current interrupt-acknowledge (INTA) sequence will require the MULTIBUS.

If the MULTIBUS is selected, the 82289 Bus Arbiter must be signalled first to request the MULTIBUS, and then enable the MULTIBUS address and data transceivers to port the remainder of the first and the second INTA cycles onto the MULTIBUS. The cascade address lines from the master 8259A Interrupt Controller ($\overline{\text{CAS0}}$, $\overline{\text{CAS1}}$, and $\overline{\text{CAS2}}$) are gated onto the local bus address lines A8, A9, and A10 (MULTIBUS address lines $\overline{\text{ADR8}}$, $\overline{\text{ADR9}}$, and $\overline{\text{ADRA}}$), respectively, using tri-state drivers.

Figure 7-5 shows an example of a circuit that performs this decoding function during interrupt-acknowledge sequences. This circuit also addresses some of the critical timing necessary in the case of a master 8259A Interrupt Controller gating a cascade address onto the MULTIBUS.

The timing of the basic interrupt-acknowledge cycle is described in Chapter Three. During the first INTA cycle, the cascade address from the master 8259A Interrupt Controller residing on the local bus becomes valid within a maximum of 565 ns following the assertion of the $\overline{\text{INTA}}$ signal from the Bus Controller. Once this address becomes valid, it must be decoded to determine whether the remainder of the INTA sequence should remain on the local bus, or should take place on the MULTIBUS. Using the cascade-decode logic shown in Figure 7-5, the decode delay adds an additional 30 ns, for a total of 595 ns from $\overline{\text{INTA}}$ to bus-select valid. The local bus Ready logic must therefore insert at least 4 wait states into the first INTA cycle before the cascade address becomes valid and the local- or MULTIBUS-select becomes valid.

If the local bus is selected for the remainder of the INTA sequence, the first INTA cycle can be terminated immediately. If the MULTIBUS is selected, however, the first INTA bus cycle must still be extended while it is ported onto the MULTIBUS in order to properly condition the slave Interrupt Controllers on the MULTIBUS.

The circuit shown in Figure 7-5 shows how the MULTIBUS 82289 Bus Arbiter and 82288 Bus Controller are selected to allow this "delayed startup" of the MULTIBUS INTA bus cycle. The CMDLY input to the 82288 is used as a select input that is sampled repetitively by the 82288; the CENL input can be tied high. Once the MULTIBUS has been selected, the MULTIBUS $\overline{\text{XACK}}$ signal should be used to terminate the bus operation.

During the second INTA bus cycle, the Master Cascade Enable (MCE) output of the 82288 Bus Controller becomes active to gate the cascade address onto address lines A8, A9, and A10. This MCE enable signal stays active one clock cycle longer than the ALE signal, allowing the cascade address to be properly captured in the MULTIBUS address latches. The MCE signal becomes active only during INTA cycles—no additional logic is required to properly enable the cascade address onto the address bus during INTA cycles.

Byte-Swapping During MULTIBUS® Byte Transfers

The MULTIBUS standard specifies that during all byte transfers, the data must be transferred on the lower-eight data lines (MULTIBUS $\overline{\text{DAT0}}$ through $\overline{\text{DAT7}}$), whether the data is associated with an even (low-byte) or odd (high-byte) address. For 16-bit systems, this requirement means that during byte transfers to odd addresses, the data byte must be

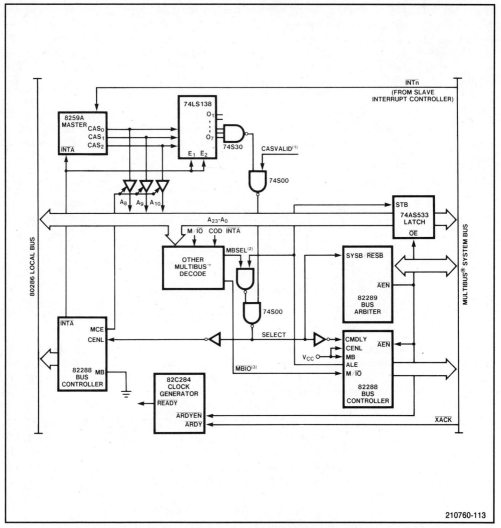

Figure 7-5. Decoding Interrupt-Acknowledge Sequences

"swapped" from the high data lines (local bus D8 through D15) onto the low data lines (D0 through D7) before being placed on the MULTIBUS, and then "swapped" back onto the high data lines when being read from the MULTIBUS. This byte-swapping requirement maintains compatibility between 8-bit and 16-bit systems sharing the same MULTIBUS.

Because of this byte-swapping requirement, the MULTIBUS $\overline{\text{BHEN}}$ signal differs in definition from the $\overline{\text{BHE}}$ signal on the 80286 local bus. Table 7-1 illustrates the differences between these two signals. Notice the difference that appears for byte transfers to odd addresses.

For 80286 systems, this MULTIBUS byte-swapping requirement is easily met by using only an additional data transceiver and necessary control logic.

Table 7-1. Local Bus and MULTIBUS® Usage of BHE/BHEN

Bus Operation	A0	$\overline{BHE}$	Transfer Occurs On	$\overline{ADR0}$	$\overline{BHEN}$	Transfer Occurs On
Word Transfer	L	L	All 16 data lines	H	L	All 16 data lines
Byte Transfer to Even Address	L	H	Lower 8 data lines	H	H	Lower 8 data lines
Byte Transfer to Odd Address	H	L	Upper 8 data lines	L	H	Lower 8 data lines

Figure 7-6 shows how this byte-swapping circuit can be implemented for the 80286 as a bus master. The three signals that control this byte-swapping function are the Data Enable (DEN), MULTIBUS Byte High Enable ($\overline{BHEN}$), and MULTIBUS Address bit 0 ($\overline{ADR0}$). The 82288 Bus Controller always disables DEN between bus cycles to allow the data transceivers to change states without bus contention. The MULTIBUS $\overline{BHEN}$ and $\overline{ADR0}$ signals are used instead of the local bus $\overline{BHE}$ and A0 because the MULTIBUS signals are latched for the duration of the bus operation. Figure 7-6 also shows the generation of the MULTIBUS $\overline{BHEN}$ Signal from the local bus $\overline{BHE}$ and A0 signals.

Implementing the Bus-Timeout Function

The MULTIBUS $\overline{XACK}$ signal terminates 80286 bus operations on the MULTIBUS by driving the $\overline{ARDY}$ input to the 82288 Bus Controller. If the 80286 should happen to address a non-existent device on the MULTIBUS, however, the $\overline{XACK}$ signal may never be activated. Without a bus-timeout protection circuit, the 80286 could wait indefinitely, tying up the MULTIBUS from use by other bus masters as well.

The bus-timeout function provides a simple means of ensuring that all MULTIBUS operations eventually terminate. Figure 7-7 shows one implementation of a bus-timeout circuit using one-shots. If the MULTIBUS $\overline{XACK}$ signal is not returned within a finite period, the bus-timeout signal is activated to terminate the bus operation.

When a bus-timeout occurs, the data read by the 80286 may not be valid. For this reason, the bus-timeout circuit may also be used to generate an interrupt to prevent software from using invalid data.

Power Failure Considerations

The MULTIBUS interface provides a means of handling power failures by defining a Power Fail Interrupt ($\overline{PFIN}$) signal and other status lines, and by making provisions for secondary or backup power supplies.

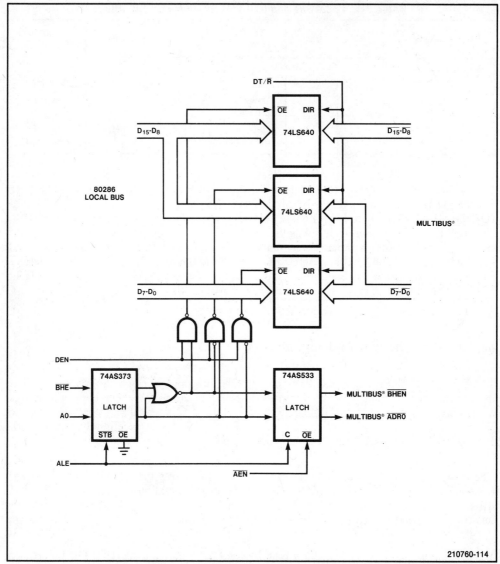

Figure 7-6. Byte-Swapping at the MULTIBUS® Interface

Typically, the Power Fail Interrupt ($\overline{\text{PFIN}}$) from the MULTIBUS is connected to the NMI interrupt request line of the CPU. When a power failure is about to occur, this interrupt enables the 80286 CPU to immediately save its environment before falling voltages and the MULTIBUS Memory Protect ($\overline{\text{MPRO}}$) signal prevent any further memory activity. In systems with memory backup power or non-volatile memory, the 80286 environment can be saved for the duration of the powerfail condition.

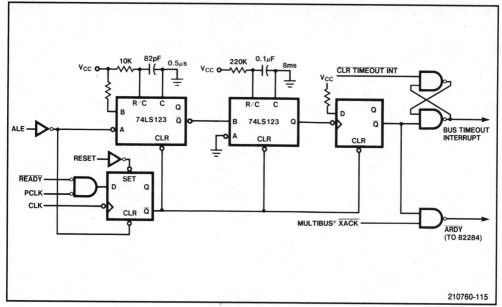

Figure 7-7. Implementing the Bus-Timeout Function

When the AC power is restored, the power-up RESET sequence of the 80286 CPU can check the status of the MULTIBUS Power Fail Sense Latch ($\overline{\text{PFSN}}$) to see if a previous power failure has occurred. If this latch is set low, the 80286 can branch to a powerup routine that resets the latch using Power Fail Sense Reset ($\overline{\text{PFSR}}$), restores its environment, and resumes execution.

Further guidelines for designing 80286 systems with power-failure features are contained in the Intel MULTIBUS Specification referred to previously.

MULTIBUS® ARBITRATION USING THE 82289 BUS ARBITER

The MULTIBUS protocols allow multiple processing elements to contend with each other for the use of common system resources. Since the 80286 does not have exclusive use of the MULTIBUS, when the 80286 processor occasionally tries to access the MULTIBUS, another bus master will already have control of the bus. When this happens, the 80286 will have to wait before accessing the bus.

The 82289 Bus Arbiter provides a compact solution to controlling access to a multi-master system bus. The Bus Arbiter directs the processor onto the bus and also allows both higher- and lower-priority bus masters to acquire the bus. The Bus Arbiter attains control of the system bus (eventually) whenever the 80286 attempts to access the bus. (The previous section reviewed some techniques to determine when the processor is attempting to access the system bus.) Once the Bus Arbiter receives control of the system bus, the 80286 can proceed to access specific resources attached to the bus. The 82289 Bus Arbiter handles this bus contention in a manner that is completely transparent to the 80286 processor.

Gaining Control of the MULTIBUS®

In an 80286 subsystem using an 82289 Bus Arbiter, the 80286 processor issues commands as though it had exclusive use of the system bus. The Bus Arbiter keeps track of whether the subsystem indeed has control of the system bus, and if not, prevents the 82288 Bus Controller and address latches from accessing the bus. The Bus Arbiter also inhibits the 82C284 Clock Generator, forcing the 82286 processor into one or more wait states.

When the Bus Arbiter receives control of the system bus, the Bus Arbiter enables the $\overline{\text{ARDY}}$ input of the Clock Generator, and enables the 82288 Bus Controller and address latches to drive the system bus. Once the system bus transfer is complete, a transfer-acknowledge ($\overline{\text{XACK}}$) signal is returned by the MULTIBUS, signalling to the processor that the transfer cycle has completed. In this manner, the Bus Arbiter multiplexes one bus master onto the multi-master bus and avoids contention between bus masters.

Since many bus masters can be on a multi-master system bus, some means must be provided for resolving priority between bus masters simultaneously requesting the bus. Figure 7-8 shows two common priority-resolution schemes: a serial-priority and a parallel-priority technique.

The serial-priority resolution technique consists of a daisy-chain of the 82289 Bus Priority In ($\overline{\text{BPRN}}$) and Bus Priority Out ($\overline{\text{BPRO}}$) signals. Due to delays in the daisy-chain, however, only a limited number of bus masters can be accommodated using this technique.

In the parallel-priority resolution technique, each 82289 Bus Arbiter makes independent bus requests using its Bus Request ($\overline{\text{BREQ}}$) signal line. An external bus-priority resolution circuit determines the highest-priority bus master requesting the bus, and grants that master control of the bus by setting $\overline{\text{BPRN}}$ low to that bus master. Any number of bus masters can be accommodated using this technique, limited only by the complexity of the external resolution circuitry.

Other priority-resolution schemes may also be used. Intel Application Note AP-51 describes in greater detail these techniques for resolving the priority of simultaneous bus requests.

Figure 7-9 shows the timing of a bus exchange for the parallel-priority resolution scheme shown in Figure 7-8. In the timing example, a higher-priority bus master requests and is granted control of the bus from a lower-priority bus master.

From the perspective of an individual MULTIBUS subsystem, the subsystem has been granted the bus when that subsystem's $\overline{\text{BPRN}}$ input from the MULTIBUS falls low (active). For the purpose of designing an 80286 sybsystem for the MULTIBUS, the $\overline{\text{BPRN}}$ signal is sufficient, and a designer need not be concerned with the particular priority-resolution technique implemented on the MULTIBUS system. The 82289 Bus Arbiter releases the bus if $\overline{\text{BPRN}}$ becomes HIGH at the end of the current bus sequence, under the control of this external arbitration device.

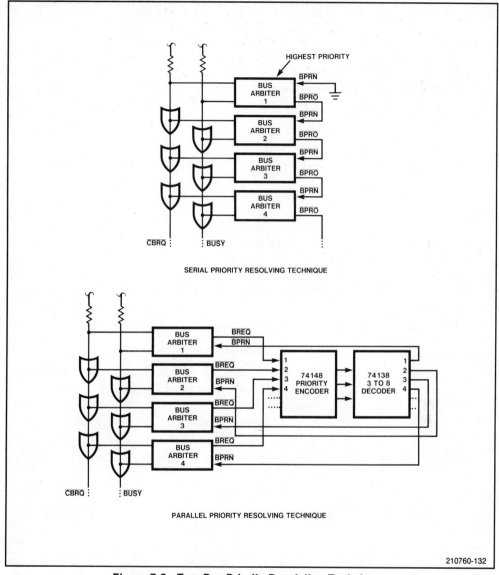

HIGHEST PRIORITY

SERIAL PRIORITY RESOLVING TECHNIQUE

PARALLEL PRIORITY RESOLVING TECHNIQUE

210760-132

Figure 7-8. Two Bus Priority-Resolution Techniques

Releasing the Bus—Three 82289 Operating Modes

Following a transfer cycle using the system bus, the 82289 Bus Arbiter can either retain control of the system bus or release the bus for use by some other bus master. The Bus Arbiter can operate in one of three operating modes, each of which defines different conditions under which the Bus Arbiter will relinquish control of the system bus.

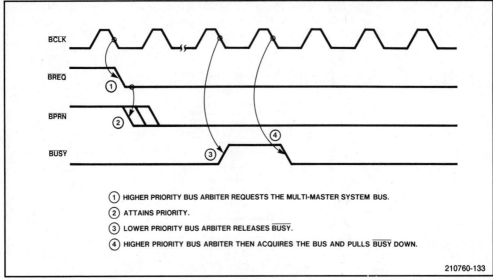

① HIGHER PRIORITY BUS ARBITER REQUESTS THE MULTI-MASTER SYSTEM BUS.

② ATTAINS PRIORITY.

③ LOWER PRIORITY BUS ARBITER RELEASES $\overline{BUSY}$.

④ HIGHER PRIORITY BUS ARBITER THEN ACQUIRES THE BUS AND PULLS $\overline{BUSY}$ DOWN.

210760-133

Figure 7-9. Bus Exchange Timing for the MULTIBUS®

Table 7-2. Three 82289 Operating Modes for Releasing the Bus

Operating Mode	Conditions under which the Bus Arbiter releases the system bus*
Mode 1	The Bus Arbiter releases the bus at the end of each transfer cycle.
Mode 2	The Bus Arbiter retains the bus until:
	• a higher-priority bus master requests the bus, driving $\overline{BPRN}$ high.
	• a lower-priority bus master requests the bus by pulling the $\overline{CBRQ}$ low.
Mode 3	The Bus Arbiter retains the bus until a higher-priority bus master requests the bus, driving BPRN high. (In this mode, the Bus Arbiter ignores the CBRQ input.

*The $\overline{LOCK}$ input to the Bus Arbiter can be used to override any of the conditions shown in the table. While LOCK is asserted, the Bus Arbiter will retain control of the system bus.

Table 7-2 defines the three operating modes of the 82289 Bus Arbiter, and describes the conditions under which the Bus Arbiter relinquishes control of the MULTIBUS. The following sections describe how to configure the Bus Arbiter in any one of these modes, and also describe a way to switch the Bus Arbiter between Modes 2 and 3 under program control from the 80286.

The decision to configure the 82289 Bus Arbiter in one of these three modes, or to configure the Bus Arbiter in a fourth manner, allowing switching between modes 2 and 3, is a choice left up to the individual designer. This choice may affect the throughput of the individual subsystem, as well as the throughput of other subsystems sharing the bus, and system throughput as a whole.

This performance impact occurs because a multi-processor system may have appreciable overhead when a processor requests and takes control of the MULTIBUS. Figure 7-10 illustrates the effect of bus set-up and hold times on bus efficiency and throughput.

When to Use the Different Modes

The various operating modes of the Bus Arbiter allow the designer to optimize a subsystem's use of the MULTIBUS to its own needs and to the needs of the system as a whole.

Mode 1, for example, would be adequate for a subsystem that needed to access the MULTIBUS only occasionally; by releasing the bus after each transfer cycle, the subsystem would minimize its impact on the throughput of other subsystems using the bus.

Mode 2 would be ideal for a subsystem that shared the MULTIBUS with a pool of other bus masters, all of roughly equal priority, and all equally likely to request the bus at any given time. The performance improvement of retaining the bus in case of a second or subsequent access to the bus would be matched to the performance impact of other bus masters, who may have to request the bus from the controlling Bus Arbiter, and thus suffer the ensuing hold delays.

Mode 3 would be ideal for a system that is likely to be using the MULTIBUS a high percentage of the time. The performance advantages of retaining control of the bus would outweigh the chances of other, lower-priority devices waiting longer periods to gain access to the MULTIBUS.

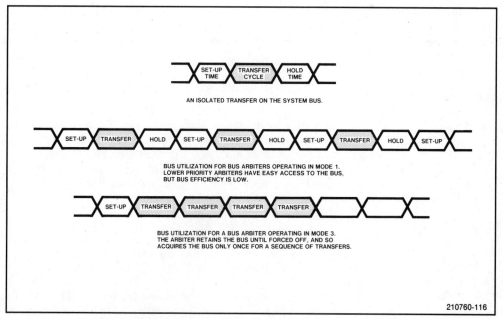

Figure 7-10. Effects of Bus Contention on Bus Efficiency

A fourth alternative, that of allowing a processor to switch its Bus Arbiter between Mode 2 and Mode 3, offers even more flexibility in optimizing system performance where such performance might be subject to experimentation, or where MULTIBUS traffic might be sporadic.

To summarize the preceeding discussion, the decision to use one or another of the four Bus Arbiter configurations depends on the relative priorities of processors sharing the bus, and on the anticipated traffic each processor may have for the bus. In order to optimize the sharing of the MULTIBUS between several bus masters, designers are urged to experiment with the different modes of each Bus Arbiter in the system.

Configuring the 82289 Operating Modes

A designer can configure the Bus Arbiter in four ways:

1. The Bus Arbiter can be configured to operate in Mode 1, releasing the bus at the end of each transfer cycle.

2. The Bus Arbiter can be configured in Mode 2, retaining the bus until either a higher- or lower-priority bus master requests the bus.

3. The Bus Arbiter can be configured in Mode 3, retaining the bus until a higher-priority bus master requests the bus.

4. The Bus Arbiter can be configured so that it can be switched between Mode 2 and Mode 3 under software control of the 80286. This last configuration is more complex than the first three, requiring that a parallel port or addressable latch be used to drive one of the strapping pins of the 82289.

Once the designer has determined which of the four bus-retention techniques to adopt, this configuration must be incorporated into the hardware design. Figure 7-11 shows the strapping configurations required to implement each of these four techniques.

Asserting the $\overline{\text{LOCK}}$ Signal

Independent of the particular operating mode of the Bus Arbiter, the 80286 processor can assert a $\overline{\text{LOCK}}$ signal during string instructions to prevent the Bus Arbiter from releasing the MULTIBUS. This software-controlled $\overline{\text{LOCK}}$ signal prevents the Bus Arbiter from surrendering the system bus to any other bus master, whether of higher- or lower-priority. $\overline{\text{LOCK}}$ is also asserted automatically by the CPU during interrupt-acknowledge cycles, the XCHG instruction, and during some descriptor accesses.

When the 80286 asserts the $\overline{\text{LOCK}}$ signal, the Bus Arbiter converts this temporary input into a level-lock signal, $\overline{\text{LLOCK}}$, which drives the MULTIBUS $\overline{\text{LOCK}}$ status line. The Bus Arbiter will continue to assert $\overline{\text{LLOCK}}$ retaining control of the MULTIBUS until the first unLOCKed bus cycle from the 80286 processor.

This $\overline{\text{LLOCK}}$ signal from the 82289 Bus Arbiter must be connected to the MULTIBUS $\overline{\text{LOCK}}$ status line through a tri-state driver. This driver is controlled by the AEN output of the Bus Arbiter.

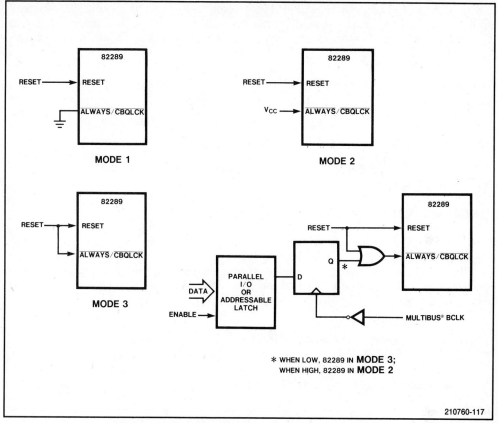

Figure 7-11. Four Different 82289 Configurations

TIMING ANALYSIS OF THE MULTIBUS® INTERFACE

The timing specifications for the MULTIBUS are explained concisely in the MULTIBUS specification, Order Number 9800683-04. To summarize these requirements as they pertain to an 80286 subsystem operating as a MULTIBUS bus master:

- The 80286 system must use one command delay when reading data from the MULTIBUS.

- The 80286 must use two command delays when writing data to the MULTIBUS.

When the 82288 Bus Controller driving the MULTIBUS is strapped in the MULTIBUS configuration (MB = 1, and CMDLY = 0), the Bus Controller automatically inserts the appropriate delays as outlined above. No further consideration is required in order to conform to the MULTIBUS timing requirements.

Table 7-3 summarizes the critical MULTIBUS parameters as they relate to the 80286 system, and shows that these parameters are satisfactorily met by a 6-MHz 80286 with one command delay during reads and two command delays during write operations. The timing parameters assume the use of 74AS533 and 74AS640 latches and transceivers.

In addition to the specific parameters defined in Table 3-1, designers must be sure that:

* To ensure sufficient access time for the slave device, bus operations must not be terminated until an $\overline{XACK}$ (transfer acknowledge) is received from the slave device.

* Following an $\overline{MRDC}$ or an $\overline{IORC}$ command, the responding slave device must disable its data drivers within 166 ns (max) following the return of the $\overline{XACK}$ signal. (All devices meeting the MULTIBUS spec. of 65 ns max meet this requirement.)

USING DUAL-PORT RAM WITH THE SYSTEM BUS

A dual-port RAM is a memory subsystem that can be accessed by the 80286 via the 80286 local bus, and can also be accessed by other processing elements via the MULTIBUS system bus. The performance advantages of using dual-port memory are described in Chapter Four. This section describes several issues that must be considered when implementing dual-port memory with a MULTIBUS interface.

Table 7-3. Required MULTIBUS® Timing for the 80286

Timing Parameter	MULTIBUS® Specification	6 MHz 80286 with: 1 CMDLY on $\overline{RD}$ 2 CMDLY on $\overline{WR}$	
t_{AS} Address Setup before command active	50 ns minimum	166.7 ns − 25 ns − 9 ns + 3 ns 135.7 ns min.	(2 CLK cycles) (ALE delay$_{max}$) (74AS533 delay$_{max}$) (Cmd delay$_{min}$)
t_{DS} Write Data Setup before command active	50 ns minimum	166.7 ns − 35 ns − 40 ns + 3 ns 94.7 ns min.	(2 CLK cycles) (DEN act. delay$_{max}$) (74LS640 delay$_{max}$) (Cmd delay$_{min}$)
t_{AH} Address Hold after command inactive	50 ns minimum	83.3 ns − 30 ns + 3 ns + 4.5 ns 60.5 ns min.	(1 CLK cycle) (Cmd inact. delay$_{max}$) (ALE act. delay$_{min}$) (74AS533 delay$_{min}$)
t_{DHW} Write Data Hold after command inactive	50 ns minimum	83.3 ns − 30 ns + 11.5 ns 64.8 ns min.	(1 CLK cycle) (Cmd inact. delay$_{max}$) (74LS640 delay$_{min}$)

Dual-port memories are a shared resource, and, like a shared bus, must address the twin issues of arbitration and mutual exclusion. Mutual exclusion addresses the case when two processors attempt to access the dual-port memory simultaneously. The MULTIBUS $\overline{\text{LOCK}}$ signal and a similar $\overline{\text{LOCK}}$ signal from the 80286 itself attempt to mediate this contention.

Chapter Four of this manual describes the techniques of addressing these two issues. This section expands on the explanation in Chapter Four and in particular discusses how to handle the two $\overline{\text{LOCK}}$ signals and avoid potential deadlock conditions that may otherwise arise.

Figure 7-12 shows a configuration where a dual-port memory is shared between an 80286 subsystem and the MULTIBUS. The $\overline{\text{LLOCK}}$ (Level-Lock) signal from the 82289 Bus Arbiter is used to provide the $\overline{\text{LOCK}}$ signal from the 80286. This $\overline{\text{LLOCK}}$ signal is not conditioned on whether the 82289 is currently selected (the SYSB/$\overline{\text{RESB}}$ input).

Avoiding Deadlock with a Dual-Port Memory

A potential deadlock situation exists for a dual-port memory when both the 80286 processor and another bus master attempt to carry out $\overline{\text{LOCK}}$ed transfers between the dual-port memory and external MULTIBUS memory or devices.

The situation can arise only when the 80286 attempts to carry out a $\overline{\text{LOCK}}$ed transfer using both the dual-port memory and the MULTIBUS. In one deadlock scenario, the 80286 processor, using the local bus, reads data from the dual-port memory and asserts the $\overline{\text{LOCK}}$ signal, preventing the dual-port memory from being accessed by another processing element on the MULTIBUS.

If, at the same time, another bus master of higher priority (or while asserting the MULTI-BUS $\overline{\text{LOCK}}$ signal) takes control of the MULTIBUS and attempts to access the dual-port memory, this bus master will be unable to access the (locked) dual-port memory and so enters a wait state, waiting for a response from the memory. At the same time, the 80286 processor will be unable to gain control of the MULTIBUS in order to complete its transfer, since the other processor gained the MULTIBUS first. The result is deadlock, and in the absence of other mechanisms, each processor stops.

Typically, both processors will eventually terminate their respective bus operations due to bus-timeout (see the earlier section on bus-timeout circuitry). If a bus timeout occurs, the processors will fail in their respective attempts to write or read data.

Since reading and/or writing improper data is to be avoided, you have two alternatives to avoid this deadlock situation:

- The first alternative is to simply avoid using $\overline{\text{LOCK}}$ed transfers from the dual-port memory in the 80286 software. No additional hardware over that shown in Figure 7-12 is required.

- The second alternative actually prevents the occurrence of $\overline{\text{LOCK}}$ed transfers between the dual-port memory and the MULTIBUS by using hardware to condition the $\overline{\text{LOCK}}$ input to the dual-port memory.

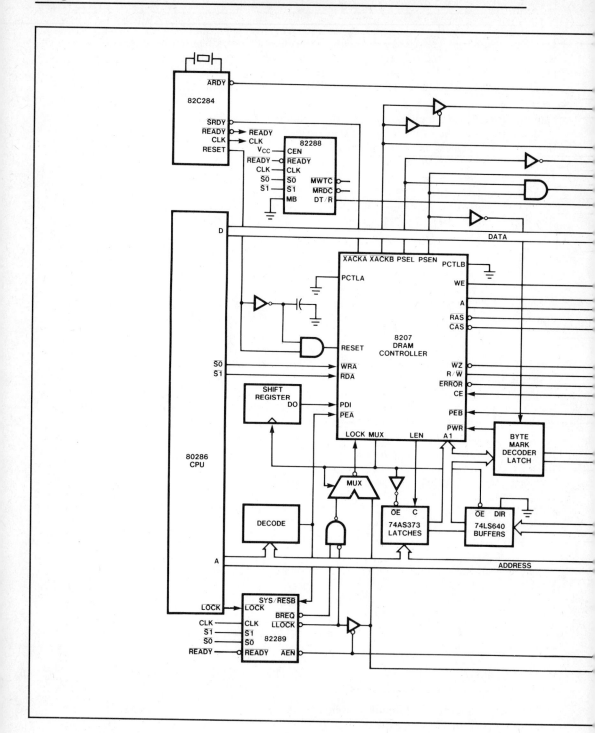

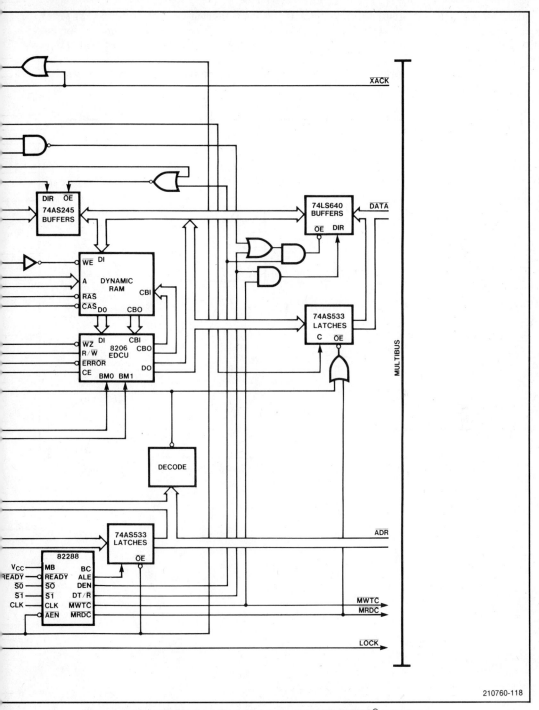

Figure 7-12. 80286 Dual-Port Memory with MULTIBUS® Interface

210760-118

Figure 7-13 shows a circuit to implement the second alternative. Bear in mind, however, that this circuit in effect destroys the $\overline{\text{LOCK}}$ condition on the dual-port memory for any transfers from the dual-port memory ending on the MULTIBUS. This fact will not be apparent from the 80286 software. Even if this alternative is implemented, software writers should be cautioned against using $\overline{\text{LOCK}}$ed transfers between the dual-port memory and the MULTIBUS.

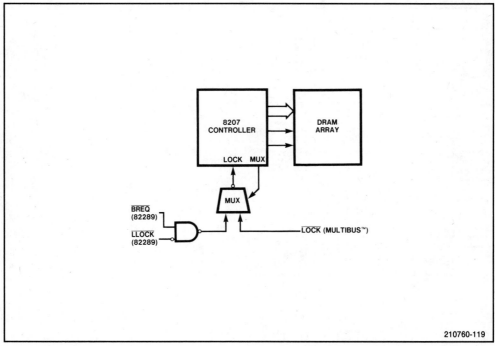

210760-119

Figure 7-13. Preventing Deadlock Between Dual-Port RAM and the MULTIBUS®

DOMESTIC SALES OFFICES

ALABAMA

Intel Corp.
5015 Bradford Drive
Suite 2
Huntsville 35805
Tel: (205) 830-4010

ARIZONA

Intel Corp.
11225 N. 28th Drive
Suite 214D
Phoenix 85029
Tel: (602) 869-4980

Intel Corp.
1161 N. El Dorado Place
Suite 301
Tucson 85715
Tel: (602) 299-6815

CALIFORNIA

Intel Corp.
21515 Vanowen Street
Suite 116
Canoga Park 91303
Tel: (818) 704-8500

Intel Corp.
2250 E. Imperial Highway
Suite 218
El Segundo 90245
Tel: (213) 640-6040

Intel Corp.
1510 Arden Way, Suite 101
Sacramento 95815
Tel: (916) 920-8096

Intel Corp.
4350 Executive Drive
Suite 105
San Diego 92121
Tel: (619) 452-5880

Intel Corp.*
400 N. Tustin Avenue
Suite 450
Santa Ana 92705
Tel: (714) 835-9642
TWX: 910-595-1114

Intel Corp.*
San Tomas 4
2700 San Tomas Expressway
Santa Clara, CA 95051
Tel: (408) 986-8086
TWX: 910-338-0255

COLORADO

Intel Corp.
4445 Northpark Drive
Suite 100
Colorado Springs 80907
Tel: (303) 594-6622

Intel Corp.*
650 S. Cherry St., Suite 915
Denver 80222
Tel: (303) 321-8086
TWX: 910-931-2289

CONNECTICUT

Intel Corp.
26 Mill Plain Road
Danbury 06811
Tel: (203) 748-3130
TWX: 710-456-1199

FLORIDA

Intel Corp.
242 N. Westmonte Dr., Suite 105
Altamonte Springs 32714
Tel: (305) 869-5588

Intel Corp.
6363 N.W. 6th Way, Suite 100
Ft. Lauderdale 33309
Tel: (305) 771-0600
TWX: 510-956-9407

Intel Corp.
11300 4th Street North
Suite 170
St. Petersburg 33702
Tel: (813) 577-2413

GEORGIA

Intel Corp.
3280 Pointe Parkway
Suite 200
Norcross 30092
Tel: (404) 449-0541

ILLINOIS

Intel Corp.*
300 N. Martingale Road, Suite 400
Schaumburg 60173
Tel: (312) 310-8031

INDIANA

Intel Corp.
8777 Purdue Road
Suite 125
Indianapolis 46268
Tel: (317) 875-0623

IOWA

Intel Corp.
St. Andrews Building
1930 St. Andrews Drive N.E.
Cedar Rapids 52402
Tel: (319) 393-5510

KANSAS

Intel Corp.
8400 W. 110th Street
Suite 170
Overland Park 66210
Tel: (913) 345-2727

MARYLAND

Intel Corp.*
7321 Parkway Drive South
Suite C
Hanover 21076
Tel: (301) 796-7500
TWX: 710-862-1944

Intel Corp.
7833 Walker Drive
Greenbelt 20770
Tel: (301) 441-1020

MASSACHUSETTS

Intel Corp.*
Westford Corp. Center
3 Carlisle Road
Westford 01886
Tel: (617) 692-3222
TWX: 710-343-6333

MICHIGAN

Intel Corp.
7071 Orchard Lake Road
Suite 100
West Bloomfield 48033
Tel: (313) 851-8096

MINNESOTA

Intel Corp.
3500 W. 80th St., Suite 360
Bloomington 55431
Tel: (612) 835-6722
TWX: 910-576-2867

MISSOURI

Intel Corp.
4203 Earth City Expressway
Suite 131
Earth City 63045
Tel: (314) 291-1990

NEW JERSEY

Intel Corp.*
Parkway 109 Office Center
328 Newman Springs Road
Red Bank 07701
Tel: (201) 747-2233

Intel Corp.
280 Corporate Center
75 Livingston Avenue
First Floor
Roseland 07068
Tel: (201) 740-0111

NEW MEXICO

Intel Corp.
8500 Menual Boulevard N.E.
Suite B 295
Albuquerque 87112
Tel: (505) 292-8086

NEW YORK

Intel Corp.
127 Main Street
Binghamton 13905
Tel: (607) 773-0337

Intel Corp.*
850 Cross Keys Office Park
Fairport 14450
Tel: (716) 425-2750
TWX: 510-253-7391

Intel Corp.
300 Motor Parkway
Hauppauge 11787
Tel: (516) 231-3300
TWX: 510-227-6236

Intel Corp.
Suite 2B Hollowbrook Park
15 Myers Corners Road
Wappinger Falls 12590
Tel: (914) 297-6161
TWX: 510-248-0060

NORTH CAROLINA

Intel Corp.
5700 Executive Center Drive
Suite 213
Charlotte 28212
Tel: (704) 568-8966

Intel Corp.
2700 Wycliff Road
Suite 102
Raleigh 27607
Tel: (919) 781-8022

OHIO

Intel Corp.*
3401 Park Center Drive
Suite 220
Dayton 45414
Tel: (513) 890-5350
TWX: 810-450-2528

Intel Corp.*
25700 Science Park Dr., Suite 100
Beachwood 44122
Tel: (216) 464-2736
TWX: 810-427-9298

OKLAHOMA

Intel Corp.
6801 N. Broadway
Suite 115
Oklahoma City 73116
Tel: (405) 848-8086

OREGON

Intel Corp.
15254 N.W. Greenbrier Parkway, Bldg. B
Beaverton 97006
Tel: (503) 645-8051
TWX: 910-467-8741

PENNSYLVANIA

Intel Corp.
1513 Cedar Cliff Drive
Camp Hill 17011
Tel: (717) 737-5035

Intel Corp.*
455 Pennsylvania Avenue
Fort Washington 19034
Tel: (215) 641-1000
TWX: 510-661-2077

Intel Corp.*
400 Penn Center Blvd., Suite 610
Pittsburgh 15235
Tel: (412) 823-4970

PUERTO RICO

Intel Microprocessor Corp.
South Industrial Park
P.O. Box 910
Las Piedras 00671
Tel: (809) 733-8616

TEXAS

Intel Corp.
313 E. Anderson Lane
Suite 314
Austin 78752
Tel: (512) 454-3628

Intel Corp.*
12300 Ford Road
Suite 380
Dallas 75234
Tel: (214) 241-8087
TWX: 910-860-5617

Intel Corp.*
7322 S.W. Freeway
Suite 1490
Houston 77074
Tel: (713) 988-8086
TWX: 910-881-2490

UTAH

Intel Corp.
5201 Green Street
Suite 290
Murray 84123
Tel: (801) 263-8051

VIRGINIA

Intel Corp.
1603 Santa Rosa Road
Suite 109
Richmond 23288
Tel: (804) 282-5668

WASHINGTON

Intel Corp.
155-108 Avenue N.E.
Suite 386
Bellevue 98004
Tel: (206) 453-8086
TWX: 910-443-3002

Intel Corp.
408 N. Mullan Road
Suite 102
Spokane 99206
Tel: (509) 928-8086

WISCONSIN

Intel Corp.
330 S. Executive Dr.
Suite 102
Brookfield 53005
Tel: (414) 784-8087
FAX: 414-796-2115

CANADA

BRITISH COLUMBIA

Intel Semiconductor of Canada, Ltd.
301-2245 W. Broadway
Vancouver V6K 2E4
Tel: (604) 738-6522

ONTARIO

Intel Semiconductor of Canada, Ltd.
2650 Queensview Drive
Suite 250
Ottawa K2B 8H6
Tel: (613) 829-9714
TLX: 053-4115

Intel Semiconductor of Canada, Ltd.
190 Attwell Drive
Suite 500
Rexdale M9W 6H8
Tel: (416) 675-2105
TLX: 06983574

QUEBEC

Intel Semiconductor of Canada, Ltd.
620 St. Jean Boulevard
Pointe Claire H9R 3K3
Tel: (514) 694-9130
TWX: 514-694-9134

*Field Application Location

CG-3/17/87

DOMESTIC DISTRIBUTORS

ALABAMA

Arrow Electronics, Inc.
1015 Henderson Road
Huntsville 35805
Tel: (205) 837-6955

†Hamilton/Avnet Electronics
4940 Research Drive
Huntsville 35805
Tel: (205) 837-7210
TWX: 810-726-2162

Pioneer/Technologies Group Inc.
4825 University Square
Huntsville 35805
Tel: (205) 837-9300
TWX: 810-726-2197

ARIZONA

†Hamilton/Avnet Electronics
505 S. Madison Drive
Tempe 85281
Tel: (602) 231-5100
TWX: 910-950-0077

Kierulff Electronics, Inc.
4134 E. Wood Street
Phoenix 85040
Tel: (602) 437-0750
TWX: 910-951-1550

Wyle Distribution Group
17855 N. Black Canyon Highway
Phoenix 85023
Tel: (602) 866-2888

CALIFORNIA

Arrow Electronics, Inc.
19748 Dearborn Street
Chatsworth 91311
Tel: (818) 701-7500
TWX: 910-493-2086

Arrow Electronics, Inc.
1502 Crocker Avenue
Hayward 94544
Tel: (408) 487-4600

Arrow Electronics, Inc.
9511 Ridgehaven Court
San Diego 92123
Tel: (619) 565-4800
TLX: 888064

†Arrow Electronics, Inc.
521 Weddell Drive
Sunnyvale 94086
Tel: (408) 745-6600
TWX: 910-339-9371

Arrow Electronics, Inc.
2961 Dow Avenue
Tustin 92680
Tel: (714) 838-5422
TWX: 910-595-2860

†Avnet Electronics
350 McCormick Avenue
Costa Mesa 92626
Tel: (714) 754-6051
TWX: 910-595-1928

Hamilton/Avnet Electronics
1175 Bordeaux Drive
Sunnyvale 94086
Tel: (408) 743-3300
TWX: 910-339-9332

†Hamilton/Avnet Electronics
4545 Viewridge Avenue
San Diego 92123
Tel: (619) 571-7500
TWX: 910-595-2638

†Hamilton/Avnet Electronics
20501 Plummer Street
Chatsworth 91311
Tel: (818) 700-6271
TWX: 910-494-2207

†Hamilton/Avnet Electronics
4103 Northgate Boulevard
Sacramento 95834
Tel: (916) 920-3150

†Hamilton/Avnet Electronics
3002 G Street
Ontario 91311
Tel: (714) 989-9411

Hamilton/Avnet Electronics
19515 So. Vermont Avenue
Torrance 90502
Tel: (213) 615-3909
TWX: 910-349-6263

Hamilton Electro Sales
9650 De Soto Avenue
Chatsworth 91311
Tel: (818) 700-6500

CALIFORNIA (Cont'd)

†Hamilton Electro Sales
10950 W. Washington Blvd.
Culver City 90230
Tel: (213) 558-2458
TWX: 910-340-6364

Hamilton Electro Sales
1361 B West 190th Street
Gardena 90248
Tel: (213) 558-2131

†Hamilton Electro Sales
3170 Pullman Street
Costa Mesa 92626
Tel: (714) 641-4150
TWX: 910-595-2638

Kierulff Electronics, Inc.
10824 Hope Street
Cypress 90430
Tel: (714) 220-6300

†Kierulff Electronics, Inc.
1180 Murphy Avenue
San Jose 95131
Tel: (408) 971-2600
TWX: 910-379-6430

†Kierulff Electronics, Inc.
14101 Franklin Avenue
Tustin 92680
Tel: (714) 731-5711
TWX: 910-595-2599

†Kierulff Electronics, Inc.
5650 Jillson Street
Commerce 90040
Tel: (213) 725-0325
TWX: 910-580-3666

Wyle Distribution Group
26560 Agoura Street
Calabasas 91302
Tel: (818) 880-9000
TWX: 818-372-0232

†Wyle Distribution Group
124 Maryland Street
El Segundo 90245
Tel: (213) 322-8100
TWX: 910-348-7140 or 7111

†Wyle Distribution Group
17872 Cowan Avenue
Irvine 92714
Tel: (714) 863-9953
TWX: 910-595-1572

Wyle Distribution Group
11151 Sun Center Drive
Rancho Cordova 95670
Tel: (916) 638-5282

†Wyle Distribution Group
9525 Chesapeake Drive
San Diego 92123
Tel: (619) 565-9171
TWX: 910-335-1590

†Wyle Distribution Group
3000 Bowers Avenue
Santa Clara 95051
Tel: (408) 727-2500
TWX: 910-338-0296

Wyle Military
18910 Teller Avenue
Irvine 92750
Tel: (714) 851-9958
TWX: 310-371-9127

Wyle Systems
7382 Lampson Avenue
Garden Grove 92641
Tel: (714) 891-1717
TWX: 910-595-2642

COLORADO

Arrow Electronics, Inc.
1390 S. Potomac Street
Suite 136
Aurora 80012
Tel: (303) 696-1111

†Hamilton/Avnet Electronics
8765 E. Orchard Road
Suite 708
Englewood 80111
Tel: (303) 740-1017
TWX: 910-935-0787

†Wyle Distribution Group
451 E. 124th Avenue
Thornton 80241
Tel: (303) 457-9953
TWX: 910-936-0770

CONNECTICUT

†Arrow Electronics, Inc.
12 Beaumont Road
Wallingford 06492
Tel: (203) 265-7741
TWX: 710-476-0162

Hamilton/Avnet Electronics
Commerce Industrial Park
Commerce Drive
Danbury 06810
Tel: (203) 797-2800
TWX: 710-456-9974

†Pioneer Northeast Electronics
112 Main Street
Norwalk 06851
Tel: (203) 853-1515
TWX: 710-468-3373

FLORIDA

†Arrow Electronics, Inc.
350 Fairway Drive
Deerfield Beach 33441
Tel: (305) 429-8200
TWX: 510-955-9456

Arrow Electronics, Inc.
1001 N.W. 62nd St., Ste. 108
Ft. Lauderdale 33309
Tel: (305) 776-7790
TWX: 510-955-9456

†Arrow Electronics, Inc.
50 Woodlake Drive W., Bldg. B
Palm Bay 32905
Tel: (305) 725-1480
TWX: 510-959-6337

†Hamilton/Avnet Electronics
6801 N.W. 15th Way
Ft. Lauderdale 33309
Tel: (305) 971-2900
TWX: 510-956-3097

Hamilton/Avnet Electronics
3197 Tech Drive North
St. Petersburg 33702
Tel: (813) 576-3930
TWX: 810-863-0374

Hamilton/Avnet Electronics
6947 University Boulevard
Winterpark 32792
Tel: (305) 628-3888
TWX: 810-853-0322

†Pioneer Electronics
337 N. Lake Blvd., Ste. 1000
Alta Monte Springs 32701
Tel: (305) 834-9090
TWX: 810-853-0284

Pioneer Electronics
674 S. Military Trail
Deerfield Beach 33442
Tel: (305) 428-8877
TWX: 510-955-9653

GEORGIA

†Arrow Electronics, Inc.
3155 Northwoods Parkway
Suite A
Norcross 30071
Tel: (404) 449-8252
TWX: 810-766-0439

Hamilton/Avnet Electronics
5825 D. Peachtree Corners
Norcross 30092
Tel: (404) 447-7500
TWX: 810-766-0432

Pioneer Electronics
3100 F. Northwoods Place
Norcross 30071
Tel: (404) 448-1711
TWX: 810-766-4515

ILLINOIS

†Arrow Electronics, Inc.
2000 E. Alonquin Street
Schaumberg 60195
Tel: (312) 397-3440
TWX: 910-291-3544

†Hamilton/Avnet Electronics
1130 Thorndale Avenue
Bensenville 60106
Tel: (312) 860-7780
TWX: 910-227-0060

Kierulff Electronics, Inc.
1140 W. Thorndale
Itasca 60143
Tel: (312) 250-0500

ILLINOIS (Cont'd)

MTI Systems Sales
1100 West Thorndale
Itasca 60143
Tel: (312) 773-2300

†Pioneer Electronics
1551 Carmen Drive
Elk Grove Village 60007
Tel: (312) 437-9680
TWX: 910-222-1834

INDIANA

†Arrow Electronics, Inc.
2495 Directors Row, Suite H
Indianapolis 46241
Tel: (317) 243-9353
TWX: 810-341-3119

Hamilton/Avnet Electronics
485 Gradle Drive
Carmel 46032
Tel: (317) 844-9333
TWX: 810-260-3966

†Pioneer Electronics
6408 Castleplace Drive
Indianapolis 46250
Tel: (317) 849-7300
TWX: 810-260-1794

KANSAS

†Hamilton/Avnet Electronics
9219 Quivera Road
Overland Park 66215
Tel: (913) 888-8900
TWX: 910-743-0005

Pioneer Electronics
10551 Lackman Rd.
Lenexa 66215
Tel: (913) 492-0500

KENTUCKY

Hamilton/Avnet Electronics
1051 D. Newton Park
Lexington 40511
Tel: (606) 259-1475

MARYLAND

Arrow Electronics, Inc.
8300 Gulford Road #H
Rivers Center
Columbia 21046
Tel: (301) 995-0003
TWX: 710-236-9005

†Hamilton/Avnet Electronics
6822 Oak Hall Lane
Columbia 21045
Tel: (301) 995-3500
TWX: 710-862-1861

†Mesa Technology Corp.
9720 Patuxentwood Dr.
Columbia 21046
Tel: (301) 720-5020
TWX: 710-828-9702

†Pioneer Electronics
9100 Gaither Road
Gaithersburg 20877
Tel: (301) 921-0660
TWX: 710-828-0545

MASSACHUSETTS

†Arrow Electronics, Inc.
1 Arrow Drive
Woburn 01801
Tel: (617) 933-8130
TWX: 710-393-6770

†Hamilton/Avnet Electronics
10D Centennial Drive
Peabody 01960
Tel: (617) 532-3701
TWX: 710-393-0382

Kierulff Electronics, Inc.
13 Fortune Dr
Billerica 01821
Tel: (617) 667-8331

MTI Systems Sales
13 Fortune Drive
Billerica 01821

Pioneer Northeast Electronics
44 Hartwell Avenue
Lexington U21/3
Tel: (617) 861-9200
TWX: 710-326-6617

MICHIGAN

Arrow Electronics, Inc.
755 Phoenix Drive
Ann Arbor 48104
Tel: (313) 971-8220
TWX: 810-223-6020

†Hamilton/Avnet Electronics
32487 Schoolcraft Road
Livonia 48150
Tel: (313) 522-4700
TWX: 810-242-8775

Hamilton/Avnet Electronics
2215 29th Street S.E.
Space A5
Grand Rapids 49508
Tel: (616) 243-8805
TWX: 810-273-6921

Pioneer Electronics
4505 Broadmoor Ave. S.E.
Grand Rapids 49508
Tel: (616) 555-1800

†Pioneer Electronics
13485 Stamford
Livonia 48150
Tel: (313) 525-1800
TWX: 810-242-3271

MINNESOTA

†Arrow Electronics, Inc.
5230 W. 73rd Street
Edina 55435
Tel: (612) 830-1800
TWX: 910-576-3125

Hamilton/Avnet Electronics
12400 White Water Drive
Minnetonka 55343
Tel: (612) 932-0600
TWX: (910) 576-2720

†Pioneer Electronics
10203 Bren Road East
Minnetonka 55343
Tel: (612) 935-5444
TWX: 910-576-2738

MISSOURI

†Arrow Electronics, Inc.
2380 Schuetz
St. Louis 63141
Tel: (314) 567-6888
TWX: 910-764-0882

†Hamilton/Avnet Electronics
13743 Shoreline Court
Earth City 63045
Tel: (314) 344-1200
TWX: 910-762-0684

Kierulff Electronics, Inc.
11804 Borman Dr.
St. Luis 63146
Tel: (314) 997-4956

NEW HAMPSHIRE

†Arrow Electronics, Inc.
3 Perimeter Road
Manchester 03103
Tel: (603) 668-6968
TWX: 710-220-1684

Hamilton/Avnet Electronics
444 E. Industrial Drive
Manchester 03104
Tel: (603) 624-9400

NEW JERSEY

†Arrow Electronics, Inc.
6000 Lincoln East
Marlton 08053
Tel: (609) 596-8000
TWX: 710-897-0829

†Arrow Electronics, Inc.
2 Industrial Road
Fairfield 07006
Tel: (201) 575-5300
TWX: 710-998-2206

†Hamilton/Avnet Electronics
1 Keystone Avenue
Bldg. 36
Cherry Hill 08003
Tel: (609) 424-0110
TWX: 710-940-0262

†Microcomputer System Technical Distributor Centers

DOMESTIC DISTRIBUTORS

NEW JERSEY (Cont'd)

†Hamilton/Avnet Electronics
10 Industrial
Fairfield 07006
Tel: (201) 575-3390
TWX: 701-734-4388

†Pioneer Northeast Electronics
45 Route 46
Pinebrook 07058
Tel: (201) 575-3510
TWX: 710-734-4382

†MTI Systems Sales
383 Route 46 W
Fairfield 07006
Tel: (201) 227-5552

NEW MEXICO

Alliance Electronics Inc.
11030 Cochiti S.E.
Albuquerque 87123
Tel: (505) 292-3360
TWX: 910-989-1151

Hamilton/Avnet Electronics
2524 Baylor Drive S.E.
Albuquerque 87106
Tel: (505) 765-1500
TWX: 910-989-0614

NEW YORK

Arrow Electronics, Inc.
25 Hub Drive
Melville 11747
Tel: (516) 694-6800
TWX: 510-224-6126

†Arrow Electronics, Inc.
3375 Brighton-Henrietta Townline Rd.
Rochester 14623
Tel: (716) 427-0300
TWX: 510-253-4766

Arrow Electronics, Inc.
7705 Maltage Drive
Liverpool 13088
Tel: (315) 652-1000
TWX: 710-545-0230

Arrow Electronics, Inc.
20 Oser Avenue
Hauppauge 11788
Tel: (516) 231-1000
TWX: 510-227-6623

Hamilton/Avnet Electronics
333 Metro Park
Rochester 14623
Tel: (716) 475-9130
TWX: 510-253-5470

†Hamilton/Avnet Electronics
103 Twin Oaks Drive
Syracuse 13206
Tel: (315) 437-2641
TWX: 710-541-1560

†Hamilton/Avnet Electronics
933 Motor Parkway
Hauppauge 11788
Tel: (516) 231-9800
TWX: 510-224-6166

†MTI Systems Sales
38 Harbor Park Drive
P.O. Box 271
Port Washington 11050
Tel: (516) 621-6200
TWX: 510-223-0846

†Pioneer Northeast Electronics
1806 Vestal Parkway East
Vestal 13850
Tel: (607) 748-8211
TWX: 510-252-0893

†Pioneer Northeast Electronics
60 Crossway Park West
Woodbury, Long Island 11797
Tel: (516) 921-8700
TWX: 510-221-2184

NEW YORK (Cont'd)

†Pioneer Northeast Electronics
840 Fairport Park
Fairport 14450
Tel: (716) 381-7070
TWX: 510-253-7001

NORTH CAROLINA

†Arrow Electronics, Inc.
5240 Greendairy Road
Raleigh 27604
Tel: (919) 876-3132
TWX: 510-928-1856

†Hamilton/Avnet Electronics
3510 Spring Forest Drive
Raleigh 27604
Tel: (919) 878-0819
TWX: 510-928-1836

Pioneer Electronics
9801 A-Southern Pine Blvd.
Charlotte 28210
Tel: (704) 527-8188
TWX: 810-621-0366

OHIO

Arrow Electronics, Inc.
7620 McEwen Road
Centerville 45459
Tel: (513) 435-5563
TWX: 810-459-1611

†Arrow Electronics, Inc.
6238 Cochran Road
Solon 44139
Tel (216) 248-3990
TWX: 810-427-9409

Hamilton/Avnet Electronics
777 Brookedge Blvd.
Westerville 43081
Tel: (614) 882-7004

†Hamilton/Avnet Electronics
954 Senate Drive
Dayton 45459
Tel: (513) 433-0610
TWX: 810-450-2531

†Hamilton/Avnet Electronics
4588 Emery Industrial Parkway
Warrensville Heights 44128
Tel: (216) 831-3500
TWX: 810-427-9452

†Pioneer Electronics
4433 Interpoint Blvd.
Dayton 45424
Tel: (513) 236-9900
TWX: 810-459-1622

†Pioneer Electronics
4800 E. 131st Street
Cleveland 44105
Tel: (216) 587-3600
TWX: 810-422-2211

OKLAHOMA

Arrow Electronics, Inc.
4719 S. Memorial Drive
Tulsa 74145
Tel: (918) 665-7700

OREGON

†Almac Electronics Corpora-
tion
1885 N.W. 169th Place
Beaverton 97006
Tel: (503) 629-8090
TWX: 910-467-8743

†Hamilton/Avnet Electronics
6024 S.W. Jean Road
Bldg. C, Suite 10
Lake Oswego 97034
Tel: (503) 635-7848
TWX: 910-455-8179

OREGON (Cont'd)

Wyle Distribution Group
5250 N.E. Elam Young Parkway
Suite 600
Hillsboro 97124
Tel: (503) 640-6000
TWX: 910-460-2203

PENNSYLVANIA

Arrow Electronics, Inc.
650 Seco Road
Monroeville 15146
Tel: (412) 856-7000

Hamilton/Avnet Electronics
2800 Liberty Ave., Bldg. E
Pittsburg 15238
Tel: (412) 281-4150

Pioneer Electronics
259 Kappa Drive
Pittsburgh 15238
Tel: (412) 782-2300
TWX: 710-795-3122

†Pioneer Electronics
261 Gibralter Road
Horsham 19044
Tel: (215) 674-4000
TWX: 510-665-6778

TEXAS

†Arrow Electronics, Inc.
3220 Commander Drive
Carrollton 75006
Tel: (214) 380-6464
TWX: 910-860-5377

†Arrow Electronics, Inc.
10899 Kinghurst
Suite 100
Houston 77099
Tel: (713) 530-4700
TWX: 910-880-4439

†Arrow Electronics, Inc.
10125 Metropolitan
Austin 78758
Tel: (512) 835-4180
TWX: 910-874-1348

†Hamilton/Avnet Electronics
2401 Rutland
Austin 78758
Tel: (512) 837-8911
TWX: 910-874-1319

†Hamilton/Avnet Electronics
2111 W. Walnut Hill Lane
Irving 75062
Tel: (214) 659-4100
TWX: 910-860-5929

†Hamilton/Avnet Electronics
4850 Wright Road #190
Stafford 77477
Tel: (713) 780-1771
TWX: 910-881-5523

Kierulff Electronics, Inc.
9610 Skillman
Dallas 75243
Tel: (214) 343-2400

†Pioneer Electronics
1826 D. Kramer Lane
Austin 78758
Tel: (512) 835-4000
TWX: 910-874-1323

†Pioneer Electronics
13710 Omega Road
Dallas 75234
Tel: (214) 386-7300
TWX: 910-850-5563

†Pioneer Electronics
5853 Point West Drive
Houston 77036
Tel: (713) 988-5555
TWX: 910-881-1606

UTAH

†Hamilton/Avnet Electronics
1585 West 2100 South
Salt Lake City 84119
Tel: (801) 972-2800
TWX: 910-925-4018

Kierulff Electronics, Inc.
1946 W. Parkway Blvd.
Salt Lake City 84119
Tel: (801) 973-6913

Wyle Distribution Group
1325 West 2200 South
Suite E
Salt Lake City 84119
Tel: (801) 974-9953

WASHINGTON

†Almac Electronics Corp.
14360 S.E. Eastgate Way
Bellevue 98007
Tel: (206) 643-9992
TWX: 910-444-2067

Arrow Electronics, Inc.
14320 N.E. 21st Street
Bellevue 98007
Tel: (206) 643-4800
TWX: 910-444-2017

Hamilton/Avnet Electronics
14212 N.E. 21st Street
Bellevue 98005
Tel: (206) 453-5874
TWX: 910-443-2469

Wyle Distribution Group
1750 132nd Ave., N.E.
Bellvue 98005
Tel: (206) 453-8300

WISCONSIN

†Arrow Electronics, Inc.
430 W. Rausson Avenue
Oakcreek 53154
Tel: (414) 764-6600
TWX: 910-262-1193

Hamilton/Avnet Electronics
2975 Moorland Road
New Berlin 53151
Tel: (414) 784-4510
TWX: 910-262-1182

Kierulff Electronics, Inc.
2238-E W. Bluemound Rd.
Waukeshaw 53186
Tel: (414) 784-8160

CANADA

ALBERTA

Hamilton/Avnet Electronics
2816 21st Street N.E.
Calgary T2E 6Z2
Tel: (403) 230-3586
TWX: 03-827-642

Hamilton/Avnet Electronics
6845 Rexwood Road Unit 6
Mississauga, Ontario L4V1R2
Tel: (416) 677-0484

†Zentronics
Bay No. 1
3300 14th Avenue N.E.
Calgary T2A 6J4
Tel: (403) 272-1021

BRITISH COLUMBIA

Hamilton/Avnet Electronics
105-2550 Boundry Road
Burmalay V5M 3Z3
Tel: (604) 272-4242

BRITISH COLUMBIA (Cont'd)

Zentronics
108-11400 Bridgeport Road
Richmond V6X 1T2
Tel: (604) 273-5575
TWX: 04-5077-89

MANITOBA

Zentronics
590 Berry Street
Winnipeg R3H OS1
Tel: (204) 775-8661

ONTARIO

Arrow Electronics Inc.
24 Martin Ross Avenue
Downsview M3J 2K9
Tel: (416) 661-0220
TLX: 06-218213

Arrow Electronics Inc.
148 Colonnade Road
Nepean K2E 7J5
Tel: (613) 226-6903

†Hamilton/Avnet Electronics
6845 Rexwood Road
Mississauga L4V 1R2
Tel: (416) 677-7432
TWX: 610-492-8867

†Hamilton/Avnet Electronics
210 Colonnade Road South
Nepean K2E 7L5
Tel: (613) 226-1700
TWX: 05-349-71

†Zentronics
8 Tilbury Court
Brampton L6T 3T4
Tel: (416) 451-9600
TWX: 06-976-78

Zentronics
564/10 Weber Street North
Waterloo N2L 5C6
Tel: (519) 884-5700

†Zentronics
155 Colonnade Road
Unit 17
Nepean K2E 7K1
Tel: (613) 225-8840
TWX: 06-976-78

QUEBEC

†Arrow Electronics Inc.
4050 Jean Talon Quest
Montreal H4P 1W1
Tel: (514) 735-5511
TLX: 05-25596

Arrow Electronics Inc.
909 Charest Blvd.
Quebec 61N 269
Tel: (418) 687-4231
TLX: 05-13388

Hamilton/Avnet Electronics
2795 Rue Halpern
St. Laurent H4S 1P8
Tel: (514) 335-1000
TWX: 610-421-3731

Zentronics
505 Locke Street
St. Laurent H4T 1X7
Tel: (514) 735-5361
TWX: 05-827-535

†Microcomputer System Technical Distributor Centers

CG-3/17/87

EUROPEAN SALES OFFICES

BELGIUM

Intel Corporation S.A.
Rue de Cottages 65
B-1180 Brussels
Tel: (02) 347-0666

DENMARK

Intel Denmark A/S*
Glentevej 61 - 3rd Floor
DK-2400 Copenhagen
Tel: (01) 19-80-33
TLX: 19567

FINLAND

Intel Finland OY
Rousilantie 2
00390 Helsinki
Tel: (8) 0544-644
TLX: 123332

FRANCE

Intel Paris
1 Rue Edison, BP 303
78054 Saint-Quentin-en-Yvelines Cedex
Tel: (33) 1-30-57-7000
TLX: 69901677

Intel Corporation, S.A.R.L.
Immeuble BBC
4 Quai des Etroits
69005 Lyon
Tel: (7) 842-4089
TLX: 305153

WEST GERMANY

Intel Semiconductor GmbH*
Seidlestrasse 27
D-8000 Muenchen 2
Tel: (89) 53891
TLX: 05-23177 INTL D

Intel Semiconductor GmbH
Verkaufsbuero Wiesbaden
Abraham-Lincoln Str. 16-18
6200 Wiesbaden
Tel: (6121) 76050
TLX: 04186183 INTW D

Intel Semiconductor GmbH
Verkaufsbuero Hannover
Hohenzollernstrasse 5
3000 Hannover 1
Tel: (511) 34-40-81
TLX: 923625 INTH D

Intel Semiconductor GmbH
Verkaufsbuero Stuttgart
Bruckstrasse 61
7012 Fellbach
Tel: (711) 58-00-82
TLX: 7254826 INTS D

ISRAEL

Intel Semiconductor Ltd*
Attidim Industrial Park
Neve Sharet
Dvora Hanevia
Bldg. No. 13, 4th Floor
P.O. Box 43202
Tel Aviv 61430
Tel: (3) 491-099, 491-098
TLX: 371215

ITALY

Intel Corporation S.P.A.*
Milanofiori, Palazzo E/4
20090 Assago (Milano)
Tel: (02) 824-4071
TLX: 341286 INTMIL

NETHERLANDS

Intel Semiconductor (Nederland) B.V.*
Alexanderpoort Building
Marten Meesweg 93
3068 Rotterdam
Tel: (10) 21-23-77
TLX: 22283

NORWAY

Intel Norway A/S
P.O. Box 92
Hvamveien 4
N-2013, Skjetten
Tel: (2) 742-420
TLX: 78018

SPAIN

Intel Iberia
Calle Zurbaran 28-IZQDA
28010 Madrid
Tel: (1) 410-4004
TLX: 46880

SWEDEN

Intel Sweden A.B.*
Dalvagen 24
S-171 36 Solna
Tel: (8) 734-0100
TLX: 12261

SWITZERLAND

Intel Semiconductor A.G.*
Talackerstrasse 17
8152 Glattbrugg
CH-8065 Zurich
Tel: (01) 829-2977
TLX: 57989 ICH CH

UNITED KINGDOM

Intel Corporation (U.K.) Ltd.*
Pipers Way
Swindon, Wiltshire SN1 1RJ
Tel: (0793) 696-000
TLX: 444447 INT SWN

*Field Application Location

EUROPEAN DISTRIBUTORS/REPRESENTATIVES

AUSTRIA

Bacher Elektronics Ges.m.b.H.
Rotenmuehlgasse 26
A-1120 Wien
Tel: (222) 835-6460
TLX: 131532

BELGIUM

Inelco Belgium S.A.
Ave. des Croix de Guerre, 94
Bruxelles 1120
Tel: (02) 216-01-60
TLX: 64475

BENELUX

Koning en Hartman Electrotechniek B.V.
Postbus 125
2600 AC Delft
Tel: (15) 609-906
TLX: 38250

DENMARK

ITT MultiKomponent
Naverland 29
DK-2600 Glostrup
Tel: (02) 456-66-45
TLX: 33355 ITTCG DK

FINLAND

Oy Fintronic AB
Melkonkatu 24A
SF-00210 Helsinki 21
Tel: (0) 692-60-22
TLX: 124224 FTRON SF

FRANCE

Generim
Zone d'Activite de Courtaboeuf
Avenue de la Baltique
91943 Les Ulis Cedex
Tel: (1) 69-07-78-78
TLX: 691700

Jermyn
73-79 Rue des Solets
Silic 585
94663 Rungis Cedex
Tel: (1) 45-60-04-00
TLX: 290967

Metrologie
Tour d'Asnieres
4, Avenue Laurent Cely
92606 Asnieres
Tel: (1) 47-90-62-40
TLX: 611448

FRANCE (Cont'd)

Tekelec Airtronic
Cite des Bruyeres
Rue Carle Vernet BP 2
92310 Sevres
Tel: (1) 45-34-75-35
TLX: 204552

WEST GERMANY

Electronic 2000 Vertriebs AG
Stahlgruberring 12
8000 Muenchen 82
Tel: (089) 42-00-10
TLX: 522561 ELEC D

Jermyn GmbH
Schulstrasse 84
6277 Bad Camberg
Tel: (064) 34-231
TLX: 415257-0 JERM D

Metrologie GmbH
Meglingerstr. 49
8000 Muenchen 71
Tel: (089) 570-940
TLX: 5213189

Metrologie GmbH
Rheinstr. 94-96
6100 Darmstadt
Tel: (06151) 33661
TLX: 176151820

Proelectron Vertriebs AG
Max-Planck-Strasse 1-3
6072 Dreieich
Tel: (06103) 3040
TLX: 417972

ITT-MultiKomponent
Bahnhofstrasse 44
7141 Moeglingen
Tel: (07141) 4879
TLX: 7264399 MUKO D

ISRAEL

Eastronics Ltd.
11 Rosanis Street
P.O. Box 39300
Tel Aviv 61392
Tel: (3) 47-51-51
TLX: 342610 DATIX IL or
33638 RONIX IL

ITALY

Eledra Componenti S.P.A.
Via Giacomo Watt, 37
20143 Milano
Tel: (02) 82821
TLX: 332332

ITALY (Cont'd)

Intesi
Milanofiori E5
20090 Assago
Tel: (02) 824701
TLX: 311351

Lasi Elettronica S.P.A.
Viale Fulvio Testi, 126
20092 Cinisello Balsamo
Tel: (02) 244-0012, 244-0212
TLX: 352040

NORWAY

Nordisk Electronik A/S
Postboks 130
N-1364 Hvalstad
Tel: (2) 846-210
TLX: 77546 NENAS N

PORTUGAL

Ditram
Avenida Marques de Tomar, 46A
Lisboa P-1000
Tel: (351-1) 734-834
TWX: (0404) 14182

SPAIN

ITT
21-3 Miguel Angel
Madrid 28010
Tel: (1) 419-54-00
TWX: 27461

A.T.D. Electronica S.A.
Pl. Ciudad de Viena 6
28040 Madrid
Tel: (1) 234-4000
TWX: 42477

SWEDEN

Nordisk Elektronik AB
Box 1409
S-171 27 Solna
Tel: (8) 734-97-70
TLX: 10547

SWITZERLAND

Industrade AG
Hertistrasse 31
CH-8304 Wallisellen
Tel: (01) 830-5040
TLX: 56788

UNITED KINGDOM

Accent Electronic Components Ltd.
Jubilee House, Jubilee Way
Letchworth, Herts SG6 1QH
England
Tel: (0462) 686666
TLX: 626923

Bytech Ltd.
Unit 2 Western Centre
Western Industrial Estate
Bracknell, Berkshire RG12 1RW
England
Tel: (0344) 482211
TLX: 848215

Comway Microsystems Ltd.
John Scott House, Market St.
Bracknell, Berkshire RJ12 1QP
England
Tel: (0344) 55333
TLX: 847201

IBR Microcomputers Ltd.
Unit 2 Western Centre
Western Industrial Estate
Bracknell, Berkshire RG12 1RW
England
Tel: (0344) 486-555
TLX: 849381

Jermyn Industries
Vestry Estate, Otford Road
Sevenoaks, Kent TN14 5EU
England
Tel: (0732) 450144
TLX: 95142

Rapid Silicon
Rapid House, Denmark St.
High Wycombe, Bucks HP11 2ER
England
Tel: (0494) 442266
TLX: 837931

Rapid Systems
Rapid House, Denmark St.
High Wycombe, Bucks HP11 2ER
England
Tel: (0494) 450244
TLX: 837931

Micro Marketing
Glenageary Office Park
Glenageary, Co. Dublin
Ireland
Tel: (0001) 856288
TLX: 31584

YUGOSLAVIA

H.R. Microelectronics Corp.
2005 De La Cruz Blvd., Ste. 223
Santa Clara, CA 95050 U.S.A.
Tel: (408) 988-0286
TLX: 387452

INTERNATIONAL SALES OFFICES

AUSTRALIA

Intel Australia Pty. Ltd.*
Spectrum Building
200 Pacific Hwy., Level 6
Crows Nest, NSW, 2065
Tel: (2) 9571-2744
TLX: 20097
FAX: (2) 923-2632

CHINA

Intel PRC Corporation
15/F, Office 1, Citic Bldg.
Jian Guo Men Wai Street
Beijing, PRC
Tel: (1) 500-4850
TLX: 22947 INTEL CN
FAX: (1) 500-2953

HONG KONG

Intel Semiconductor Ltd.*
1701-3 Connaught Centre
1 Connaught Road
Tel: (5) 844-4555
TWX: 63869 ISLHK HX
FAX: (5) 294-589

JAPAN

Intel Japan K.K.
5-6 Tokodai Toyosato-machi
Tsukuba-gun, Ibaraki-ken 300-26
Tel: (02) 97-47-8511
TLX: 03656-160

Intel Japan K.K.*
Daiichi Mitsugi Bldg.
1-8889 Fuchu-cho
Fuchu-shi, Tokyo 183
Tel: (04) 23-60-7871

Intel Japan K.K.
Flower-Hill Shin-machi Bldg.
1-23-9 Shinmachi
Setagaya-ku, Tokyo 154
Tel: (03) 426-2231

Intel Japan K.K.*
Kumagaya Bldg.
2-69 Hon-cho
Kumagaya, Saitama 360
Tel: (04) 85-24-6871

Intel Japan K.K.
Mishima Tokyo-Kaijo Bldg.
1-1 Shibahon-cho, Mishima-shi
Shizuoka-ken 411
Tel: (05) 59-72-2141

JAPAN (Cont'd)

Intel Japan K.K.*
Mitsui-Seimei Musashi-Kosugi Bldg.
915-20 Shinmaruko, Nakahara-ku
Kawasaki-shi, Kanagawa 211
Tel: (04) 47-33-7011

Intel Japan K.K.
Nihon Seimei Bldg.
1-12 Asahi-cho
Atsugi, Kanagawa 243
Tel: (04) 62-23-3511

Intel Japan K.K.*
Ryokuchi-Station Bldg.
2-4-1 Terauchi
Toyonaka, Osaka 560
Tel: (06) 863-1091

Intel Japan K.K.
Shinmaru Bldg.
1-5-1 Marunouchi
Chiyoda-ku, Tokyo 100
Tel: (03) 201-3621

KOREA

Intel Technology Asia Ltd.
Room 906, Singsong Bldg.
25-4, Yoido-Dong, Youngdeungpo-ku
Seoul 150
Tel: (2) 784-8186
TLX: 29312 INTELKO
FAX: (2) 784-8096

SINGAPORE

Intel Singapore Technology, Ltd.
1-1 Thomson Road
#21-06 Goldhill Square
Singapore 1130
Tel: 250-7811
TLX: 39921 INTEL
FAX: 250-9256

TAIWAN

Intel Technology (Far East) Ltd.
Taiwan Branch
10/F., No. 205, Tun Hua N. Road
Taipei, R.O.C.
Tel: (02) 716-9660
TLX: 13159 INTELTWN
FAX: (02) 717-2455

*Field Application Location

INTERNATIONAL
DISTRIBUTORS / REPRESENTATIVES

ARGENTINA

VLC S.R.L. Bartalome Mitre 1711
3 Piso
1037 Buenos Aires
Tel: 54-1-49-2092
TLX: 17575 EDARG-AR

AUSTRALIA

Total Electronics
Private Bag 250
9 Harker Street
Burwood, Victoria 3125
Tel: 61-3-288-4044
TLX: AA 31261

Total Electronics
P.O. Box 139
Artamon, N.S.W. 2064
Tel: 61-02-438-1855
TLX: 26297

BRAZIL

Elebra Microelectronica S/A
Geraldo Flausino Gomes, 78
9 Andar
04575 - Sao Paulo - S.P.
Tel: 55-11-534-9600
TLX: 3911125131 ELBR BR
FAX: 55-11-534-9424

CHILE

DIN Instruments
Suecia 2323
Casilla 6055, Correo 22
Santiago
Tel: 56-2-225-8139
TLX: 440422 RUDY CZ

CHINA

Novel Precision Machinery Co., Ltd.
Flat D, 20 Kingsford Ind. Bldg.
Phase I, 26 Kwai Hei Street
N.T., Nowloon
Hong Kong
Tel: 852-0-223-222
TWX: 39114 JINMI HX
FAX: 852-0-261-602

CHINA (Cont'd)

Schmidt & Co. Ltd.
18/F Great Eagle Centre
23 Harbour Road
Wanchai, Hong Kong
Tel: 852-5-833-0222
TWX: 74766 SCHMC HX
FAX: 852-5-891-8754

INDIA

Micronic Devices
Arun Complex
No. 65 D.V.G. Road
Basavanagudi
Bangalore 560 004
Tel: 91-812-600-631
TLX: 0845-8332 MD BG IN

Micronic Devices
403, Gagan Deep
12, Rajendra Place
New Delhi 110 008
Tel: 91-58-97-71
TLX: 03163235 MDND IN

Micronic Devices
No. 516 5th Floor
Swastik Chambers
Sion, Chambray Road
Bombay 400 071
Tel: 91-52-39-63
TLX: 9531 171447 MDEV IN

JAPAN

Asahi Electronics Co. Ltd.
KMM Bldg. 2-14-1 Asano
Kokurakita-ku
Kitakyushu-shi 802
Tel: 093-511-6471
FAX: 093-551-7861

C. Itoh Techno-Science Co., Ltd.
C. Itoh Bldg., 2-5-1 Kita-Aoyama
Minato-ku, Tokyo 107
Tel: 03-497-4840
FAX: 03-497-4969

JAPAN (Cont'd)

Dia Semicon Systems, Inc.
Wacore 64, 1-37-8 Sangenjaya
Setagaya-ku, Tokyo 154
Tel: 03-487-0386
FAX: 03-487-8088

Okaya Koki
2-4-18 Sakae
Naka-ku, Nagoya-shi 460
Tel: 052-204-2911
FAX: 052-204-2901

Ryoyo Electro Corp.
Konwa Bldg.
1-12-22 Tsukiji
Chuo-ku, Tokyo 104
Tel: 03-546-5011
FAX: 03-546-5044

KOREA

J-Tek Corporation
6th Floor, Government Pension Bldg.
24-3 Yoido-Dong
Youngdeungpo-ku
Seoul 150
Tel: 82-2-782-8039
TLX: 25299 KODIGIT
FAX: 82-2-784-8391

Samsung Semiconductor &
Telecommunications Co., Ltd.
150, 2-KA, Tafpyung-ro, Chung-ku
Seoul 100
Tel: 82-2-751-3987
TLX: 27970 KORSST
FAX: 82-2-753-0967

MEXICO

Dicopel S.A.
Tochtli 368 Fracc. Ind. San Antonio
Azcapotzalco
C.P. 02760-Mexico, D.F.
Tel: 52-5-561-3211
TLX: 1773790 DICOME

NEW ZEALAND

Northrup Instruments & Systems Ltd.
459 Kyber Pass Road
P.O. Box 9464, Newmarket
Auckland 1
Tel: 64-9-501-219, 501-801
TLX: 21570 THERMAL

Northrup Instruments & Systems Ltd.
P.O. Box 2406
Wellington 856658
Tel: 64-4-856-658
TLX: NZ3380
FAX: 64-4-857276

SINGAPORE

Francotone Electronics Pte Ltd.
17 Harvey Road #04-01
Singapore 1336
Tel: 283-0888, 289-1618
TWX: 56541 FRELS
FAX: 2895327

SOUTH AFRICA

Electronic Building Elements, Pty. Ltd.
P.O. Box 4609
Pine Square, 18th Street
Hazelwood, Pretoria 0001
Tel: 27-12-469921
TLX: 3-227786 SA

TAIWAN

Mitac Corporation
No. 585, Ming Shen East Rd.
Taipei, R.O.C.
Tel: 886-2-501-8231
FAX: 886-2-501-4265

VENEZUELA

P. Benavides S/A
Avilanes a Rio
Residencias Kamarata
Locales 4 A17
La Candelaria, Caracas
Tel: 58-2-571-0396
TLX: 28450 PBVEN VC
FAX: 58-2-572-3321

*Field Application Location

DOMESTIC SERVICE OFFICES

ALABAMA

Intel Corp.
5015 Bradford Drive, #2
Huntsville 35805
Tel: (205) 830-4010

ARIZONA

Intel Corp.
11225 N. 28th Dr. #D214
Phoenix 85029
Tel: (602) 869-4980

Intel Corp.
500 E. Fry Blvd., Suite M-15
Sierra Vista 85635
Tel: (602) 459-5010

ARKANSAS

Intel Corp.
P.O. Box 206
Ulm 72170
Tel: (501) 241-3264

CALIFORNIA

Intel Corp.
21515 Vanowen
Suite 116
Canoga Park 91303
Tel: (818) 704-8500

Intel Corp.
2250 E. Imperial Highway
Suite 218
El Segundo 90245
Tel: 1-800-468-3548

Intel Corp.
1900 Prairie City Rd.
Folsom 95630-9597
Tel: (916) 351-6143

Intel Corp.
2000 E. 4th Street
Suite 110
Santa Ana 92705
Tel: (714) 835-5789
TWX: 910-595-2475

Intel Corp.
2700 San Tomas Expressway
Santa Clara 95051
Tel: (408) 970-1740

Intel Corp.
4350 Executive Drive
Suite 150
San Diego 92121
Tel: (619) 452-5880

COLORADO

Intel Corp.
650 South Cherry
Suite 915
Denver 80222
Tel: (303) 321-8086
TWX: 910-931-2289

CONNECTICUT

Intel Corp.
26 Mill Plain Road
Danbury 06811
Tel: (203) 748-3130

FLORIDA

Intel Corp.
1500 N.W. 62, Suite 104
Ft. Lauderdale 33309
Tel: (305) 771-0600
TWX: 510-956-9407

Intel Corp.
242 N. Westmonte Drive
Suite 105
Altamonte Springs 32714
Tel: (305) 869-5588

GEORGIA

Intel Corp.
3280 Pointe Parkway
Suite 200
Norcross 30092
Tel: (404) 441-1171

ILLINOIS

Intel Corp.
300 N. Martingale Rd.
Suite 300
Schaumburg 60194
Tel: (312) 310-5733

INDIANA

Intel Corp.
8777 Purdue Rd., #125
Indianapolis 46268
Tel: (317) 875-0623

KANSAS

Intel Corp.
8400 W. 110th Street
Suite 170
Overland Park 66210
Tel: (913) 345-2727

KENTUCKY

Intel Corp.
3525 Tatescreek Road,
#51
Lexington 40502
Tel: (606) 272-6745

MARYLAND

Intel Corp.
5th Floor
7833 Walker Drive
Greenbelt 20770
Tel: (301) 441-1020

MASSACHUSETTS

Intel Corp.
3 Carlisle Road
Westford 01886
Tel: (617) 692-1060

MICHIGAN

Intel Corp.
7071 Orchard Lake Road
Suite 100
West Bloomfield 48033
Tel: (313) 851-8905

MISSOURI

Intel Corp.
4203 Earth City Expressway
Suite 143
Earth City 63045
Tel: (314) 291-2015

NEW JERSEY

Intel Corp.
385 Sylvan Avenue
Englewood Cliffs 07632
Tel: (201) 567-0821
TWX: 710-991-8593

Intel Corp.
Raritan Plaza III
Raritan Center
Edison 08817
Tel: (201) 225-3000

NORTH CAROLINA

Intel Corp.
2306 W. Meadowview Road
Suite 206
Greensboro 27407
Tel: (919) 294-1541

Intel Corp.
2700 Trycliff Rd, Suite 102
Raleigh 27607
Tel: (919) 781-8022

OHIO

Intel Corp.
Chagrin-Brainard Bldg.
Suite 305
28001 Chagrin Boulevard
Cleveland 44122
Tel: (216) 464-6915
TWX: 810-427-9298

Intel Corp.
6500 Poe
Dayton 45414
Tel: (513) 890-5350

OREGON

Intel Corp.
15254 N.W. Greenbrier
Beaverton 01886
Tel: (503) 645-8051
TWX: 910-467-8741

Intel Corp.
5200 N.E. Elam Young Parkway
Hillsboro 97123
Tel: (503) 681-8080

PENNSYLVANIA

Intel Corp.
201 Penn Center Boulevard
Suite 301 W
Pittsburgh 15235
Tel: (313) 354-1540

TEXAS

Intel Corp.
313 E. Anderson Lane
Suite 314
Austin 78752
Tel: (512) 454-3628
TWX: 910-874-1347

Intel Corp.
12300 Ford Road
Suite 380
Dallas 75234
Tel: (214) 241-2820
TWX: 910-860-5617

Intel Corp.
8815 Dyer St., Suite 225
El Paso 79904
Tel: (915) 751-0186

VIRGINIA

Intel Corp
1603 Sar ., Rosa Rd., #109
Richmor J 23288
Tel: (804) 282-5668

WASHINGTON

Intel Corp.
110 110th Avenue N.E.
Suite 510
Bellevue 98004
Tel: 1-800-468-3548
TWX: 910-443-3002

WISCONSIN

Intel Corp.
450 N. Sunnyslope Road
Suite 130
Brookfield 53005
Tel: (414) 784-8087

CANADA

Intel Corp.
190 Attwell Drive, Suite 103
Rexdale, Ontario
Canada K2H 8R2
Tel: (416) 675-2105

Intel Corp.
620 St. Jean Blvd.
Pointe Claire, Quebec
Canada H9R 3K2
Tel: (514) 694-9130

Intel Corp.
2650 Queensview Drive, #250
Ottawa, Ontario,
Canada K2B 8H6
Tel: (613) 829-9714

CUSTOMER TRAINING CENTERS

CALIFORNIA

2700 San Tomas Expressway
Santa Clara 95051
Tel: (408) 970-1700

ILLINOIS

300 N. Martingale, #300
Schaumburg 60173
Tel: (312) 310-5700

MASSACHUSETTS

3 Carlisle Road
Westford 01886
Tel: (617) 692-1000

MARYLAND

7833 Walker Dr., 4th Floor
Greenbelt 20770
Tel: (301) 220-3380

SYSTEMS ENGINEERING OFFICES

CALIFORNIA

2700 San Tomas Expressway
Santa Clara 95051
Tel: (408) 986-808f.

ILLINOIS

300 N. Martingale, #300
Schaumburg 60173
Tel: (312) 310-8031

MASSACHUSETTS

3 Carlisle Road
Westford 01886
Tel: (617) 692-3222

NEW YORK

300 Motor Parkway
Hauppauge 11788
Tel: (516) 231-3300